To

Miss Linna E. Bresette

Sincerely

Mary Nestor

Wom

Leader

BELLEVUE BOOKS PUBLISHING CO.
ROCKFORD, ILLINOIS

Woman's

Labor Leader

AN AUTOBIOGRAPHY OF AGNES NESTOR

Thomas Nestor

572

Anna McEwen Nestor

≈≈≈≈≈≈≈ Acknowledgment ≈≈≈≈≈≈≈

Grateful acknowledgment with thanks is hereby offered to the following persons and organizations whose kindnesses have greatly facilitated the issuing of this book:

To Mr. Lee Ettelson, editor of the *Chicago American,* for his kind permission for our reprinting herein certain articles which appeared first in that newspaper.

Likewise, to Mr. John S. Knight, editor of the *Chicago Daily News,* for his kind permission for the reprinting herein of certain articles which appeared first in that newspaper.

To Mr. Daniel De Falco, head resident of the University of Chicago Settlement, for unearthing for our use the striking picture (page 62) of Mary E. McDowell at work at the turn of the century and at the very beginning of the Women's Trade Union League movement.

To Rockford College for providing us with the fine photograph of Jane Addams, an early graduate of that institution.

To the Chicago Waitresses Union, Local No. 484, for the use of the rare portrait of Elizabeth Maloney.

The title for the book has been adopted by the publishers from the usual newspaper references to Miss Nestor.

THE EDITOR

Contents

1-The
Early
Struggle

AGNES NESTOR
PHOTOGRAPH FROM AN OIL PAINTING BY F. ZAKHAROV

Chicago, 1897

IT WAS the spring of 1897, the year of financial panic, that my mother, my sister Mary, my brother Owen, and I set out from our home in Grand Rapids for Chicago.

Father, obliged to go where he might find work at his old trade of machinist, had left for Chicago right after Christmas. It had been a happy Christmas, our last in Grand Rapids, with our elder brother Arthur home all the way from New York where he had a job. After the holidays, we had begun packing up all our furniture to be sent ahead to Chicago, had given up our home and divided the family to stay with friends, and in March had enjoyed a round of farewell parties. Now we were setting forth.

I was overjoyed at the idea of the great adventure — life in the great city of Chicago! Mary, however, was in tears. She had heard that Chicago was an unfriendly city where no one knew his next-door neighbor, and she was sure that we would never be happy away from Grand Rapids.

In Chicago the next morning, Father met us at the depot, and we boarded the cable car to go to our new home. As we passed through the business section, the city seemed strangely silent. It was Sunday morning, and few people were on the streets.

Our new home was on the third floor of a large apartment house on the north side of the city. The house had no porch, and there was no yard. We had never felt so boxed up in all our lives.

After a few weeks, to Mary's surprise, we found the neighbors very friendly. Most of them owned and lived in frame cottages with high outside steps leading to the second floors.

Owen started at the Mulligan School at the end of our street and soon made many friends. Mary got a job in a candy factory. One hot day in August, my mother accompanied me as I set out to look for work.

We went first to places near by. At a fringe factory on Clybourn Avenue, no girls were needed. At a yeast factory on North Ashland Avenue we saw a sign in the window, "No help wanted," so we turned away. I had noticed a glove factory in this vicinity and had decided that there was where I would really like to work, the Eisendrath Glove Factory. We went in with high hope.

There was a tiny woman, evidently the bookkeeper, in the outer office. She referred me to the superintendent sitting near by. He looked me over and asked gruffly:

"How old are you?"

I was small for my age and wore my hair down my back in two long braids. When I said, "Fourteen," he snapped:

"You look younger than that!"

I said that my mother would corroborate my statement. She did, very earnestly.

"Well, give your name and address to the bookkeeper there," he said. "We will send for you if we need a girl."

As we left the factory, I could hardly speak, I was so filled with disappointment.

"It was just a way to get rid of me," I said, gulping down a sob.

"No," my mother tried to console me, "the little woman said they would send for you."

But I still did not believe that they would.

A few days later the early morning mail brought a postcard directing me to report prepared for work and to bring with me shears and an apron. I hurried over to the factory and was assigned to work in the knitting department. The knitting department was a small room in a corner of the shipping department on the factory's first floor.

I was put to work on a winding machine, winding the yarn onto cones. If a thread broke, that stopped the whole operation, and I would get a reproving look from the boy who worked with me.

Around me in the small room there was the clicking of the knitting machines, the humming of the sewing machines, but all this did not distract me. My own machine ran quietly and steadily. I concentrated on my work and was happy all day long. At five-thirty the whistle blew — the end of the working day.

I walked home with one of the older girls from another department. I asked her how long she had worked at the factory.

"Seven years," she replied.

I fairly gasped. *Seven years!*

That evening at supper I said to the family: "Just think, I walked home tonight with a girl who has worked at that place seven years!" Little did I think that I would work there ten years!

That night, when I had told her how a broken thread stopped my winding operation, my mother showed me how to make a small knot which would fit into the machine. She had worked in a cotton mill in her childhood and was able to give me many such practical aids.

MY REGIME at the factory began that week in August. Leaving home every morning at six-thirty, after a hurried breakfast at six, I began work at seven o'clock. At nine-thirty each day the whistle blew for a five-minute lunch period — just time enough to eat a sandwich brought from home.

We had only a half-hour at noon. It was a sight then to see the men from the tanneries opposite running across the way to the saloon and back with long sticks from which beer pails were suspended.

Saturday was our short day. On Saturday we worked only nine hours. We looked forward to that day because it was also payday.

The weekly pay for beginners was three dollars. At least that was what was agreed on. But a new foreman figured that as the rate was five cents an hour, for a forty-nine-hour week the pay should amount to only two dollars and ninety-five cents. This calculation took effect the first week I was there. The older girls, who also had their pay docked for that missing hour, made a great fuss. But in the end they had to accept the new scale or lose their jobs.

When Labor Day came around, a notice was posted that we must work. Without letting me know their plans, the older girls stayed away. In our department, only a few showed up for work, so we few were sent home. On my way home, I met the superintendent. He asked why I was not at work. When I told him, he did not say a word but hurried on to the factory.

I was surprised that Labor Day had not much significance

to Chicago employers. My father had told me that as early as 1894 Labor Day had been established by law as a national holiday. Peter J. Maguire, executive secretary of the Brotherhood of Carpenters and Joiners of America, a pioneer labor leader of New York City, had been the founder, he having first proposed it to a labor convention in 1882.

My earliest recollection of Labor Day in Grand Rapids had been of hearing a band playing in the distance and of running with a crowd of other children down Leonard Street to Canal Street to see the parade. We were always impressed by the group of stalwart blacksmiths wearing red flannel shirts. There was usually a large group of these men because the trade of horse-shoeing was flourishing in our city at the time. The parade usually ended up with a big picnic. How little I had thought back there in Grand Rapids what that word "labor" would mean to me in a few years!

Shortly after Labor Day we moved to a two-story flat-building on Clifton Avenue between Garfield and Webster. There we had a back porch and a large yard. It was a homelike neighborhood consisting chiefly of two-flat dwellings; but the buildings were packed close together, and my father did not like the idea of this congestion. He used to say that where the sunshine does not enter in, the doctor does. So after a year we moved to the West Side far out on Maplewood Avenue. This was a great distance from our work; we girls wanted to move north again, but this did not happen until some years later.

Meanwhile, I was learning a new kind of work. From the winder I was promoted to mending the knit wrists of gloves. For this work I used a small hook to pick up the dropped stitches. It was concentrated, monotonous work; but as there were several other girls sitting with me, we used to vie with each other to see who could do the quickest job. We did not realize that the foreman was counting the individual output of the workers.

Whenever our output fell below a certain amount, the foreman would ask why we had not produced as much as on some other day. I admit that sitting together in a group we did quite a bit of talking. Seeing this, the foreman reprimanded us for wasting time. But we had become so dexterous that we could work and talk without the talk interfering. None of the other girls answered the foreman. But I looked up and said:

"It's no fun sitting here working all way and not saying a word!"

"You don't come here to have fun, do you?" asked he, icily.

I had no reply ready, and after that we kept silent when we knew that he was around.

After a while I was promoted to the sewing machine. My job was to feed work into the machine that sewed the knit wrists on to mittens. I liked this work and had no trouble running the machine all day. I worked so enthusiastically that I began to make a record. At the end of one ten-hour day the foreman asked me:

"How do you like working on this machine?"

Like the foolish girl I was then, I replied, "Oh, I never get tired of sewing on it!"

"Good," he said. "Remember that a few years from now."

As the years went by and I was still sewing at the machine, I remembered this remark and realized that the encouragement from the foreman had been only a ruse to make me speed up more. I was sewing over a hundred dozen pairs of wristbands in a day. One day the foreman asked:

"Agnes, how many dozen have you sewed today?"

Proudly I replied, "One hundred and ten dozen."

"Not enough," said he. "Mary Wiggins, who sewed on this

machine before you, sewed over one hundred and seventeen dozen."

"What then?" asked I.

"Well, you will have made a record of sewing the most that was ever sewed on this machine if you can make it one hundred and twenty dozen."

As I walked home with the girl who had worked there for seven years, I repeated the conversation.

"My dear girl," she warned me, "don't make any record you can't live up to. Once you sew that many you'll have to keep it up."

I soon learned that it was best to set a certain steady speed and to keep that pace without breaking any records.

In the washroom one day I happened to hear a glove-operator complaining that her machine was out of order and that in consequence her pay would be curtailed and she would receive only five dollars that week.

Five dollars! thought I. *My! I wish I could make that much in a week!* I asked the girl what was the usual full-time pay of a glove-operator. When I heard it was the magnificent sum of twelve dollars a week, I went to my foreman and said that I wanted to work upstairs in the glove department.

I had not reasoned that by moving upstairs to work I would be undermining the whole organization of the downstairs knitting department. But that was what the foreman gave me to understand. Were he to let me go upstairs to work, said he, the whole downstairs group would want to go too, and he would not be able to keep anyone in his department. "Anyone taking your place," said he, "might ask, 'Where is the girl who used to do this work?' I would have to say that she is upstairs making gloves, and then the new girl would want to go up there too."

I was tired of being held back when I knew I was expert and worth more money. I told the foreman that I was leaving, that I was going to the Burnham factory where they were hiring girls for regular glove work. The foreman said that I might as well try it, but that he knew I would not like it at Burnham's and would be glad to come back to Eisendrath's.

Determined at least to try for a better-paying job, I took a day off and applied at the Burnham glove factory downtown.

I was given a job at "banding." This consisted of hemming bands, then sewing them on work gloves before the gloves were closed, then sewing the gores at the sides. It was piecework at six cents per dozen pairs. When I agreed to the price, I had no idea that I would sit around for hours waiting for work. So this was the trouble with a piecework job! But I determined to stick to it. The forelady was very nice, which helped — some. Some days I would be given only a dozen pairs, then would be sent home having earned only six cents. I would walk the three miles home; I had already spent five cents for carfare to get to work.

I knew that I could go back to my old job at the Eisendrath factory; but I was too proud to let the foreman know that what he had said had proven true — that I would not like the arrangements at Burnham's.

Three weeks before Christmas, when the work was slack, I was laid off. It was not a pleasant prospect looking toward Christmas, which our family had always happily celebrated with gifts and gala preparations.

The next day I searched the "Want Ads." There was one asking for girls to make wreaths of evergreen for the Christmas trade. That sounded like the Christmas spirit, so I went to apply for the job. I was hired to begin work the next day.

What a dismal disappointment the job proved to be! Instead

of sitting in a warm conservatory surrounded by Christmas trees, as I had imagined, a half-dozen of us who had applied for temporary work were relegated to a large, bare, unheated loft. When lunch time came it was impossible to eat the cold lunches we had brought, for we were chilled through although we had kept our coats and overshoes on. At the end of the day we were told our work was over and that we could come back the next day for our pay, which amounted to fifty cents. That meant that I had cleared twenty cents! Thirty cents had gone for carfare — ten cents for the trip back and forth in applying for the job, ten cents to and from work, and ten cents back and forth to collect my pay. For twenty cents all one long day I had sat in a cold room twining stiff greens with fingers numb with cold.

Christmas was near, and I had bought no presents. Father was working hard to pay the rent and other household bills. Mary was doing her share working long hours in a candy factory. I had to find something to do!

After wasting shoe leather and carfare, as a last resort I went to the "Five-and-Dime" and was put in the toy department. From the beginning I knew that it would be a terrific grind, standing behind the counter all day, making change, keeping track of the merchandise — all this responsibility and slavery for three dollars a week. But my gloomy anticipation did not come up to the awful reality. I had to work overtime every night, although this brought my pay up to three dollars and fifty cents. I carried two lunches, one for noon, the other for evening. The first night, after a gruelling day, tired and hungry, I went for my lunch. It was gone — eaten by the rats which infested the place. I managed to slip out to a fruit stand near by and buy a little fruit. After that supperless night, I hid my lunches in the sleeve of my coat. We had no lockers, just some nails in the basement wall for our hats and coats.

How I ever finished my two weeks there I do not know, because during the last week I was so tired that it was only by the greatest effort that I could force myself out of bed in the mornings to go to work. The last week, the manager, seeing that some of us looked sick, allowed us to take turns coming an hour late every other day. But we worked later and later at night, cleaning up and arranging the stock for the next day. Every night my poor mother stayed close to the window at home anxiously awaiting my safe arrival.

We had heard that some firms gave bonuses to their help at Christmas. On Christmas Eve, after an unusually hectic day, and after working until near midnight getting the stock ready for inventory, I received a half-pound box of stale chocolate creams accompanied by a note saying that my services were no longer required. I arrived home at midnight. My dear mother had been at the window for hours and was nearly sick with worry.

We had a happy Christmas after all, though. Mother and Father were their usual cheerful selves and had some little surprises for each of us. But I could not forget the carefree life we had had at Grand Rapids and the lovely Christmas times we had spent when we had been children.

2

Farewell to Childhood

WHAT a different life I had led up to the age of fourteen! The factory girl of Chicago seemed an entirely different person from the little girl I had been in Grand Rapids.

My family had been in good circumstances at the time when I was born. Father then had a grocery store in Grand Rapids at the corner of Coldbrook and Iona Streets. Over the store was a nice apartment to which he had brought Mother as a bride. Here I was born, the third child; my brother Arthur and my sister Mary had preceded me. We lived opposite the Old School No. 7, and in addition to his grocery trade Father received a good profit from his candy business.

Father had come to America from Ireland. He had been born in Stradbally, in Galway. Mother had been born in the historic Mohawk Valley in New York State. They had met and married in Grand Rapids.

My earliest recollection is of my mother's being ill and confined to her room with chronic asthma. All other remedies having failed to relieve her, our old family physician, Dr. Wood, suggested that she take a trip out West. But Mother did not want to go away among strangers. She wanted to visit some old friends back East in East Troy, New York. She asked if a complete rest in the East might not do.

Dr. Wood consented to her wishes. I can remember the struggle it was to get Mother ready for the trip, especially those times when she had to stand up to have a new dress fitted by Lizzie McMahon, the housekeeper who also did all the family sewing. I remember, too, how the neighbors said that my mother would not survive the long trip and how hard it was for them to tell her good-bye. They were feeling that they would never see her alive again.

Mary and I went along with Mother. I remember little about the trip, except the excitement of our having linen dusters, which grown ladies wore in those days to keep their dresses clean while travelling.

In East Troy we visited Katie Coleman and her family. Katie had been a girlhood friend of Mother's and had worked with Mother in the Harmony Cotton Mills in Cohoes, directly across the river.

We stayed in East Troy six weeks. Mother had hoped to visit her brother Charlie in Gloversville, a short distance from East Troy, but she was not able to make the trip; she was miserable all during our visit. Uncle Charlie came over to see her and to meet his two little nieces.

Mother's friends in East Troy used to give Mary and me money to buy candy. I remember going to a certain candy store, where, because I took such a long time to make my choice, I must have been a very troublesome customer. "How many for a cent?" I would ask, as I pointed to almost every kind of candy in the store. One day in exasperation the storekeeper handed me a single stick of candy! "Go home," he said, "and do not come here any more!" I wonder now if this was a foreshadowing of my later bargaining propensities when I dealt in labor relations instead of sweets.

As we were leaving East Troy, her kind friends wept over

Mother, feeling that it was a last farewell. But, surprisingly, on the trip home her asthma attacks were not nearly so violent as they had been before, and when we reached home she seemed in better health. At home she continued to grow stronger, and it was not long before she was able to do things about the house. Gradually she became entirely well, and the asthma did not trouble her again until very late in life.

Faithful Lizzie McMahon stayed with us for several years more, taking full responsibility of the household. Even after she left to take a position as seamstress, she continued to sew for us.

Meanwhile, while we children were still very young, Father went into politics and was elected alderman of the old Fifth Ward. Two terms he served in this office and then was elected city marshal. He sold his grocery business, in order to give all his time to this latter office.

We moved then to a house at 111 East Leonard Street in the north end of the city, and here we lived for ten years. The house sat on a high terrace with a view down past the old railroad depot, the first depot built in Grand Rapids. It had been built in 1859 at what was then the extreme north of the town. The engineers laying out the tracks had used the line of least resistance and had routed the trains around the hill.

It never occurred to us to wonder whether we lived on the right or the wrong side of the tracks, for our high location gave us the finest vantage point in the city. We liked being near to the depot because we saw so many interesting sights. We could see the trains arriving, and when there was a train-load of Dutch immigrants coming in we would hurry down to the depot to see these foreigners who had come directly from Holland to Grand Rapids. They still wore their native cos-tumes and clumping wooden shoes. They came to work in the Grand Rapids furniture factories and they brought along their families. Most of them settled far out on Leonard Street.

I know at least one furniture manufacturer (and no doubt there were others) went directly to Holland to contract for this cheap labor. This was before the Federal Government outlawed contract labor.

Rising up in direct view from our house was a great hill which to us looked like a mountain. We used to climb this hill to see the balloon ascensions at Reed Lake where we often went for family picnics and which in those days was considered to be a very remote part of the city. It is now called Ramona. In those days we had to take a dummy railroad from the end of the streetcar line to get there.

On top of the hill was a plateau, since made into a city park, called Lookout Park because of its fine view in all directions. In the old city records I found that my father proposed that site for a park while he was alderman but that the city council thought the plan not feasible. From the valley side of the city, there were two hundred steps leading up the steep hill, and these steps we children loved to count as we climbed.

I can truly say that I attended the "Little Red Schoolhouse." It was Public School No. 7, my first school. We lived just across the street! Built in 1860 of red brick, it was called the "Old School" and was a two-story structure with a schoolroom on each floor. It was heated by a large wood-burning stove with a zinc screen which was shifted if any part of the room became too warm. The building, situated on a hill surrounded by woods, had the appearance of a real country school. Its actual name was the Leonard Street School, but it had been started as a district school when there were few others in Grand Rapids. The land had cost only $300 and the building $1500, but it must have been well built because it served the children of the neighborhood for many years. It has since been replaced by a modern school.

Lucy Bettes, who came from a teaching family, was our principal. She, her sister Anna, and a cadet made up the teaching staff. Anna Bettes was my first teacher and, eventually, my last, at the Old Central Grammar School.

The time came when I left the Old School. A stretch of land on our street, just beyond the block where we lived, was purchased by Bishop Henry J. Richter for the Catholic Diocese. The Redemptorist Order began to build their new church, St. Alphonsus. When completed, the first floor was used as a school, and church services were held upstairs. The dedication was a great occasion with the Knights of Labor heading the parade.

Mary and I were transferred to this school which opened with about 180 children. The Dominican Sisters were in charge headed by the brilliant young principal, Sister Cyprian. She also taught the high-school grades in what was called the High Room. My teacher was Sister Ignatius for whom I always had great affection.

In the next block the Bishop built St. John's Orphan Asylum, using a fund left by a benevolent citizen, John Clancy. My mother had a special place in her heart for orphans because she had been raised in a Catholic orphanage. The first three orphans, the Meredith children, were taken at once into Mother's heart and often visited at our home. We children regarded all the orphans as our personal friends even as the institution grew in numbers. We were always invited to their parties and special programs.

One of my saddest memories of the orphanage asylum was during the diphtheria epidemic which one summer took a toll of seven lives — six of the children and one Sister. It was

AGNES, OWEN, AND MARY NESTOR

AGNES NESTOR'S BIRTHPLACE IN GRAND RAPIDS

before the discovery of antitoxin for this disease. Too often a little white hearse passed our home and we felt so sorry to know that another child was a victim of the dreadful scourge. When Sister Isabella, the youngest of the nuns, died, we stood on our hill to watch the pathetic litle funeral leaving the orphanage at dusk.

But sorrow was turned into joy in our household about that time because a baby brother was born. My father announced that his name would begin with an "O," so my mother guessed at once that he would be called "Owen," after my father's brother. It was a family name with the Nestors.

With her growing family my mother again needed household help and had the good fortune to get a fine young girl recently come from Holland who became our "hired girl," as domestic help was then called. She stayed with us for several years, until my mother could manage alone.

As Easter approached, my mother began to wonder whether the children at the orphanage would be given eggs. From her own experience she knew that people always remembered orphans at Christmas, but what about Easter?

Mary and I were told to ask our classmates at St. Alphonsus School to ask their mothers to donate a dozen eggs each. By Holy Saturday, Mother had collected a bushel of eggs, which we children, happy in knowing that there were enough eggs for a good feast, carted to the asylum. My mother kept up this practice every Easter until we left Grand Rapids, even extending the donation by collecting money for hams and by interesting other women in working at this charity. Mother often accomplished a great deal in her quiet way.

HOW DIFFERENT our Christmas holidays had been then from the bleak discouraging days of that first Christmas season in Chicago!

During the Christmas holidays we coasted and skated. In those days Grand Rapids was a wonderful place for winter sports. Coasting on the many hills was our delight. On Saturdays, Bridge Street, now Michigan Street, was closed to all traffic so that the children could coast there. On other days we used the hill near our house. Starting near the school, we flew down across the tracks and across Plainfield Avenue without fear of traffic dangers, using bobsleds which were long enough for a dozen or more to straddle. When we moved to Palmer Street, our last home in Grand Rapids, we had even better coasting. Fairbanks Street near by was the steepest hill in the city and everyone came to coast there.

Not far from our home, near the hill, there was a swamp where we got black dirt for our flower gardens. The old reservoir there was our skating pond in winter.

When we were not coasting or skating, we had afternoon parties and dancing parties and taffy-pulls in our kitchen and Mother allowed us to call in the neighborhood children.

Christmas was the great day at our house with presents galore and feasting. Birthdays too were celebrated not only in our family but also among the neighboring children.

I remember when a schoolmate, Jennie Hoban, wanted to have a birthday party but her mother told her that eggs were too expensive to make the cakes. Jennie's mother was preparing a surprise party, inviting all Jennie's friends to come to the house and not letting Jennie know that refreshments had been prepared. When we had all assembled, a big open sleigh drawn by a team of horses stopped in front of the house and Mrs. Hoban announced, "Get ready for a sleigh ride!" Soon we were all tucked into the straw and blankets and away we went into the country. On our return, a fine hot supper awaited us — and plenty of cake too!

SPRING BROUGHT its own joys in those days. Leonard Street stretched out into the country where we had May parties in the woods. How we loved finding the early spring flowers!

We used to drive out to a distant relative's farm — Uncle Pat Bird's — on Sundays. We would pass an old tollgate, and it would seem like ancient days when the gatekeeper collected pennies from the driver. These small sums were used to keep up the roads, which, in those days would otherwise be too muddy and difficult for horse and buggy and farm wagon to pass over.

Summer was the time when we put on shows in our back yard, using the space between our woodshed and the lot of our neighbor, the Fergusons. Mrs. Brinkman, another neighbor, would lend us sheets for the curtain.

Harriet Ferguson was taking elocution lessons, so she always played the star parts in our plays. Strangely, she was a shy, timid girl who would not go on an errand alone but would always stop at our door to ask one of us girls to go with her.

We had learned how to stage shows from seeing the children trained for "exhibitions" for the Closing Exercises at St. Alphonsus School. My sister Mary was in the Wand Drill for the first Closing Exercises, which were held at Redmond's Opera House. I thought she had the most important part in the whole entertainment. She said afterwards that, as she led the procession from the wings, she had the most terrible stage fright, but that when she heard the music she got over her fright and then went through the whole drill without a mistake.

When Mary and I were permitted to go to dancing parties, we felt that we were growing up, for we were then allowed to stay at the parties until eight o'clock in the evening! At the Carews', who like the Algiers, had a very large house, they rolled back the rugs for dancing parties. Mr. Carew would play the violin and one of his daughters the piano.

Our family was very fond of dancing. Father had been a great dancer in his youth, and my elder brother, Arthur, seemed to take after him in this. Arthur used to practice his steps in our summer kitchen, almost wearing out the floor with his jigging. He taught our younger brother, Owen, to dance, and if Arthur had remained at home the two might have made a great dancing team.

Arthur also took up the piccolo and played in a small orchestra of North-End boys who practiced at each other's houses. At our house they used the diningroom for rehearsals, always closing and locking the door. We girls often tried to get in to these band practices, but we were always shooed away. Some of these boys became professional musicians, two of them later on getting to have orchestras of their own. One, Johnny Taylor, became one of the greatest drummers in the country, travelling with the Rogers Brothers Circus. Arthur, however, did not persist in the musical field. He announced one day that he wanted to leave high school.

"You will either continue in school or go to work," my father said in answer to this.

Arthur said he would go to work. He got a job with an old neighbor from Coldbrook Street, Joseph Cargill, who had a photoengraving company. Mr. Cargill took Arthur on as an apprentice making woodcuts. Arthur worked at the trade a few months, and then he received an offer of a job with a wood-vulcanizing company in New York. He took the New York job and remained there, eventually becoming manager of the company.

I remember vividly when the circus came to town. We went down to see the parade of costumed performers headed by the elephant and the band. The parade satisfied me; after the parade, I didn't care about going to see the circus.

We always attended the county and state fairs, taking our lunch along because we always stayed all day. We would come home loaded with things which had been given away.

I often compare now our simple amusements with the more complex ones of the modern child. The other day during a visit with the daughter of an old friend of my mother's, Teresa Donovan, she and her young son took me for a drive. While Teresa and I talked about old times, the boy listened to the car radio. Suddenly he broke into our conversation, asking, "What would we do without the radio, the car, and the movies?"

I told him that his mother and I had grown up without these things and had had a very good time.

"What did you do to have a good time?" he asked, with sincere curiosity.

I tried to tell him, but I know he did not understand.

I HAD ALWAYS BEEN a delicate child. One summer my mother decided to send me to visit at Uncle Pat Bird's farm in the hope that country air might benefit me. Farmers who were neighbors to Uncle Bird often passed our house, so Mother said that I might "catch" a ride if I recognized any of Uncle Bird's neighbors driving back to their homes.

With this hope, Mary and I sat on a little hill at our corner one day watching to see some farmer come by whom we might know. But as wagon after wagon rolled by I could only shake my head at each and say to Mary, "No, I don't know him."

Finally Mary's patience gave out. "Aggie," she said, "you'll never get to the country this way. Unless you hail the next farmer who is going the right direction, you may be here for hours."

When the next wagon came along, Mary motioned at him to stop and went over to talk with him. Then she beckoned to me.

"He goes near Bird's," said she. "Get in."

I mounted to the seat beside the farmer, and off we went. Mary returned home feeling that she had done her duty. But when Mother asked her who had given me the ride and Mary replied that she did not know, Mother was alarmed. Then when Father came home that evening and was told that I had gone off with a stranger, he became so worried that he made arrangements to drive out to the farm with Mother. They found me at the Bird farm safe and sound.

As it had happened, the farmer had let me off a bit short of the Bird farm, and I had had to walk a long half-mile under a burning sun along a rough country road and carrying my heavy luggage. It had been a weary trudge for a little girl. There were in those days no telephones, except in a few business houses, or I would have sent word back to my parents.

I thoroughly enjoyed that summer on the farm. I liked to dig potatoes and to hunt for eggs. It was a thrill for me a city child to find a whole nest of eggs. But I drew the line at berry-picking after just one day under the hot sun, and I refused to go again with the other children.

I had often wondered how butter was made. I shall never forget the time that I solved the mystery. While the cream was splashing in the big churn, I opened the lid and was splashed with buttermilk from head to foot.

It was a great time when all the farmers of the neighborhood came to thresh the wheat. This was, of course, before the improved threshing machinery had been devised. The farm women came along, too, to help with the meals, for cooking for a large group of hungry men who had been out in the field all day was a big job.

I returned home from the farm much improved in health and ready for school again.

ONE DAY while I was still at the Old School, Miss Bettes asked if anyone could bring a flag to school for Decoration Day. Boldly I raised my hand. I was hoping to get one, and a great big one indeed, from Mr. Perry, the mayor of Grand Rapids. My father had by this time become assistant city treasurer, and his association with Mr. Perry had ripened into a warm friendship. I went to see Mr. Perry, and the next day a beautiful American flag arrived at our school.

That same day Mr. Perry said to my father: "Your little girl asked for that flag just in time. The Wealthy Avenue School sent over for it last night."

The title, "Wealthy Avenue," was used to describe the street where the rich people of that time lived.

When my father told me this, it made the flag doubly precious, and on the day of our program, proudly I said to my classmates:

"Wealthy Avenue School wanted that flag, but *we* got it!"

Perhaps back there for the first time I was learning how satisfying it can be to obtain things for one's group.

MY FATHER continued as city treasurer under the next mayor, Dr. Hake. Then he ran for sheriff. When I asked my mother what a sheriff was, she tried to explain as simply as possible by saying that when prisoners ran away the sheriff had to go out to find them. This seemed such a dangerous job that I prayed hard that Father wouldn't get it. To my great relief, he was defeated.

When he went out of public office, Father was without a cent. Politics to him had been costly, for he was a man of that kind who puts everything into a job and takes nothing out. Meanwhile factories were shutting down, and times were getting bad. Father went to work, but not at the kind of job that suited him, and often he would come home saying that things were getting so bad that he might soon have to go elsewhere to look for work. Finally he went to Chicago and found a job. He returned to spend Christmas with us; then back to Chicago he went, and we made plans to follow him. I was fourteen; childhood was over; soon I, too, would be at work.

3

I Become a Striker

OUR FIRST CHRISTMAS in Chicago had just passed. Mary was still working long hours at the candy factory. I, without work, was almost fifteen, in this year of 1898, and it seemed that all my dreams of learning some trade and rising rapidly to the top in it had gone up in smoke! In the big metropolis of Chicago, our visions of becoming important wage-earners had not fructified as we had hoped.

Back now I went to Burnham's where I had been laid off just before the holidays. There had been changes in the shop. The nice forelady was gone. I missed her. However, I had had a nice rest and was filled with new determination. I was put in the banding department — piecework again! — work for a few hours one day and then nothing the next.

As Washington's Birthday would be a holiday at Burnham's, I planned that on that day I would go back to Eisendrath's. I would brave it out; I would go boldly to the glove department upstairs and ask for a job there. I would not go back to the knitting room!

I went to Eisendrath's glove department and waited a long, long time for the foreman. I knew that he had stopped to consult with my former foreman before interviewing me. To my surprise he hired me to begin work the next day. Again it was piecework, but here the work was continuous.

Our machines were on long tables in large rooms, and we operators sat on both sides of the tables. At last I was where I had longed to be, and here I worked for ten years. I was earning fairly good pay for those times, and I was happy. We would mark out the quantity of our work and keep account of our earnings. I still have that little book in which I kept my accounts. It is interesting to see how I gradually increased my weekly pay.

To drown the monotony of work, we used to sing. This was allowed because the foreman could see that the rhythm kept us going at high speed. We sang *A Bicycle Built for Two* and other popular songs.

Before we began to sing we used to talk very loudly so as to be heard above the roar of the machines. We knew we must not stop our work just to hear what someone was saying; to stop work even for a minute meant a reduction in pay.

We did want to do a little talking, though. In order not to lose time by it, we worked out a plan. We all chipped in and bought a dollar alarm clock which we hung on the wall. We figured that we could do a dozen pairs of gloves in an hour. That meant five minutes for a pair. As we worked we could watch the clock to see if we were on schedule. If we saw ourselves falling behind, we could rush to catch up with our own time. No one was watching us or pushing us for production. It was our strategem for getting the most out of the piecework system. We wanted to earn as much as we possibly could.

But, though we all seemed happy at first, gradually it dawned dimly within us that we were not beating the piecework system; it was beating us. There were always "pacemakers," a few girls who could work faster than the rest, and they were the ones to get the new work before the price was set. Their rate of work had to be the rate for all of us, if we were to earn a decent wage. It kept us tensed to continual hurry.

Also, there were some unjust practices, outgrowths from another era, which nettled us because they whittled away at our weekly pay. We were charged fifty cents a week for the power furnished our machines. At first we were tolerant of the charge and called it "our machine rent." But after a time that check-off of fifty cents from our weekly pay made us indignant.

We were obliged, besides, to buy our own needles. If you broke one, you were charged for a new one to replace it. We had, also, to buy our own machine oil. It was expensive; and to make matters worse, we had to go to certain out-of-the-way places to obtain it.

But this was not all. Every time a new foreman came in, he demonstrated his authority by inaugurating a new set of petty rules which seemed designed merely to irritate us. One such rule was that no girl must leave her own sewing room at noon to eat lunch with a girl in another room. My sister Mary had now come into the factory, and we were in the habit of grouping at lunch time with friends from other departments. But even two sisters from different departments were not permitted to eat lunch together. Mary was in a different department at the time, and this regulation seemed too ridiculous to be borne. Consequently, whenever the foreman had left the room at noon, we went where we pleased to eat our lunch. Sometimes he spied on us and ordered us "Back where you belong!"

In the face of all this, any new method which the company sought to put into effect and disturb our work routine seemed to inflame the deep indignation already burning inside us.

Thus, when a procedure was suggested for subdividing our work, so that each operator would do a smaller part of each glove, and thus perhaps increase the overall production — but also increase the monotony of the work, and perhaps also decrease our rate of pay — we began to think of fighting back.

The management evidently heard the rumblings of a threatened revolt. Our department was the "glove-closers." A representative of the company sent for a group from another department, the "banders," asking them to give this new method of subdividing the work a trial and promising an adjustment if the workers' earnings were found to be reduced. The group agreed to try out the new method; but when they got back to their department and told the banders about it, the banders revolted, refused to work the new way on trial, and walked out.

We of our department felt that we should be loyal to the girls who had walked out, and we told the foreman that if the company tried to put new girls in the places of the banders, we would walk out, too!

We had taken a bold step. Almost with spontaneity we had acted in support of one another. Now we all felt tremulous, vulnerable, exposed. With no regular organization, without even a qualified spokesman, how long would such unified action last? If anyone ever needed the protection of a firm organization, I for one at that moment felt keenly that we certainly did.

The glove-cutters, all men, had a union which had existed for about a year. The girl who sat next to me told me about it. She had a boy friend in this union, but she was always careful not to let anyone hear her talk about it because in those days unions were taboo. She said that the cutters — all men — had talked of trying to get the girls to join the union and had wanted to approach our plant to suggest it, but that some of the members had said, "You'll never get those girls to join a union. They'll stand for anything up there!"

The banders had been smart. They had walked out on Saturday. One of their number decided to get publicity about their grievances and she gave the newspapers the full story about their strike.

The Chicago Federation of Labor was having a meeting that day, and the glove-cutters from our shop had special delegates there. A labor reporter went to these delegates asking for details about the walk-out of the banders. It was the first the delegates had heard of the matter. But, learning that the banders of their own factory had struck, they decided to try to get all the girls to join the union.

On Monday the president of the union tried to arrange a meeting with our group. But it was too late. During the week end, the boss had decided to abandon the new system. Workers had been sent word to come back and everything would be all right, that they could work as before. We felt that now we had a certain power and were delighted over what seemed to us a moral victory. Monday morning found us back at work.

All was not settled, however. On Monday the glove-cutters' union rented a hall within a block of the factory. As we came out from work that afternoon, members of the glove-cutters' union met us telling us to go to a union meeting at this hall.

Israel Solon was one of these men. Sometimes, if a girl hesitated about going to the hall, he would urge:

"Don't be afraid of the boss; protect yourself! Go to the union meeting!"

I was only too anxious to go and did not care who saw me. It seemed legitimate to protect one's self from unjust rules. I went without hesitation.

The meeting was a great success; workers packed the hall,

and many non-members signed for membership. The work of organizing continued for three evenings, until most of the shop had been persuaded to join.

Toward the end of the week, there was a disturbance in the cutting department. It leaked through to us that a cutter had been discharged and that the cutters were organizing a protest strike. We were young and inexperienced in union procedure; and, as I look back now, I see that because of that lack of experience, and because we were newly organized and therefore anxious to use our new organization, we did a rash thing. We started a strike movement in protest at the discharge of the cutter and also for the redress of our own grievances. We even celebrated the event with a birthday party for one of our girls and had a feast with lemon cream pie at lunch time. During the feast we formulated our plan. We decided it would be cowardly to walk out at noon. We would wait until the whistle blew for us to resume work, and then, as the power started up on the machines, we would begin our exodus.

Somehow the foreman got wind of our plan. We were forming a line when reinforcements from the foremen's division scattered around the room ordering us to go back to our places. We began to chant: "We are not going to pay rent for our machines!" We repeated it over and over, for that was our chief grievance.

The foreman retorted: "They pay for their machines in the East!"

That was the last straw. I shouted back at him: "Well, we are in Chicago! We don't care what they do in the East!"

We walked out. We did not use the near-by stairs but walked through the next room in order that the girls there might see us leaving. The girls there were busily at work quite unconscious of our strike movement. I knew that our cause was lost unless we got those girls to join us. When we got out to the street, I told my companions that all was lost unless we could get those others to walk out too. We lined up across the street shouting "Come on out!" and calling out the names of some of the girls. We kept this up until a few did obey us. Gradually others followed until the shop was almost emptied. Then we paraded to the hall on Leavitt Street for the meeting with the union leaders.

At the meeting we were called upon to state our demands. We gave them: no more machine rent; no paying for needles; free machine oil; union shop; raises for the cutters who were paid the lowest wages.

The man at the head of the table asked:

"What else do you want?"

"Nothing else. If we get those things that is all we will ever want!"

Evidently the union officers thought I was a ringleader, for when the committee was appointed to represent our group, my name was called. When Mary heard it, she said:

"Why did they put Agnes on? She can't talk!"

This seems amusing to me now; also to certain of my friends who were present at that meeting, for they assure me that I have been talking ever since.

Our commtitee went back to the shop that afternoon, and I asked to speak with the heads of the company. The superintendent was the only one who came to meet with us, and he was in no mood to talk of a settlement. He told us that it was too soon, that it would take some time to consider our demands which I, as representative, had proceeded to explain to him. We were determined and fearless, because we knew our demands were just.

We joined the picket line again and held meetings every day

and evening in the hall the cutters had rented. How important we felt! Speakers sent to our evening meetings were furnished by the Chicago Federation of Labor Organization Committee headed by John Fitzpatrick. One evening they sent Sophie Becker of the Boot and Shoe Workers Union, the only woman on the organization committee. I am afraid that I was a great hero-worshipper in those days! I was so thrilled with her speech that as she left the hall I leaned over just to touch her. Then I leaned back satisfied because I had got that close to her.

All this was happening at the same time that streetcar conductors were being discharged because it became known that they were forming a union. Some of the conductors, as they passed our picket line, would throw us handsful of buttons which read:

ORGANIZE. I'M WITH YOU!

We wore those buttons on our coats, and when we boarded the cars we would watch the expression on each conductor's face to find out whether or not he had joined the union.

Chicago was fast becoming quite a union city during that spring of 1898. No such wave of organization did I see again until much later during the NRA. John Fitzpatrick, later to become one of the outstanding labor leaders of the country, and his committee were kept busy going from meeting to meeting.

The second week of our strike began. About the middle of the week, we girls on the picket line each received a letter from the company urging us to come back to work and promising that if we reported upon receipt of the letter our old places would be restored to us, that there would be no more machine rent or "power charge," as they called it, that needles would be furnished at cost, that machine oil would be furnished free, and that the cutters would receive a dollar a week raise. But no mention was made of our demand for a union shop.

We talked it all over with misgivings, lest some of the girls be misled by these promises. Without a company recognition of our union, we might all be lured back to work, the more progressive and outspoken of us discharged one by one, and all the old practices put back in force, perhaps even more tightly than ever. Such things had happened before. Our safety and our future, we knew, lay in our union. We decided not to return to work just yet. Meanwhile we doubled our picket line, determined that none of our group should falter.

We had hoped to get all the girls in the factory into our union, but we had had trouble with the girls of the kid glove department. Only a few of these "aristocrats" had ventured to walk out with us. The rest had remained aloof. Like the gloves they made, the kid glove makers felt that they were superior to the rest of us and used to refer haughtily to the rest of us as the "horsehide girls."

During one of the last days of our strike, one of these kid glove girls passed along our picket line on her way to work. We told her that she wasn't going in; we formed a circle around her and took her to the streetcar a block away and waited to see that she went home. We stood waiting for the car beside a long water trough where teamsters watered their horses. One girl who was holding tightly to the kid glove maker threatened, "Before I let go of you, I will duck you in that water trough." It was only an idle threat; of course she did not intend doing it.

Newspapermen were on hand trying to get stories about the strike. Luke Grant, a veteran labor reporter, was watching as we put the girl on the streetcar.

Next morning a front-page story appeared headlined,

"STRIKERS DUCK GIRL IN WATER TROUGH." Other newspapers carried the same fiction and played it up for several days, some even with cartoons of the fictitious event.

This trough incident became the favorite story of John Fitzpatrick. The story got better each time he told it; also worse, because I was made the culprit, the girl who had done *the ducking!* Mr. Fitzpatrick expanded the story, adding a policeman who, after pushing our strikers around, was ducked in the horse-trough by Agnes Nestor! I did not mind the joke, which was doubly incongruous because I was small for my age and frail-looking at that time.

Perhaps because of this newspaper publicity — and Luke Grant always insisted that his story won the day for us — or perhaps because it looked as though we girls would refuse forever to return to work unless all our demands were met, the management agreed to our union shop and to the redress of all our grievances. We went back to work the following Monday with, as we said, "flying colors." Our union shop, we felt, was our most important gain.

ABOUT THIS TIME I broke into print. For a small journal I wrote an article which might prove a clarification for those who think strikers merely "troublemakers" and "disturbers of the peace." The article has since been reprinted in the *Women's Trade Union League of Chicago Year Book,* the *Union Labor Advocate,* the *Chicago Daily Socialist* and the *Brotherhood of Railroad Trainmen's Magazine.*

◆

A DAY'S WORK MAKING GLOVES
Agnes Nestor
Glovemakers' Union, Chicago

The whistle blows at 7 A. M. but the piece workers have until 7.30 to come in to work. The penalty for coming late (after 7.30 A. M.) is the loss of a half day as the girls cannot then report to work until noon. This rule is enforced to induce the girls to come early but it often works a hardship on them when they are unavoidably delayed on account of the cars, etc. Stormy weather is the only excuse.

All the work in the sewing department is piece work so the wages depend upon the speed of the operator. The gloves are made by the dozen and each class of operators has a particular part of them to make. After they are cut they go to the silker, who does the fancy stitching on the backs; then to the closer, who sews in the thumbs and joins the pieces to the palms to form the backs; they then go to several operators each of whom does a small part of the banding; then the gloves come back to the closer to be closed around the fingers. This finishes most of the bandtop gloves but the gauntlets have to go to the binder or hemmer who finishes the tops. Nearly all of the gloves are finished on the wrong side and have to go to another department to be turned and layed off on a heated iron form; this is the finishing process. This is the making of the heavy working and driving gloves.

A few years ago most of the gloves were made throughout by one operator, but by degrees the manufacturers have divided the work into sections until now the closers and girls making the finer driving and fancy gauntlets are the only girls who really have a trade to learn. The other work is very straight and requires more speed than skill.

It is only through our union that we have been able to have the closing work made throughout by the one operator. The employers claim that their object in wanting to have this work done in sections is to make it easier for girls to learn and to make possible a better system in giving out the work. They offered to divide the total price proportionally among the different operators so that there would be no reduction by this arrangement. There was always some reduction in the other sectional work; for instance, a girl received thirty-three cents a dozen for doing all the banding on a certain style of glove. By having this work made in sections and with improved machinery the total price is seventeen cents, necessarily involving a reduction in some sections. We believe we are justified in refusing to have our "closing" work made in sections, if for no other reason than that one part of the "closing" work is very heavy and hard, and when a girl does it all day she is completely tired out, while the putting in thumbs and backing is much lighter and easier work which it is a sort of a rest to do part of the day. So when it is a question of our strength to us and not dollars or cents to the employer, so he claims, then why should we not insist an making our gloves throughout. I am not bringing in the question of breaking up our trade or the monotony and other disagreeable features of section work. One employer even offered us an increased price on the harder part of the work to induce us to accept his system, but even this we refused. You see there is a human as well as a financial question involved in this for us and I think the human is the greater of the two.

It is a curious sight to go through a factory and see in

spaces between the windows and on the posts at certain distances apart, eighty-five-cent alarm clocks. The clocks are bought as the result of a collection, which means that each girl puts in five or ten cents.

I have heard and read criticisms of the men who work watching the clock, ready to drop their tools on the minute of quitting time. But the reason our girls buy and watch the clocks is not to see how soon they can quit work, but to see that they do not lose time. It is easy to lose a few minutes and not notice it until the end of the day when we count up our work and pay. Every girl knows just how long it takes her to make any part of the glove. We figure that we can make a pair in a certain number of minutes so we watch the clock to see that we will come out on time with our dozen.

When we begin our day's work we never know what our day's pay will be. We have to figure to make up for time we lose. Although it is not our fault it is at our expense. For instance: a dozen gloves may be cut from very heavy leather and very difficult to sew; or perhaps when we go to the desk for work we may have to stand waiting in line ten to twenty minutes; or the belt of our machine may break and we may have to walk around the factory two or three times before we find the belt boy who, perhaps, is hidden under a table fixing a belt, and then we have to wait our turn; or we go to another desk to get our supplies such as needles, thread, welt, etc. But what we dread most of all is the machine breaking down as we do not know how long it will take to repair it. For this work the machinist takes our name and again we have to wait our turn. The foreman is very willing to allow us to use another machine, but when a girl is accustomed to her own machine it is not an easy matter to sew on any other. For each kind of leather and style of glove we use a different color and number of thread and size of needle; each of these requires a certain tension so that in changing the thread, needles and machine for the various kinds of work again time is taken, our time. Each glove has to be stamped with the girl's number so that a glove can always be traced back to the maker and all "busters" brought to her to repair.

I remember a certain style of glove of which I found I could make a dozen in one hour and a half. There happened to be a large order for this work going through, so that I had a great amount of it. At the end of the day, nine and a half hours, I found that I had only five dozens made. The next day I watched the clock very closely to see where the two hours went the day before. I finished each dozen on "scheduled time" but at the end of this day I found I still had only my five dozens made. I tried this every day for a week, each day trying to work harder, only with the same result and to find myself completely tired out.

A great many employers give as their reason for preferring the piece-work system and establishing it as much as possible, that they are only paying for the work they receive and have more work turned out in a day. This no doubt is true; but it is too often at the expense of the girl. For she pays not only the loss of time but the loss of health too. I am one of the many who are very much against this system for I have seen too many awful results from it. We have a certain amount of strength and energy and if this is to be used up the first few years at the trade what is to become of the workers after that? This system, moreover, encourages a girl to do more than her physical strength will allow her to do continuously. Piece work is worry as well as work.

When I started in the trade and saw the girls working at that dreadful pace every minute, I wondered how they could keep up the speed. But it is not until you become one of them that you can understand. The younger girls are usually very anxious to operate a machine. I remember the first day that I sewed, making the heavy linings. The foreman came to me late in the day and asked how I liked the work. "Oh," I said, "I could never get tired sewing on this machine." But he had seen too many girls "get tired," so he said "Remember those words a few years from now if you stay," and I have.

At half-past nine the whistle blows again and we have five minutes for a light lunch. This time we have to make up so we work until 5:35 P. M. At noon we have only half an hour, which means that the girls have to bring cold lunches. The firm heats a large boiler of water so the girls can make tea or coffee. While half an hour seems a short time for lunch still a great many girls take ten or fifteen minutes of this to trim their gloves or whatever work they can do while the power is shut down. The girls all eat at their places, two or three grouping together. I believe a lunch-room should be provided where we could eat without the sight of gloves and the smell of leather.

There is a big army of foremen, forewomen, and others employed by the various manufacturers just to study and plan how they can save a few cents here and there for the firm. Their methods of saving too often result in a "cut" here and there. As these "cuts" continue to come one after another, the girls must work faster and faster to make up for them, until they have to give up, and then there are other girls ready to take their places in the race. They all have to compete with the "pacemaker." There is only one way of resisting this and that is through the united efforts of the workers in their trade union.

Employers frequently complain about the big expense of "breaking in so much help." If they spent some of this money to make the factory conditions better it would not be necessary to break in so many workers. I believe it would pay them in the end.

One of the valuable features of our trade union is that the workers have an opportunity to meet their employer. It is only by representatives of both employers and employed sitting around the table and talking matters over that they can both recognize and understand each other's rights and interests.

The International
Glove Workers Union

THE STRIKE had lasted ten days. We returned to work triumphant, because we had won all our demands.

The girls who had not joined in our strike were not very friendly, but we could afford to be generous with them; for under the agreement they were all to join the union within a specified time.

Meanwhile, it seemed important that we begin at once to strengthen our new union. I tried to induce the older girls to accept offices in the union in order to give it stability. I am sure that I didn't know even the meaning of the term then, though; and there were many other things of which we all were ignorant. Few of us had ever been to a business meeting and we were all ignorant of parliamentary procedure. At our first meeting after the strike, we were so green as to applaud when the minutes were read.

But we learned quickly. One great aid for me was my father. As an alderman back in Grand Rapids, he had made himself into an excellent parliamentarian. On matters in this field I could consult with him.

On matters concerning labor unions I could consult with him, too. My father had come from Stradbally, in Galway, on the west coast of Ireland, where, so they say, life is so hard that those who live in that rugged region face life with a stronger will than those who come from parts where living is easier.

When he was very young, his mother had brought him to Baltimore, him the youngest of her brood of four, when she had come to America to join her husband. The husband had died while the children were still young, and the mother had had a difficult time raising her little family.

Thomas, my father, had done all sorts of odd jobs as he grew up, the outstanding one, of course, being that of apple-boy at Ford's Theatre. When he had grown old enough, he had become a machinist's apprentice. Back in 1863, at the time of the Civil War, he had joined a machinist's union, a local organization which the next year at a meeting in Cincinnati was brought with many other such scattered locals under the International Union of Machinists and Blacksmiths of North America. My father often said that he could never understand why they had grouped machinists and blacksmiths together.

That union had endured only ten years, but he felt sure that the seed sown back there helped the later organizations, and he often spoke of meeting some of the "old boys" in the shops.

In comparing his old union with the one of later years in Chicago, my father said that the same arguments against unions were being used by the bosses as in the early days. Also, that the men usually had the same excuses for not joining.

My father, in the early days, had also been a member of the Knights of Labor. I still have an old book he owned, a book published in 1881, *The History of Labor*. It is a volume which he used to read and reread. I myself began delving into it when I was old enough to think of settling on a career, and we had used to have long talks about labor problems.

As our glove-operators' organization now began to take form, I felt it not a good thing for us to be in such a large union as that of the glove-cutters', an organization numbering hundreds of members of whom we operators formed only a small group. To my mind such a large organization seemed unwieldy. Also, so many of our problems were different from those of the glove-cutters.

I spoke of this, and finally one of the men suggested that the operators form their own local. A night was set for the work of organization and the election of our own officers. The officers of the glove-cutters' union were present to lend a helping hand. All went well until we came to the election of a treasurer. The cutters said that we need not have a treasurer, that they would take care of our money. I suggested that we leave that point "on the table."

John Fitzpatrick was my great friend and counsellor. I went to his office and told him that the cutters wanted to take "all our money."

"Would you let anyone take your purse?" asked he.

"No, sir."

"Well, then, those cutters can't take your local's money either."

At our next meeting, following a motion to elect our own treasurer, we proceeded to elect her.

All this was in 1902 when there was talk of the formation of an "International Union of Glove Workers of America" to bring into one organization all the glove-worker unions then in existence. Seventeen such unions had been chartered directly by the A. F. of L. Many of these were in the Midwest — in Chicago, Rockford, Kewanee, and DeKalb, Illinois; in Milwaukee and Ripon, Wisconsin; in St. Paul, Minnesota; in Des

Moines, Iowa, and Detroit, Michigan. Five of these seventeen were in New York State, and there were two in California. In addition to these, there were other glove-worker unions without A. F. of L. charters. Under the auspices of the A. F. of L., a convention of delegates from all these various unions was planned to take place in December in Washington, D. C., to work out the formation of the new international union. I was elected one of the two delegates to represent our union at the proposed convention.

We of our union were operating under a charter issued directly from the A. F. of L., with our own official charter number, 9039, and the designation, "Glove Workers Union, Local of Operators, No. 2." In our union there were only women. But there was also another group of women glove-operators belonging to the cutters' union. I consulted with John Fitzpatrick about this matter, and he referred me to A. F. of L. Vice-President Thomas Kidd of Chicago. With the help of Mr. Kidd we worked out an agreement between the two groups concerning representation at the convention. Though I was thus greatly concerned about our status in regard to the forthcoming convention, my co-delegate, Josie Butler, and I could scarcely contain ourselves at the prospect of going to Washington, D. C.

In order to keep down expenses for our union which paid our travelling and hotel bills, we rode in the day coach all the way and when we got to Washington checked in at the Keystone Hotel on Pennsylvania Avenue, a hotel we had heard was inexpensive. It was a very old-fashioned hotel with its office on the second floor.

The convention was called to order by Frank Morrison, secretary of the A. F. of L., and later it was addressed by A. F. of L. President Samuel Gompers. The convention lasted four days, every day crowded with business. When the convention was not in session, Josie Butler and I spent our time across the street from our hotel at the National Hotel visiting with the delegates from Gloversville, New York.

There is one place in America which is famous for the making of gloves — Gloversville, New York. Glovemaking is an industry whose origin is lost in antiquity, and gloves have been made the world over. In America the industry dates back to pre-Revolution days. In 1760, Sir William Johnson, then chief agent of King George with the North American Indians, brought over several families from Perthshire, Scotland, and settled them along a small creek in what is now the eastern part of Fulton County in New York State. Many of these settlers were glovers, for Perth was then a great glovemaking center and had a glove guild whose charter dated back to 1390. To America these settlers had brought with them their glove patterns and the proper needles and threads of their trade. They began almost at once to make gloves, first leather mittens which they sold to the farmers round about; then, as their markets expanded, heavy work gloves and gloves of fine kid. This first settlement was called Johnstown.

About 1830 a new town was founded by settlers from Johnstown at a place a few miles away then called "Stump City." This new town, whose principal industry was the making of gloves, and which soon outgrew Johnstown itself, was renamed in honor of the glove — "Gloversville." With this early start, Gloversville became and remained the center of the glovemaking industry of America. Thus, the delegates from Gloversville, old in the trade and experienced in organization, were to us justifiably impressive.

Though prior to the convention, only four of the unions of Gloversville and Johnstown had been chartered by the A. F.

of L., all of the glove-worker unions from that region were represented, and they comprised two-thirds of the convention delegates.

Outstandingly impressive among the Gloversville delegates was one George H. Taylor, an able and experienced man who was heading the International Table Cutters Union, a well-organized group of whom all had learned their trade abroad. At the start of the convention, George H. Taylor was seated as temporary chairman. Later he was elected general president of the new International Glove Workers Union of America which the convention formed. A. H. Cosselman, another outstanding figure from Gloversville, and a man who later was to give our Chicago union much assistance, was elected general secretary. I was offered a place on the executive board. I said that I might be able to accept such a position later on, but that I did not feel equal to it just then.

As the convention drew to a close, it voted to hold the next convention at Gloversville, where the headquarters of our newly-formed International Glove Workers Union was to be.

There had been little time for sight-seeing in Washington, D. C. This was a great disappointment to me. But on the way back to Chicago, the train would stop at Baltimore, and I had arranged to stop over to visit with my father's brother, Patrick Nestor, and his family, none of whom I had ever seen.

Patrick Nestor was my father's oldest brother. After their mother's death, Patrick had remained in Baltimore, while my own father had set out for Michigan. Two other children there had been in that family; Owen, a roving sort of fellow who had died young, and Mary, who had died at nineteen.

Josie Butler was stopping over in Baltimore with me. We would spend the week end there and then be back in Chicago in time for Christmas, which I knew I could not possibly spend away from home.

5

Gloversville and Cohoes

THE CONVENTION held in Gloversville in 1903 was larger than the one which had been held in Washington the preceding year. There were large delegations not only from Gloversville but also from the neighboring glove city, Johnstown. Our local was brought into prominence because we, an organization which had been in existence little more than a year, had managed to send full delegations to both conventions, each a great distance from our own city. Josie Butler and I, and a third delegate, Mrs. Mages, were our representatives.

Gloversville was then a city of 15,000. But in Gloversville glovemaking so overshadowed every other industry that the county had become known as the glovemaking center of America. Gloversville manufactured fine glove and leather novelties. It had glove-leather dressing plants, knitting mills, and shoe-leather tanneries. It was fascinating to see the number of people who worked in these leather and glove industries.

In our Chicago local there had been a matter which had plagued us since our organization. It was a jurisdictional affair. Most of the glove-operators in our factory belonged to our local. But a few at the very beginning of our early strike had joined with the cutters in their local and had remained there. I had been instructed to bring up at the convention the question: *"Should our local have the right to take in all glove-operators in our factory?"*

On the evening that this question was to be proposed for vote, we were at Mrs. Cora B. Hogan's for dinner, and I, in great uneasiness, walked the floor waiting for the time when we would start for the convention. I felt we could not go home without this burning question settled. It *was* settled, and to our satisfaction. A provision was written into the constitution covering jurisdiction of locals.

It was at this convention that I made my first public speech. At a great mass meeting of glove workers, the delegates wanted to hear a representative from the Middle West, and I was selected.

I was nervous, but Israel Solon, always helpful, gave me simple instructions:

"Tell them," said he, "how you glove-operators organized in Chicago and conducted your first strike. Forget about yourself and just tell your story."

It was an ordeal at first to face a great audience of complete strangers. But I followed Mr. Solon's advice and soon became so absorbed that I completely forgot I was making a speech.

Before the convention closed, we found out that we were going to have trouble that year with the manufacturers. President Taylor advised the delegates that the employers were getting ready to force the issue of the so-called "open shop," and that this would have to be resisted in Fulton County by the Table Cutters Union.

We were happy, though, over the convention, for we felt that it was added prestige that the convention had voted to hold its next meeting, in 1905, in Chicago, and also that I had been elected a vice-president on the executive board.

IN ADDITION to being present at the convention, I had had two other reasons for wanting to come to Gloversville. My mother had a brother, Charles, who lived there. I had met him once when I had been very small, and I wanted to see him again. The other reason was that Gloversville was only about ten or fifteen miles from Cohoes where my mother had worked as a child millhand.

The convention over, I renewed my acquaintance with Uncle Charlie and met his family; then I boarded the train which would take me to Cohoes.

My mother, whose maiden name was Anna McEwen, had been one of a family of four children, two boys and two girls, all born at Tribes Hill in the historic Mohawk Valley in Upper New York. She, however, had no recollection at all of her life at Tribes Hill. She did not even remember her father, who had died young. Her mother had moved to East Troy, where she was forced to put the two little girls, Anna, my mother, aged six, and Mary Elizabeth, aged nine, in the St. Vincent's Orphanage Asylum. The boys, James, thirteen, and Charles, seven, had been "farmed out" to a family, the Putnams, at Tribes Hill.

Within three years the four children were complete orphans. My mother remembered the nuns of the orphanage taking her and her sister Mary Elizabeth to Tribes Hill for their mother's funeral; and she remembered that aunts came down from Canada. But that was all that she ever knew of her family, because after the funeral she and her sister were brought back to the orphanage.

In that day, when a girl reached the age of twelve at the orphanage, she was given to some family to work her way. Mary Elizabeth was soon twelve, and she was sent to live with a woman at East Troy, now Watervliet. A little more

time, and my mother was sent to Schuylerville to live with a
Mr. and Mrs. Stephens.

One day, anxious to see her older sister, little Anna made
her way to East Troy, a distance of thirty-three miles. When
she reached the house where Mary was supposed to be, she
was told that Mary was not at home. Little Anna made as
though to go away, then slipped around to the rear of the
house, where she discovered Mary working turning collars
by hand.

They were able to talk only a few minutes, and Anna left
terribly saddened. Mary had told her that she was practically
a prisoner, seeing no one, not allowed to go out, and kept
stitching all day long and sometimes into the night, hand-
stitching the collars for the big collar factory at Troy.

The brothers were working at Gloversville, and at last they,
too, went to Schuylerville to see Anna. When they heard from
Anna about Mary's hard life they said they would go and
take Mary away. Following Anna's advice, they entered by the
back way and found Mary hard at work. They told the woman
at the house that they wanted to take their sister for a walk,
and, in spite of the woman's objections, took Mary by force
and brought her to Gloversville to live with them. But Mary
did not live long; she died at the age of nineteen.

Shortly after the visit from her brothers, Anna left Schuylerville and went to work at the Harmony Mills at Cohoes. There
she had to go to work at five in the morning and would rush
out in the dark of that hour with a shawl over her head
because she had had no time to comb her hair. When she
had got her loom started, she would comb her hair to be
ready to go out to breakfast at seven o'clock. She worked
then until nightfall. These long working hours prevailed in
all the mill towns, and many a child worked a fourteen-hour

day. When my mother used to tell me of her hard life at Cohoes, it made a deep impression on me.

My mother had not been at the factory long when the workers went on strike. As the child workers were running down the stairs they met the superintendent who was coming up to investigate.

'What's going on?" he asked gruffly. Then when they tried to tell him, he roughly pushed the group aside, saying scornfully, "I'm not going to talk to children!"

In those days children who worked were not supposed to have grievances, were not supposed to demand shorter hours for back-breaking work.

But even before my mother's time there had been protests against working standards and conditions among mill workers. New Hampshire had passed a ten-hour-day law for women as early as 1847. In the mill-workers' publication, *Voice of Industry,* an article appeared the day after the mill-workers' strike of May 8, 1847, with the headline, "All hail to New Hampshire; the Ten-Hour Bill passed the House by 144 Majority."

But that victory was short-lived; the law contained a joker called "A saving clause" which permitted women to work longer than ten hours. That clause nullified the law. It seems that notice was given to work more than ten hours *or else not at all.*

New Jersey and Pennsylvania followed suit with their laws all having a contract clause.

Horace Greeley, in his *New York Weekly Tribune,* protested this legal farce. He wrote: "If you work thirteen hours per day, or as we may think fit, you can stay; if not, you can have your walking papers; and well you know that no one else hereabout will hire you! — is it not most egregious flummery?"

So, despite the law, my mother had to keep working her long hours. It was fifty years before anything was done by legislation to limit the working hours for women and children.

My mother was still working at the mill when the Civil War began. Her older brother James enlisted in August of 1864, served two years, then re-enlisted in the 10th Regiment of the New York Volunteers. He returned broken in health and was taken to the hospital at Albany. One day while working at her loom, she glanced out the window and saw her younger brother Charles riding on horseback toward the mill. She knew that her brother James must be near death. She and Charles rode back to the hospital and remained with James until he died.

During his last days James, concerned about his younger sister, had wanted my mother to live with Charles at Gloversville. But my mother, of an independent disposition, wanted to stay with her friends in Cohoes.

Under the long hours in the cotton mill, her own health began to fail. She tried working in a box factory, but that was too hard for a tired-out girl. She was invited by her friend Mary McEniry to join her in New York. There she stayed a year, working in a candy store on Seventh Avenue. She returned to Cohoes refreshed and went back to work at the mill.

Mary McEniry now decided to go to Grand Rapids, Michigan, where her family was now living. She urged my mother to join her. My mother did, and thus she escaped forever from the cotton mills.

In Grand Rapids, Mary McEniry, a milliner by trade, opened a shop, and my mother worked for a while with her. Then one night at the McEniry home she met my father, and a little later they were married.

As I entered the town of Cohoes, the big Harmony Mills,

where my mother had worked as a little girl, loomed up before me. It was like seeing an awful ghost rising up out of the past.

A few years later, when I was again in Gloversville, I journeyed the few miles over to Tribes Hill to see where my mother had been born and to find, if possible, some trace of her relatives.

The little village of Tribes Hill sits on a considerable elevation. Once it was the site of the Sa-Da-Go tribal village of the Mohawk Indians. Its name it had derived from the practice of various Indian tribes assembling there from the old Mohawk Turnpike. Fort Hunter, an early British fort, and later an American one across the Mohawk River, was linked with this hill all during the early days of warfare against the Indians.

At Tribes Hill I went out to the village cemetery and searched about for the name "McEwen." It could not be found. I did find the Putnam lot, that of the family that had raised my uncles. There was a large stone with names and dates going back to the early part of the eighteenth century. But the sexton said that no records had been kept of burials since about 1800. An early resident, he told me, had purchased a large section in the cemetery and provided that any Tribes Hill resident could be buried there. The section seemed large enough to take care of the whole village. But I could find in it no McEwen family.

At Tribes Hill I had at last seen the village in which life for my mother had begun. I wanted now to add one more link with our past — to visit my brother, Arthur, who lived near New York City, at Perth Amboy, where the factory he managed was located.

From Cohoes I set off for New York, where Arthur met my train. He knew how gleefully I reacted to sight-seeing, so he hired a hansom cab, one of those two-wheelers with the driver

ARTHUR

NESTOR

OWEN

NESTOR

seated high at the back, and we drove down Broadway. This being my first view of New York, he asked me what I wanted to see first. When I told him the Flatiron Building, he was both surprised and amused. We rode past the building and looked at it from all sides, and he admitted that he had never realized it was such an interesting structure.

That evening he took me on the ferry across to the Jersey side. It was a novel experience. The next day we went sightseeing again in New York, and on Sunday Arthur hired a horse and buggy and we went driving around the Jersey countryside. It was a memorable vacation. But it had not completely wiped from my mind the memories of Cohoes.

THAT FALL our union agreement with the Eisendrath Glove Company expired, and a new agreement had to be worked out. Mr. Cosselman, whom I had met at the conventions, came from Gloversville to get us started on the right path. He was experienced in such negotiations. The important thing in organizing our committee, said he, was to elect a good spokesman.

Our committee was to be a joint one with both the operators' and the cutters' locals represented. The agreement was presented and ratified by the joint membership, and I was selected to be spokesman for our committee. We proceeded then to negotiate our wage adjustments and further agreements about price levels for piecework.

The machine operators' work was piecework, and our aim was to adjust prices. Our girls held up prices fairly well, but it was the men workers, the wax-threaders for work gloves, who earned the highest wages. That work had been changed to the regular sewing-machine section run by the women and was called now the dry-thread work. The output was not as great as had been turned out by the men of the wax-thread division, but in our agreement we asked for a raise. It took several weeks to reach a settlement agreeable to all parties concerned.

MEANWHILE, news came to us in December of that year, 1903, that over in Fulton County, New York, the glove-worker unions of Gloversville and Johnstown were meeting with great difficulties.

In Gloversville and Johnstown the International Table Cutters Union had determined to lead the fight for the "closed shop," or "union" shop, as the term was intended to signify.

Trouble over the issue was of course expected. At the annual meeting of the executive committee of the union and a committee from the Glove Manufacturers Association, the manufacturers' committee informed the union that before any business could be transacted pertaining to the schedule for the ensuing year, the union would have first to consent to an agreement containing a clause prohibiting any discrimination against non-union labor.

To this the International Table Cutters Union would not agree, and the schedule which that union presented to the manufacturers on December 21, of course, did not contain any such clause.

The manufacturers responded with a lockout. The workmen were simply told *there was no more work!*

The American Table Cutters Union, composed of those cutters in Fulton County who had learned their trade in this country, immediately joined in the fight; and thus the entire glove industry of the region was tied up.

The lockout lasted for six months, until June of 1904!

We felt sorry for our friends in Johnstown and Gloversville.

A GROUP OF WORKERS AT THE EISENDRATH FACTORY AROUND 1903

DELEGATES TO THE FIRST GLOVE WORKERS CONVENTION IN WASHINGTON, I

We knew they were having a hard struggle through the long winter months. Our International Glove Workers Union was then but a young and struggling organization whose limited resources could not begin to support a strike involving the greater portion of its membership over so long a period.

Many felt that our organization was the first to meet this so-called "open shop" attack by the employers. They felt that this lock-out in Fulton County, New York, was a challenge to the labor movement and that the labor movement should have financed the strike to win against this first attack. Of course, the A. F. of L. sent out delegations of our Fulton County members to solicit funds with their credentials and aided in many other ways. But the labor movement was not then as powerful as it is today. Our own International Glove Workers Union made as good a fight as some of the older and better-established unions probably could have made. But, nevertheless, the struggle met with defeat.

The Fulton County glove workers, however, though they had lost their fight, refused to go back to work as individuals. Seeing that after their long struggle, they had to accept defeat, they marched back in a body, describing their return, not as a defeat, but as a "glorious surrender."

This unsuccessful fight of the glove workers of Johnstown and Gloversville all but wrecked their union. Many of the members became discouraged, and when we held the convention in Chicago the next year, there were no delegates from Johnstown or Gloversville except the officers of the International Glove Workers Union, Taylor and Cosselman. We remained loyal to our defeated partners and re-elected Taylor and Cosselman to their offices.

During this period we had general strikes in the smaller glove shops in Chicago, and many glove manufacturers threatened that they would leave the city rather than deal with workers' unions. Chambers of commerce in various towns of the region invited the manufacturers to locate in their communities, offering various inducements to the employers, promising no labor troubles, and even offering buildings, and in some cases bonuses. Three factories did move to smaller towns — two to Wisconsin and one to Indiana. But even so, our union meanwhile was growing in membership and stability.

2-In the
Thick of
the Fight

MARY E. McDOWELL

FIRST PRESIDENT OF THE WOMEN'S TRADE UNION LEAGUE OF CHICAGO

6

The Women's Trade Union League

IN THE SUMMER of 1904, there was a great strike of the Chicago stockyard workers. Nearly three thousand women worked in these stockyards. They worked in the canneries, in the chipped beef rooms, in the packing rooms, packing, weighing, and painting cans, and sewing the bags for the hams. They had been working long hours for meager pay. On strike they were destitute.

In the newspapers, in connection with the strike, I read of the beneficent activities of a Mary McDowell, president of a new organization called the National Women's Trade Union League. As head also of the University of Chicago Settlement, this Mary McDowell was said "to live on the very doorsteps of the strikers."

I became more and more interested in this league as I heard more and more of what it was doing for the women strikers. Then one day a woman from Boston came to see me. She was a member of the Women's Trade Union League of Boston, and she was making a study of women's trade unions. She told me a great deal about the league; she said that the Women's Trade Union League of Chicago wanted me, as president of our glove-workers' local, together with some of our members, to attend their next meeting.

I was too shy to attend that next meeting, for I knew I would be called on "to say something." But when a second invitation came, I did accept. The meeting was at Hull House, where the league was giving a party for the women strikers from the stockyards. I went to the meeting with a group of our union members, and, sure enough, I was asked "to say something." I got through my little talk somehow.

At that meeting we girls from our union met some fascinating personages — Miss Mary McDowell, Miss Jane Addams, Miss Ellen Gates Starr. We liked them tremendously. We left the meeting so enthusiastic about the Women's Trade Union League that we immediately applied for membership.

The Women's Trade Union League was an unusual, and destined to be a powerful, organization. It had been but recently organized. Its aim was to secure the organization of all women workers of the United States into trade unions, in the hope of thus gaining for these women better working conditions, a reduced working day, a living wage, and full citizenship as women. Into its membership the league admitted all working women whether trade-unionists or not, and women who, though not of the working class, were interested in the purposes of the league. This was not a movement which had begun at the bottom among the lowly. Sparking the organization were women like Mary McDowell and Jane Addams, women who had the advantages of cultural background and high social standing, but who were also motivated by a high sense of social justice and an unselfishness of purpose. They were women of great vision and high courage.

Mary McDowell I particularly admired, and the more I got to know her the better I liked her. She was of Irish and Scotch descent, and this seemed to have given her a delicious sense of humor and wit which could take the dullness out of any kind of meeting. Her warm, friendly manner captured my heart at our first meeting, as she captured the heart of everyone who met her. She had been one of the group who, back in 1903 when the A. F. of L. was holding its convention in Boston, had issued the call for the formation of the Women's Trade Union League.

The league had been organized from the top downward, with first a national organization, then state organizations, and finally organizations in the larger cities. At one of the early anniversary celebrations of the league, John Fitzpatrick, president of the Chicago Federation of Labor, said that the one thing he particularly liked about the league was that it was not afraid to blaze new trails. At the first league national convention, Samuel Gompers, president of the A. F. of L., a guest speaker, sounded a warning. It was easy, said he, for an organization such as the league to go along when everything was peaceful. The real test of the organization would come, said he, when the group found it had to take a stand. The real test would come, said he, when we had to decide whether we would support strikes.

Our Women's Trade Union League of Chicago took its "stand" by supporting the strike of the corset workers of Aurora, Illinois. League officers sent letters to every woman's club in Illinois asking their members not to buy a certain make of corset manufactured in Aurora. Lovely, gentle Mrs. Charles H. Henrotin, a leader in women's clubs, a social leader in Chicago, and an aristocrat by birth and breeding, was treasurer of the league. She became a staunch supporter of the strike.

An attorney for the corset company threatened to sue the league officers for their boycott letters. Anna Nicholes carried the matter before the Illinois State Federation of Women's Clubs, and this brought so much publicity that the corset company dropped all threat of suit.

At the next convention of the Illinois State Federation of Women's Clubs the members voted to amend their constitution to permit an organization such as our league to affiliate. Not all of the clubwomen felt kindly toward the league, however, and one was heard to say:

"Isn't it dreadful! I suppose next year we'll have those corset workers here as members!"

IN THE EARLY 1900's, it was a bold step to suggest that a member of a trade-union league give a talk on trade-unionism before a convention of the Illinois State Federation of Women's Clubs. This was indeed blazing new trails. Mary McDowell, chairman of the Industrial Program Committee for the clubwomen's convention for that year, conferred with the league officers about the matter and about the choice of a speaker.

It happened that about this time Margaret Dreier of New York was coming to Chicago as the bride of Raymond Robins, the well-known head of Northwestern University Settlement. Margaret Dreier had been the first president of the Women's Trade Union League of New York. She had a firsthand knowledge of the industrial woman and her problems. She was, moreover, charming and beautiful, with a background of wealth and culture. Mary McDowell invited her to be the principal speaker at the convention with the subject, "Household Employment." With her radiant personality, Margaret Dreier Robins was certain to win over the clubwomen!

That point settled, the next question which faced the league officers was how the clubwomen would receive trade-union women from the factories. At a preliminary conference on the matter, Mary McDowell, in her usual forceful way, announced:

"The clubwomen must sometime hear something from women in industry. Let them have it now!"

Catherine Finnegan, a girl from the bindery women's union, and I were selected for the task.

The convention was held in Joliet, Illinois. That summer of 1905 I had been busy making new agreements with the glove manufacturers and negotiating with the Eisendrath Glove Company in behalf of our local union. Mr. Joseph Eisendrath had two sisters-in-law, Mrs. Henry Solomon and Mrs. William Kuh, who were active in club work, very well known, and very fine women. In one of our conferences Mr. Eisendrath, who had read in the newspapers about my part in the coming convention, jokingly said to me:

"You had better be careful what you say, Agnes, because I am going to have two reporters there who will give me an account of every word."

I knew he meant Mrs. Solomon and Mrs. Kuh, because he added that he wanted me to meet his two sisters-in-law. I promised him that I would look for them.

That conversation took place at the evening session on the day before the convention. I was making new recommendations for our shopwork and trying to adjust the new agreements. The meeting lasted until a late hour but was ended satisfactorily, with the company agreeing to most of my suggestions.

Before I could go home, I had a very important errand. I had to call at the dressmaker's where I was having a new blouse made for the great occasion next day. I must describe that blouse, in view of what a reporter at the convention wrote of my appearance. The blouse was of white mercerized silk trimmed at the top of the collar with rose-colored velvet and surrounded by a belt of velvet rose-colored too. The next day when I put it on and went to the convention in Joliet I thought I looked as gay as a butterfly.

Considering the affair a red-letter day in our lives, a large group of glove-operators, including my sister Mary and Elisabeth Christman, had taken the day off and travelled down to Joliet to hear me speak. At the last minute, Catherine Finnegan had found herself unable to come, so I was the only trade-union girl on the program.

As I got up to speak, I believe I was more concerned about pleasing my little delegation of glove-operators than I was about pleasing the clubwomen. I was determined to make good for those loyal friends who had come there to hear me!

My speech made the following headline in a Chicago morning paper: "CLUBWOMEN EXTEND HAND TO TOILERS." Another paper headlined the story, "WOMEN FOR CLOSED SHOP," and reported that the closed shop idea received hearty applause, adding that the convention "tackled questions regarding social and industrial conditions the mere mention of which a few years ago would have been deemed anarchistic if brought up at a clubwomen's convention."

The newspapers gave an account of the resolution which came up before the convention asking for an investigation by the Federal Government of the conditions under which women all over the country were compelled to work.

But the crowning touch was a reporter's description of me — so typical of the times!

"Before the resolution was presented to the convention," he wrote, "a factory girl, simply dressed, stepped to the platform and began telling her story. She was a small figure, dressed in black with a touch of white around her neck, and with a voice with the ring of refinement in it. As the girl began speaking, the clubwomen glanced at their programs and read, 'The Story of the Glove Makers, by Miss Agnes Nestor.' There was an outburst of applause and then deep silence. The clubwomen wanted to hear the story."

The newspaper quoted my speech. But I was disappointed as I read the description of my appearance, because the pretty white blouse with touches of rose was utterly ignored and I was described as looking like what a working girl was supposed to look like in those days, dark and shabby, "dressed in black with a touch of white around her neck."

After my speech that night at the convention, I told Mary McDowell that I wanted to meet Mrs. Solomon and Mrs. Kuh. When I was introduced to Mrs. Solomon she said that I had left out two important persons from my speech — my employer as an employer, and myself as a worker.

I tried to be as tactful as possible in my remarks on the subject.

But not so the newspapers, for they had not finished yet. Back at work finishing the agreements with the company the next day, I never dreamed that I, a working girl, was making news. A reporter had gone to my home for a follow-up story and had asked where I could be reached. My mother could not tell him. So he interviewed *her.* His story was printed in the same paper which had described me as dressed so drably. The reporter had asked about my work, saying, in order to draw my mother out:

"I wouldn't think Miss Nestor's employers would like her going around talking about her early struggles."

To this my mother had replied:

"My daughter is doing all she can to advance the interests of all working girls, and I am glad the clubwomen are giving her their sympathy. Mr. Eisendrath is a fine man, and most of the managers of the factories try to do the right thing by their girls; but they don't always see the real needs of the employees; so this club movement will do much good, I am sure. I believe the world is growing better and the girls in factories some day will have as many advantages as those who do not have to toil."

This interview was printed in the Sunday edition. I was very proud of the way my mother had handled the interview, and when I read it I laughed and said:

"I know how proud Mr. Eisendrath will be to be spoken of so highly!"

I thought to myself that those who read the article would consider that I had given a good account of my employer to my mother.

Another meeting with the heads of the company had been set for the next week. I told the girls serving with me on our committee:

"Wait until you hear what Mr. Eisendrath says about that newspaper story!"

We were hardly seated at the meeting when Mr. Eisendrath turned to me and said:

"Agnes, your mother is all right!"

Then he proceeded to tell me how his friends had kept calling him all day, saying, "I hear you're a fine man!" and then ringing off. Not having seen the story in the paper, he had finally said to one phone-caller:

"What under the sun are you talking about?"

"Why, Miss Nestor says you are a fine man — read your Sunday paper!" he was told.

He had found the paper and the mystery was solved. I will say that he was not displeased. He chuckled as he said to me:

"You know, a fellow likes to read something like that once in a while. So often an employer is pictured as just a slave driver!"

The echoes of that convention went on reverberating for some time. Even now, more than forty years later, some of the women who were very young back there tell me that they remember my speech.

JOHN MITCHELL

IN 1905, our National Women's Trade Union League sent Mary McDowell to Washington, D. C., to bring before Congress the league's campaign for an investigation into the working conditions of women and children in industry. I felt a very personal interest in that campaign, for I knew the childhood of my mother and my Aunt Mary, the collar worker of Troy. That year, 1905, for the first time the subject of working conditions for women was brought to the floor of the Congress.

It is hard now to believe that "Uncle Joe" Cannon, the Speaker of the House, backed the opposition. He wanted the Census Bureau to make the investigation. (There was no Labor Department at that time.) But our league committee stood firm in the demand that the investigation be undertaken by the Bureau of Labor Statistics. Mary McDowell spoke out:

"We don't want just a count made," said she. "We want facts about conditions!"

She immediately sought the support of John Mitchell, then president of the United Mine Workers of America. Mr. Mitchell promptly wired all of his district presidents for co-operation, and their telegrams poured in to the Congressmen.

This was at the time when the United Mine Workers were out on their first general strike, and the Chicago Federation of Labor was holding a great mass meeting in a downtown Chicago theatre with John Mitchell as speaker. I attended the mass meeting and was so impressed with him that henceforth John Mitchell became my great idol in the labor movement.

After the program, the members filed up to meet John

Mitchell. A man of finely-modeled features and a mien of great dignity, he looked almost priest-like in his straight white collar much like a Roman collar. He had been a coal miner at the age of thirteen and now had risen to one of the highest offices in labor leadership. The great coal strike of 1902 had brought him into national prominence as an outstanding champion of justice.

As I was introduced to him, John Mitchell said, "Why, I have heard of you from your employer, Henry Greenbaum." Mr. Greenbaum was at that time manager of the Eisendrath Glove Company.

I left the platform walking on air. To think that the great John Mitchell knew my name and at once associated me with my Glove Workers Union!

In later years I came to know John Mitchell well, for I worked with him on committees. My high esteem of him never lessened. All those who were associated with him held him in the same high regard. Mrs. East, who was a reporter for the United Mine Workers' conventions and other labor activities, and who later opened a business school in Washington, D. C.; Harriet Reid, who was in his office when John Mitchell was New York State Commissioner of Labor; and Mary Morris, who was John Mitchell's secretary for a long time; these are some others I knew who came under John Mitchell's magnetic influence and felt the impact of his strong character.

HOUSEWORK OR FACTORY?

IN JUNE OF 1906, the General Federation of Women's Clubs was holding its biennial convention in Minneapolis, and Rheta Childe Dorr, the writer, chairman of the Industrial Program Committee for the convention, had asked Mary McDowell to present to the convention the need for an investigation survey of the working conditions of women and to bring along two trade-union girls to speak also. Josephine Casey of the Elevated Railway Employees' Union and I were selected.

I was getting ready to leave on the Sunday before the convention when I became so exhausted that I had to leave off packing and tumble into bed. When I got up late that evening to catch the train to Minneapolis, my father looked at me and shook his head, saying:

"If they want to see a tired-out working girl, they will surely see one. For you are a good specimen."

Nevertheless I went and bore up under the four days of the convention. Looking over a scrapbook recently I came across this excerpt from an article written by Effie Leese Scott in a Tucson, Arizona, newspaper of February 18, 1932, twenty-four years afterwards:

"Some years ago," wrote Effie Leese Scott, "while reporting a national convention of clubwomen, at a time when women's clubs were looking askance at such problems as those which concerned the factory women, Miss Nestor, fresh from her own machine in a glove factory, came before 2,000 clubwomen to plead with them to help the working women to obtain an eight-hour standardized working day in every state.

"Miss Nestor soon found herself in the midst of a word battle, the bomb coming from a New York woman who asked, 'If the working women don't like the way the manufacturers treat them, why don't they come into our homes and work? We pay good wages, give them their room and board, and yet we have difficulty in getting enough help to run our houses!'

"Then little Miss Nestor gave a talk on behalf of the working woman that went around the world."

In answer to that New York woman's question, Josephine

Casey, who was rather sharp in her replies, got up and said, "If the clubwomen are not capable of running their own homes, why do they expect the working girls to do it for them?" A hot discussion followed.

After the discussion was over, a woman came up to me and felt the material of my white blouse, the same blouse I had worn at the Joliet convention — my dress-up blouse.

"You're not a real working girl," said she. "Look at the good blouse you are wearing!"

At least this time I had the satisfaction that the blouse was recognized for what it was and was not called "a black dress with a touch of white around the neck."

Next morning the Minneapolis newspapers carried big stories with the heading, "THE CLUBWOMAN VERSUS THE SERVANT GIRL PROBLEM," crowding out most of the other convention news. One paper had a cartoon depicting a clubwoman on her knees, the maid ready to leave, and her friend, the policeman, waiting outside the door. Another paper praised the two working girls who had "put life in the convention." Our pictures were reprinted in the Chicago papers with added stories.

Josephine and I bought a number of newspapers at the newsstand in our hotel. The man in charge inquired, "Are you the girls?" We admitted that we were.

On the train for Chicago, when the conductor began talking to us about "the two working women at the Minnesota clubwomen's convention," we had to admit that we were the two miscreants who had created the storm.

The whole disturbance seems almost unbelievable now. But back there in 1906 it was quite real, and not long afterwards I found myself in another such predicament.

I had been scheduled to speak at a prominent woman's club

THE MYSTERY EXPLAINED

At the meeting of the Federation of Woman's Clubs a delegate explained the existence of the servant problem by saying that "working girls do not intend to run homes for women who are too lazy or incompetent to do it for themselves."

on the subject, "Changes in Industry." Just before the meeting I was met at the door by an excited chairwoman who explained that after my subject had been announced there had been such a commotion among the members that they had had to invite the secretary of the Illinois Manufacturers' Association to attend also so that he might reply to my talk.

"You see," the agitated chairwoman went on, "they were afraid you were going to talk about trade unions. You are not going to, are you?"

I replied that I would keep to my subject, "Changes in Industry," but that I intended to be critical of industry.

When the question period came after my talk, I was surprised that all the questions were about trade unions, the very subject the chairwoman had told me was not to be brought up!

We had a frank and satisfactory discussion, and the secretary of the Illinois Manufacturers' Association slipped away without meeting me. I guess he felt the women were capable of taking care of themselves and that I might be considered quite harmless and not a dangerous firebrand.

Clubwomen now have broadened their views and their programs. They are no longer afraid of those subjects. The Chicago Woman's Club, one of the oldest of that city's clubs, has sent a delegate to our Women's Trade Union League meetings for years. This delegate has a place on the clubwomen's program at their annual meeting and makes her report on the Women's Trade Union League activities. But it is only by knowing what happened in the years gone by that we can appreciate the distance we have come and the gains we have made in public relations.

7

Officer of an International Trade Union

I LL WHEN I had started for the General Federation of Women's Clubs convention in Minneapolis, I returned to Chicago after that convention and collapsed. I remained ill all that summer of 1906. I tried going back to the factory, but I did not have the strength for the work.

I did, however, keep up my work and interest in our glove-operator's union, and by mid-August when the International Glove Workers Union held its convention in Milwaukee, I felt strong enough to attend. That convention changed the whole course of my life. For at that convention I was elected secretary-treasurer of the International Glove Workers Union.

After the failure of the glove-workers' strike in Johnstown and Gloversville, New York, the locals in that region had all but lost their organizations. Realizing that the office of secretary-treasurer now rightly belonged to the Middle West where a large membership now was, Mr. Cosselman sent word from Fulton County that he was retiring from the office. I was proposed for the office and elected. I resigned from the presidency of our Chicago local and Elisabeth Christman succeeded me in that office.

It was hard to believe, I a young member of a young organization in the position of secretary-treasurer of the International

Glove Workers Union! But I did have some background for my new work. I had attended, during my years of membership, all the conventions, and I had served on the union's executive board. Also, I was young enough to have the courage to launch out in new directions in this new office. I soon found I was going to need both that experience and that courage.

I was not to take office until December of the year. My mother advised me to take time off to build up my strength and thus to be ready when my new duties should begin. Meanwhile, that summer the Milwaukee Avenue Bank of Chicago, where our local's funds were kept, closed its doors. The president of the bank fled.

The bank was located in a neighborhood of people who had worked hard for their savings. It was a tragic situation and served to revive the movement for the U. S. Postal Savings Banks. Poor people felt they needed a safer place for their savings. Late that summer, the bank's former depositors and other interested parties held a mass meeting at Turner Hall, and, because our union had lost all its funds in the bank's failure, I was asked to speak. It was an impressive meeting. Mayor Edward F. Dunne presided, and the principal speaker was Senator William Mason. Dr. Graham Taylor, head of the Chicago Commons, and Raymond Robins, both of whom lived in the heart of the district where the bank was located, spoke also. I remember Senator Mason speaking for the U. S. Parcel Post as well as for the U. S. Postal Savings Bill and telling us that the five chief opponents of the Parcel Post Bill were the five express companies. My mother attended the meeting, the first time she had ever heard me speak in public.

WE MAY THINK LITTLE of it now, but forty years ago a woman labor leader was a rarity. Getting ready for my secretary-treasurer position in the International Glove Workers Union, I rented an office in the Bush Temple of Music at 800 North Clark Street where many other international unions had headquarters. Bert Lowe, a wax-threader from Milwaukee, had been elected president of our International Glove Workers Union, and together, with a good executive board, we set to work to strengthen our organization.

That October when I went down to Streator, Illinois, with Mary McDowell, to the Illinois State Federation of Labor convention, we found ourselves the only women delegates. We were escorted to the convention platform to sit and we both were asked to address the convention. The convention, small in those days, was held in a lodge hall. Now, of course, the conventions are much, much larger. In 1947 there were a thousand delegates, of which ninety-three were women. But back in 1906 women delegates to the convention were indeed few.

The next year, 1907, Mary McDowell, Mary Kenny O'Sullivan, and I were delegates from the Women's Trade Union League to the A. F. of L. convention in Norfolk, Virginia, that delightful old city with its tang of salty ocean air. Our mission was to present to the convention a resolution asking that a woman organizer be appointed to serve on the A. F. of L. staff. As soon as we had arrived at Norfolk, I introduced myself to Frank Morrison, secretary of the A. F. of L. I had corresponded with him as secretary of our International Glove Workers Union. Our meeting was amusing.

"What!" he exclaimed. "You are not Agnes Nestor! Impossible! You are too young!"

He seemed surprised also that a woman held the position of secretary-treasurer of an international union.

Our resolution, when brought before the convention's resolutions committee, created much opposition. Some years before, a young woman organizer for the A. F. of L. had had an unfortunate experience. It was therefore felt by many that to be on the road organizing was not a proper job for a woman.

We asked the committee to allow us to select the woman for the job, adding that we would be responsible for her. But even that did not satisfy. The committee's report recommended that the whole matter be taken up by the executive council. We decided not to object to this, but meanwhile to put on our own women organizers and thus to demonstrate that women could do the work.

Following the convention's adoption of the committee's report, a message came to me from Mr. Samuel Gompers, president of the A. F. of L., saying that he wanted me on the platform. I went to him on the platform, and Mr. Gompers rose and handed me his gavel. "Please preside," said he, and then he walked away. He wished to show the convention that a woman was capable of handling the business of the unions.

As president I had presided at the meetings of our local union back in Chicago. But this sudden request to preside at a great A. F. of L. convention seemed for a moment quite a different matter. Just at that time a committee was reporting. When the committee chairman had concluded, I put a motion, and, after the vote had been taken, banged down the gavel. I was taken off my feet when the entire hall applauded my little performance. I think what pleased the delegates most was that I had made special effort to have those in the rear seats hear me. There were, of course, no loudspeakers in those days.

Mr. Gompers returned to the chair, and I went back to my seat attended by more applause — and cheers! The incident made the newspapers all over the country with the headline, "WOMAN PRESIDES AT A. F. OF L. CONVENTION."

I met Mr. Gompers many times after that and must say that he was always noted for doing graceful things.

That Norfolk convention of 1907 brought up issues and alignments which were new to me and which seemed to come to a climax at that meeting. One of these was the matter of old-age pensions. John Walker, a young man from Illinois, pleaded in an impassioned speech for a group of resolutions, including pensions for the aged. Many of the delegates were deeply impressed. But the resolutions were referred back to committee. Mary McDowell then rose and asked the chairman:

"Why do you oppose these resolutions? You know you are for the things that they propose?"

"And give *them* the credit?" snapped the chairman, meaning by "them" a group in the convention which was opposed to him and his alignments.

But that was all long ago.

During the mid-session of the convention, Mr. Gompers announced that as a matter of personal privilege he would like time set aside that afternoon to present a certain matter. The import of his message was that certain representatives of the manufacturers had tried to bribe him to come over to their camp. Following his recital, the delegates rose and cheered Mr. Gompers in a great demonstration.

The next memorable event of that great convention came when Samuel Gompers was nominated to succeed himself once again as president of the A. F. of L. Victor Berger, a newspaper publisher of Milwaukee and the leader of a Socialist-minded group within the A. F. of L., had for years opposed Mr. Gompers. But this time, contrary to his usual procedures, Mr. Berger rose and made a motion that the election of Mr. Gompers be unanimous. The effect was electrical. The motion was greeted with cheers which rocked the convention hall.

SAMUEL

GOMPERS

JOHN

FITZPATRICK

The convention was now solidified. All stood as one man behind Mr. Gompers.

That was the last A. F. of L. convention attended by Mr. Berger. He was missed by us all.

INDUSTRIAL EDUCATION

IN 1908, the A. F. of L. held its convention in Denver, Colorado. I attended, in the delightful company of Mr. and Mrs. Robins, the latter the delegate from the Women's Trade Union League. I had never been in the West before, and between sessions, I enjoyed many a horseback ride in the mountains.

It had long been a dream of mine to help to bring supplementary education to the workers deprived of this opportunity for a broader life. I was secretly thrilled, therefore, when I was appointed at this convention to serve as secretary on a Committee on Industrial Education, with Joseph P. Valentine of the Molders' Union as chairman.

The unions at that time were skeptical of trade schools, even openly opposed to them, for fear that through them students might be trained as strikebreakers. The report of our committee led to the appointment of a larger committee to study more thoroughly the whole question.

To this larger Committee on Industrial Education Mrs. Robins and I were appointed, the only women members. John Mitchell was named chairman, and serving with us was Congressman William B. Wilson, secretary of the United Mine Workers Union. Our committee made its report at the Toronto convention of 1909. Our report covered 114 pages. It was considered important enough to be introduced by Senator Carroll S. Page in the 62nd Congress and made a Senate document.

The welfare of America, our report stated, depends largely upon the industrial training of our young workers to a high standard of efficiency. Heads, however, as well as hands, must be educated, we recommended, in order to enable the young workers to earn livings in selected vocations and to acquire intelligent understandings of their duties of citizenship. We recommended supplemental education for trades, and we pointed to some of the unions which had already undertaken this project.

We recommended the establishment of industrial courses or schools in connection with the public school system where boys and girls between the ages of fourteen and sixteen could be taught the principles of the trades and the necessary technical knowledge to work at them. But we strongly urged that such schools be not a private but a public function, the cost to be a public expense.

MY TRIP to Toronto for that convention had a melodramatic ending. I had heard that a local union of glove workers at Bowmanville, a town not far from Toronto, was having difficulties. The convention over, I went to Bowmanville, set up headquarters in an old-fashioned hotel there, and sent word to the local committee of glove workers that I was in town. They came to the hotel, we went over their affairs, and I agreed to go the next morning to the plant where they were employed.

On the way back to my room that night, I noticed that the large, wood-burning stove in the hall outside my door seemed overheated. Remembering the caution my mother had used at home in Grand Rapids in caring for stoves at night, I felt somewhat perturbed and so slept very lightly. At two o'clock in the morning I heard a commotion in the hotel. I opened my door and saw that the pipe-hole in the ceiling of the hallway was burning! I hurried into my clothes, picked up my few pieces of baggage, and was ready to leave when someone knocked on my door to warn me that the place was on fire.

Down on the first floor I found that I was the only "lady guest," as they called me, and everyone, especially one very kindly gentleman, was concerned about finding me shelter. During the night a rain had turned to sleet and everything outside was frozen over. There was a butcher shop across the way, and several of us went there. But the kindly gentleman insisted that they must find "the lady guest" some more suitable place for the rest of the night. A room was secured for me in a hotel next door. But I did not go to bed. I stood with the other guests at the window and watched my own hotel burn to the ground. It was my one hotel fire experience. It gave me an uneasy feeling, being driven out of a warm shelter in a strange town on a cold night.

Next morning, as I sat in the dining room of my second hotel looking out the window and waiting for the president of the local union to come by to take me to his plant, I could see people across the street looking at the burned hotel and wondering about survivors. But, thank heavens, no one had been hurt.

Presently I saw the president of the local union come up the street and stop dead before the ruined hotel. When I went out to meet him, the poor man was pale and shaken. He had known nothing of the fire until reaching the smoldering ashes. Until some bystander had told him that "the lady guest" was safe, he had had the feeling that I must have perished in the holocaust.

When I got to the plant that morning, I found that the plant superintendent was the same kindly gentleman who had been so concerned for my welfare the night before.

I RETURNED TO CHICAGO still fired with the enthusiasm which the Toronto convention had nurtured concerning industrial education. But in a few weeks I was off on a more presently vital endeavor. In the matter of the shorter working day for working women, a U. S. Supreme Court ruling on an Oregon law of 1903 had made it look as though proper legislation could now at last be achieved. In Illinois we of the Women's Trade Union League and other interested organizations were preparing an exhibit to show the sweatshop conditions and overlong working day the working women of Illinois were forced to accept.

8

The Fight for the
Shorter Working Day

FOR MANY YEARS attempts had been made by various labor groups in many states to get enacted legislation to protect women workers from overlong working hours, from the dangers of unprotected machinery, and from sweatshop working conditions.

Back in 1893, while John P. Altgeld was Governor, Illinois had enacted an eight-hour-day and forty-eight-hour-week law for women employed "in any factory or workshop." But this law, like other similar laws passed by other states, had been nullified by the U. S. Supreme Court, on the grounds that they violated "freedom of contract" — by which was meant "freedom to work long hours or be denied a job." In 1895, when the Ritchie Box Company brought suit in Illinois contesting the 1893 law and the Illinois Supreme Court decided in favor of the manufacturers, that was the end of the eight-hour day for working women in Illinois for over forty years. Women were forced to work fourteen, even sixteen hours a day in restaurants, machine shops, and factories, and under deplorable factory and home-workshop conditions.

Then in 1908, the U. S. Supreme Court had upheld the constitutionality of the state of Oregon's Ten-Hour-Day Law for working women. That Oregon law had been passed in 1903 —

as a health measure — to protect from exploitation the health of the mothers and future mothers of the race. Now at long last, to us who were working for the rights of working women in Illinois and elsewhere, it looked as though the long fight for the shorter working day for women could be won!

In Illinois we had been working for three years gathering reports on the conditions under which women were working. Women who did factory work in their own homes were unorganized. There was no standard of wages. Payment ranged, for instance, from one-and-a-half cents to fourteen cents per garment for home "finishers" of men's trousers. The poorer the women, the worse the bargain. In conjunction with a conference held jointly by the Women's Trade Union League and the Chicago Federation of Labor, we hoped by an exhibit to bring to light the tragedies which otherwise would stay buried in reports.

Our first exhibit, which was called "Exhibit to Dynamite Sweatshops," we set up in Brook's Casino in Chicago. Our Industrial Exhibit, sponsored by a representative group of citizens, with Mrs. Charles Henrotin as chairman, was intended to demonstrate such a need for proper legislation that an economic investigation would be certain to follow. We set up facsimilies of sweatshops we had discovered in homes — as for instance, a woman in the last stages of tuberculosis shelling nuts, these nuts to be sold commercially. Luther Bradley, the well-known cartoonist of the *Chicago Daily News,* donated a fine drawing entitled "Sacred Motherhood." It depicted a mother in a sweatshop home trying to nurse her baby while she worked at her sewing machine. The initial letter "S" in the word "Sacred" was printed with the dollar sign ($).

Governor Charles S. Deneen presided at the conference's opening session on industrial legislation. John Mitchell came

to speak at another session, as did also Charles P. Neill, U. S. Commissioner of Labor, and Professor O. Ross from the University of Wisconsin. Mary Macarthur came from England to represent the British Women's Trade Union League. Miss S. P. Breckinridge spoke on one program on "Equal Wage," the subject we became familiar with later as "Equal Pay for Equal Work."

The conference ended with a great mass meeting presided over by Mrs. Robins and held jointly by the Women's Trade Union League and the Chicago Federation of Labor. I was in the audience this last day and sitting in the balcony, when I saw and recognized William Jennings Bryan entering the hall. He came in unnoticed by the audience and slipped quietly into a seat. I rushed down the stairs and up to the platform where I whispered to Mrs. Robins that Bryan was there — a "surprise visitor." He was, of course, brought to the platform and asked to address the meeting.

The outcome of our exhibit was that Governor Deneen appointed a commission to study the need for a health, safety, and comfort law for working women and to recommend any needed legislation at the biennial session of the Illinois General Assembly the next year (1909).

Meanwhile, Louis D. Brandeis, assisted by Miss Josephine Goldmark, publications secretary for the Consumer's League, had prepared a brief. It was called *The Case for the Shorter Work Day*. It presented hundreds of pages of medical testimony pointing out the dangers of the long working day and the relation of fatigue to disease and to production output.

We had determined to seek the eventual enactment of an eight-hour-day law for working women in the state of Illinois. At a conference called by Mrs. Robins, we discussed what action first to take — whether to seek first a ten-hour-day law as more likely to be obtained, or whether to plead at the onset for the desired eight-hour-day law. Present at this conference were many friends of the proposed measure — Mary McDowell, Jane Addams, Edith Abbott, Miss S. P. Breckinridge, Edith Wyatt, and a host of other league women. Also present were Anna Willard and Elizabeth Maloney from the Chicago Waitresses Union, Local No. 484. The consensus of opinion was that we should try first for a ten-hour-day law, as a measure more likely to be obtained. But Elizabeth Maloney, a gallant fighter, did not like this half-measure.

"If this group does not want to introduce an eight-hour-day bill, my waitresses' union will introduce it!" she announced.

And with that, she and Anna Willard left the conference.

At the office of the waitresses' union, they secured a copy of the Oregon law and had it typed. Then they took a train for Springfield believing that somehow they could get their bill introduced and passed by the Illinois Legislature. Having no political experience, they had no idea of the difficulties they would encounter.

The Illinois Legislature meets for six months, from January to June, each odd-numbered year. A bill may be introduced in either the house or the senate. Passed by one of these two legislative bodies, it then goes for consideration to the other. Passed by both houses, it then goes to the Governor for his approval or veto. Approved and signed by the Governor, the bill becomes a law on the following July 1. But getting a bill introduced and passed by the Illinois Legislature is no easy matter.

In either legislative body, a bill must be read three times, on three different days. The first reading is by title only and is merely notification that the measure is being introduced for consideration. The bill is then printed by the Illinois State

Printing Office and made a part of the legislative record. It is also referred to an appropriate committee for study. This committee meets to examine the bill, to hear arguments from proponents and opponents of the measure, and finally to return the bill to its house of origin with recommendations "that it do pass," or "that it do not pass." The committee may also recommend amendments to the bill.

A bill may not merely be unfavorably recommended by the committee; it may even not be recommended at all. It may simply "die in committee." A bill not recommended out of committee by the close of the legislative session becomes then a dead bill. To have it considered at the next session, it must be introduced again, in which case it starts back with the committee.

A bill recommended out of committee and for legislative consideration, has its second reading. This is the stage at which amendments to the bill may be voted. Often amendments may negate the whole purpose of a bill, or may restrict the bill till its usefulness becomes severely limited or even destroyed, or may make its enforcement impossible.

At its third reading, a bill is open for debate and finally for passage or non-passage. On all but emergency measures, a majority vote is necessary for passage — 26 votes in the senate, 77 in the house.

Passed by one legislative body, the bill must go through the same procedure in the other.

At Springfield, Elizabeth Maloney and Anna Willard did manage to corral the speaker of the house, who turned them over to one of the least influential and most irresponsible members of the house, and this member promised to introduce their bill. Their bill called for an eight-hour-working-day law for all women employed in any manufacturing or mercantile or mechanical establishment, or laundry, or hotel, or restaurant. It was introduced in the house on March 31, 1909, "was taken up, read by title, ordered printed, and referred to the Committee on Labor and Industrial Affairs," and never came forth from the committee again.

Meanwhile, Mrs. Robins and we of the league were preparing a similar bill, and we, too, were asking now for an eight-hour-day law. Mrs. Robins was concerned that the right kind of bill be introduced, and also that it be sponsored in the legislature by some member interested enough and influential enough to gain for the measure a chance of enactment. It was important, too, that the bill be presented as a health measure, because it was on that ground that the U. S. Supreme Court had upheld the Oregon law.

Mrs. Robins asked her attorney and friend, Harold L. Ickes, to draft the measure, and he followed this through by seeing Governor Deneen, who was a friend of his, and who in turn asked his senate leader, Senator Walter Clyde Jones, one of the ablest members of the legislature, to introduce the bill in the senate.

Our bill was presented to the senate on May 6, was read by title and referred first to the Judiciary Committee, then, on the advice of Senator Jones, taken from this committee and referred to the Committee on Labor, Mines and Mining. Like the bill which had been presented to the house, our bill asked for an eight-hour-day law for working women employed in "any mechanical establishment, or factory, or laundry, or hotel, or restaurant."

Over a bill to limit the workday for working women, we knew we would meet the stiffest opposition from emloyers and manufacturers every step of the way. We knew, too, that even should the enactment of such a law be obtained, we would still face the prospect of having all our efforts nullified by an unfavorable decision from the Illinois or the U. S. Supreme Court. Understandable, therefore, was our concern that the bill be properly drawn, properly introduced, and vigorously sponsored.

Anna Willard and Elizabeth Maloney of the waitresses' union, Lulu Holley of the laundry workers' union, and I were sent down by our Women's Trade Union League to campaign for the bill. Down to Springfield also came representatives of manufacturers and other employers to object to the bill and to keep it, if possible, from ever being voted out of committee for its second reading.

The voiced objections of the manufacturers and employers to the bill were frantic and involved and various and many. Their real objection was simple and plain. It lay in one simple fact of life: the minimum wage which may be paid a working woman is the amount which will support her so that she may work tomorrow. This minimum holds whether the worker works eight hours a day or twenty. Forced thus to pay this minimum, the employers sought greedily to drain out of the working woman every last ounce of energy — even though it broke her health so that she became old before her time, even though it left her no leisure of her own to enjoy or improve her life, even though it forced her to drag inefficiently through an overlong working day.

It allowed him, on the other hand, to be lazy. Working his help overlong hours kept him from having to improve his machinery, his methods, his business acumen.

This was the manufacturers and employers' real objection to the bill. But their rationalized objections reached almost to the stars. John Glenn, secretary of the Illinois Manufacturers' Association, was our main opponent. He tried at first to belittle me at the committee hearing.

"Miss Nestor," he wanted to know, "how long is it since you worked in a factory?"

"I have been out of the factory for two years," I replied. "I had to leave the factory work because it brought on a breakdown of my health."

I had not expected that this admission would occasion the effect it did. The members of the committee began to sit up more attentively. One could almost hear the comment: "There is a little working girl asking for an eight-hour-day law. She broke down under the long hours." One could feel that a dramatic moment had been reached. The three other girls with me testified, and they scored too. We then left the chamber so that the committee could take action. They voted the bill out for its second reading.

In the senate we had won the first step. We — Elizabeth Maloney, Anna Willard, Lulu Holley, and I — returned to Chicago.

The next week when the employers discovered the bill on the calendar for action, they deluged Senator Jones with telegrams begging that the bill be referred back to committee and that they be given a further hearing. Senator Jones stood firm. He did agree to give them a hearing before the senate meeting as a committee of the whole. But he refused to allow the bill to be sent back to committee.

Senator Jones sent for our group to come back to Springfield for the second reading of the bill. We went back — fourteen times we went back, each time to be confronted with another hearing. After the other side, the manufacturers and employers, had been heard, we would be called on to testify.

At one of these hearings, Elizabeth Maloney in her testimony said that it had been ascertained in a study that a waitress on duty for ten hours walked ten miles. And she added:

"Don't you think that *eight* miles is enough for any waitress to walk in a day?"

That drove home her point, and she was applauded.

We always appeared at the hearings without an attorney. We did not need one, for who knew better than we *why* we wanted the shorter working day? Our testimony was simple but effective. Arthur Evans, a veteran newswriter for the *Chicago Tribune* and who was covering the legislative session for his paper, told me afterwards that he used to marvel at us, battling as we were against prominent corporation lawyers at these hearings. "But," he added, "you girls always came out on top!"

After fourteen weeks' struggle, Senator Jones became convinced that our bill in its original form could not pass. He advised us that to get the bill through at all, we would have, as had been done in Oregon, to exclude the hotel and restaurant workers from the protection of the proposed law, and to accept a ten- instead of an eight-hour working day.

It was not so difficult to give up for the time our dream of the eight-hour day, for we saw that it could not at one stroke be gained. But the other seemed a heartbreaking concession. It meant leaving out our loyal fellow workers who had fought by our side so valiantly, waiting on tables right up to the last minute before train times, and resuming their duties immediately upon their returns from Springfield. Mr. Ickes and Mr. Robins came down to Springfield to advise us to accept these compromises; and the waitresses agreed to continue to work for the bill even though they would now be excluded from the protection of the law the bill sought to have enacted.

We assented to the amendments of the bill. But our opposition in the senate was determined that no limitation of working hours for women was to be established by law. They tried an old and obvious trick. When we sought to amend our bill and ask for a ten- instead of an eight-hour day, they moved to table our amendment, arrogantly pretending that they were for the eight-hour law which they knew could not be passed.

But we were not deceived. One day in the elevator, one of this crowd called out to us, "We will give you eight hours or nothing!"

"Heavy on the *nothing!*" I gave back to them.

Towards the end of the legislative session we got our ten-hour bill advanced and passed by the senate. Then a new fight began.

THE FIGHT IN THE HOUSE

OUR BILL went to the house, and the few remaining days of the session brought back the manufacturers and employers who had left the previous week believing our bill to be dead. It brought in, too, more employers, such as the larger laundry owners, who began now to fear that our bill might actually be passed. Jokingly I asked some of these lobbyists where they had been, adding that we had missed them, and saying, "You should have been here last week, because we passed some important bills while you were gone."

Our bill saw its first reading in the house May 27 and was referred to committee. Two days before the legislative session was to end the bill had still not been reported out of committee for its second reading. It had not been reported out because the chairman of the committee to which it had been referred had gone on a drunken celebration, had forgot all about the bill, and was nowhere to be found. The bill had to be read the next day or it could not be passed that session and would be dead.

John Sonsteby, later a chief justice in the Chicago courts, was in Springfield at the time working on a teachers' bill. He located the chairman of the committee for us and got a suggestion as to what to do. The suggestion was that we draw up a petition and get it signed by the majority of the committee members showing that they recommended the consideration of our bill.

We got the petition drawn up, and we girls were at the State House bright and early the next morning before the doors were opened. As the members of the committee came in, we got them to sign the petition. When the chairman came along I told him that we had a great many signatures but that we could get more. He snatched the document from me, looked it over, and snarled, "Why, that was the majority at the meetings!" The bill was reported in and on its way.

On the second reading of the bill all went well, until we were approached with the proposal to amend the bill to include stores and certain other businesses. It was a trick to line up further opposition to the measure. But we were not deceived. "Oh, yes," I cried out, "include all that, and it will kill our bill!"

The amendment was voted down, and our bill advanced for final roll call on the following day.

No one is allowed now on the floor while the house is in session. But in those days there was a space behind a railing where lobbyists could stand and talk to the seated members on the floor. We stood at the railing all day anxiously waiting. About six o'clock in the evening our bill was called up. It passed with six votes to spare. Our long vigil, we felt, was ended. The Governor, we felt sure, was on our side and would sign the bill. We had established, we felt, a limitation on the length of the working day for women in Illinois!

THE DAY FOLLOWING the big event, three weary girl lobbyists returned to Chicago feeling that the fight had been won. We were resting on our laurels when word came to us that certain merchants had asked the Governor for a hearing before he acted on the bill. Hurriedly we got together a delegation — Mary McDowell, Lulu Holley, and I — to go to Springfield again.

We surmised that the constitutionality of the bill would be attacked. It was decided to ask Professor Ernst Freund, head of the Law Department of the University of Chicago, to go to Springfield with us to defend the bill. Professor Freund made it clear that he would not speak unless the question of the constitutionality of the bill were raised.

He sat through the hearing and listened to the merchants' protests against the ten-hour limitation on a woman's working day; then finally he leaned over to us and announced that he was going to talk. He rose and made a stirring plea to the Governor to sign the bill. Mary McDowell, Lulu Holley, and I each made our pleas as well. The Governor signed the bill.

We felt sorry for two older women, matrons, who had been sent down by the Chicago Elevated Company to plead that the bill be vetoed. They had been told by the company that they would lose their jobs if the bill became a law.

As Mary McDowell, Lulu Holley, and I left the State House we saw these two old women trudging dejectedly back toward their train little realizing that they had been duped into protesting a law that would cut the drudgery of their twelve-hour-day, seven-day-week working routine. I am glad to say that they did not lose their jobs and that, much later, they secured an eight-hour working day through their own union.

A ten-hour working day for working women in Illniois may not now seem much for us to have gained. But even that much had been secured only by defeating for the moment the heaviest opposition. And even at that, all working women in the state had not been included under the bill. Exceptions, concessions, had had to be made to get a ten-hour-day bill through at all. Even the waitresses, who had fought so hard and so gallantly beside us, were not covered under the law. And, further, the law contained no limitation on weekly working hours. Under the law, an employer could work his women help a seventy-hour week! — a full ten-hour day for a full seven-day week! Our task was not finished in more ways than one.

Quickly the law was challenged. The Ritchie Box Company attacked again, carrying the attack again to the Illinois Supreme Court. A woman employee of that company was persuaded to petition the court for an injunction against the enforcement of the law, on the grounds, as she told the court, that she could not earn enough money to support herself if she were not allowed to work more than a ten-hour day. The law was upheld — and once again Illinois had taken a step forward in labor legislation. We took new heart in the fight for our cherished goal — a forty-hour week and an eight-hour day.

WE CONTINUE THE FIGHT

EXCEPT THAT it established the principle in the state of Illinois that the state could by statute secure a fair workday for women workers, we of the Women's Trade Union League were not at all satisfied with the Illinois Ten-Hour-Day Law of 1909. Consequently, the 1911 session of the Illinois Legislature found us again at Springfield.

The 1909 law had been worded to cover women employed "in any mechanical establishment, or factory, or laundry."

We were now asking that that law be amended to read:

"That no female shall be employed in any mechanical or mercantile establishment, or factory, or laundry, *or hotel, or restaurant, or telegraph or telephone establishment or office thereof, or in any place of amusement, or by any person or firm or corporation engaged in any express or transportation or public utility business, or by any common carrier, or in any public institution, incorporated or unincorporated in this State,* more than ten hours during any day."

We were also asking that the hours of work for women in any one week be limited to fifty-four.

And we were asking that each employer, under penalty of $25.00 for each omission, be directed to keep a time book showing for each day the hours worked by each female in his employ.

Senator Charles F. Hurburgh, supported by Senator Walter Clyde Jones, and Senator Frank W. Burton, introduced the bill in the senate on February 23, 1911, as Senate Bill No. 241. The bill was referred to the Committee on Labor, Mines and Mining, and the above three senators were appointed a subcommittee to redraft the bill. They argued that while the constitutionality of the daily hour-limit for women working in certain employments was established, the weekly hour-limit would bring up a different question for the courts to decide. We deferred to their advice, and the committee reported the bill back to the senate. The senate passed the bill in this new form on the 28th of April, and the bill went to the house.

In the house we knew we were again in for a rough fight. Representative Burnett M. Chiperfield was our sponsor in the house, and when he tried to call up the bill for its second reading it was finally necessary to get a roll-call vote for permission to do so.

The opposition we were meeting now represented not only

the manufacturers, but also the large merchants and the utility operators. Their next step, we knew, would be to try to amend the bill in such a manner as to destroy all its effectiveness. I was sitting in the gallery with Elizabeth Maloney and Mary McEnerney. With the bill about to come up for debate and possibly amendment, Mr. Chiperfield walked down the aisle beckoning to me to come down to the house floor. This was an unusual procedure. When I tried to get to the floor of the house, the doorkeeper stopped me, as was his right. He told me afterward that he thought I had lost my mind and was rushing in to try to save my bill. "Some fellows do that," said he, "when they see their bills being killed on the floor."

Mr. Chiperfield waved his hand to the house and announced that he hoped there would be no objection to my being seated on the floor at this moment, as he needed to confer with me during the coming consideration of the bill. No objection was made, and I went and sat next to him.

And now the battle was on! The opposition's first move was to make a motion that the bill be amended to read, "That no female be employed over ten hours in any one day *except for a 90-day period during each year.*"

What a law that would have made! Shades of the Christmas rush at the Five-and-Ten! This was the merchants' group and some others trying to put through exemptions for themselves. I whispered to Mr. Chiperfield, and he moved that the motion be tabled.

Our motion carried. The amendment was tabled.

The opposition's next move was to motion that SECTION 5, that part of the bill which would force the employer to keep a time book of hours worked by female employees, be deleted from the bill.

This would have made the bill unenforceable. I whispered

to Mr. Chiperfield, and he moved that this amendment be tabled also.

Our motion carried. The amendment was tabled. Section 5 remained in the bill.

The opposition's third move was to motion for an amendment cutting out the ten-hour day limitation and substituting instead a sixty-hour week limitation. Such a change would have taken the heart out of the bill and killed its whole purpose. I advised Mr. Chiperfield to move that this motion also be tabled.

Now there was confusion on the floor. Several representatives who were on our side came to me to ask me what to do. I was not confused. "Vote against the amendment!" I said.

A member who favored the proposed ninety-day amendment came to me to ask me to subscribe to this last amendment on the sixty-hour week. "No!" I told him indignantly.

Mr. Chiperfield was growing a little panicky and whispered to me:

"Unless you agree to some of these amendments, you'll lose your bill!"

"I am against any amendment to the bill!" firmly I declared.

Mr. Chiperfield moved that the motion before the house be tabled. His motion was *not* carried. The amendment was *not* tabled. The sixty-hour-week amendment stood. In this mutilated form our bill would now, upon its third reading, come up for a vote. And if it passed, gone would be the effectiveness of our ten-hour-day law.

I felt pretty wilted, but I held my head high as I tried to walk bravely from the floor of the house back to the gallery where Elizabeth Maloney and Mary McEnerney were waiting for me. They told me they had been afraid I would yield when they saw all the pressure being brought to bear upon me. We tried to figure out what to do.

While we sat talking, two men who had come to lobby for legislation for longer sheets in beds in hotels for travelling men came over to talk with us. They asked how our bill had fared in the senate. We told them the majority of the senate was on our side. "Then," said they, "bad as your bill now is, let it stand and pass. Then get the senate to refuse to concur to the house amendments and to ask the house to recede from these said amendments. The house will then go back and pass your original senate bill."

This looked like hopeful strategy. We went to talk it over with our senate friends.

In its mutilated form we allowed the bill to be voted on by the house. It passed. We were watching as the house clerk came out carrying our bill over to the senate in his basket. Elizabeth Maloney walked back of him all the way to the senate to see that our bill remained safe. She feared some member of the opposition might grab it from the basket.

The senate refused to concur in the house amendments, and once more our bill came back to the house. All during the house recess we went about explaining to house members the effects the amendments would have on our Women's Ten-Hour Law. It was nearly midnight, at the close of the session, when our bill was called up again. Representative William P. Holaday, a good friend of ours, put a motion to the house to recede from the amendments, and the matter came to a vote. As the roll was called, first fear, then anxiety, then exultation suffused us. Our bill had passed, and another step had been taken toward our goal!

9

Uprising of the Twenty Thousand

O N NOVEMBER 22, 1909, in New York City, the shirtwaist workers, unorganized, poured out of the factories by the thousands — a spontaneous protest against sweatshop conditions. This protest became known as "The Uprising of the Twenty Thousand." It was the largest strike of women up to this time. The discontent was chiefly against the workers' being forced to pay for straps for their machines, for power, and for needles.

The strike attracted nationwide attention and soon spread. A month later, December 20, a similar strike was declared in Philadelphia. The International Ladies' Garment Workers' Union, a small organization at that time, was thus faced with the problem of handling at the same time two general strikes involving thousands of unorganized workers. It had neither the staff nor the funds for such a task.

The Women's Trade Union League of New York gave valiant service to the strikers there, raising funds, picketing, organizing meetings, and bringing in the support of prominent New York women to the cause. Mrs. Robins, president of our National Women's Trade Union League at the time, was appealed to by Abe Rosenberg, president of the International Ladies' Garment Workers' Union, to help out in Philadelphia.

When Mrs. Robins telephoned me about this, I felt like a soldier being called to duty. It was hard to leave home with Christmas only five days away, but there was only one thing for me to say; I agreed to go.

We had to leave at once. As we rode to Philadelphia we made our plans. Mrs. Robins was to try to win financial assistance and public support, while I was to help in the necessary organization work. Mr. Rosenberg, who was in charge of the strike, expressed great relief at our arrival.

We were both invited to stay at the College Settlement, where Miss Anna Davis was head resident. It was a good arrangement, because we were free to come and go as we pleased, and we found friends at the settlement who proved sympathetic to the strike and helpful.

I was barely settled when a newspaperman came to me with a tale of how extravagantly Mr. Rosenberg was living, while the poor strikers were starving! I was aware of the tactics the reporter was trying to use to aid his paper in discrediting the strike. I knew that poor Mr. Rosenberg had to count his every penny. I gave the reporter the facts.

Mrs. Robins set about at once to arrange a downtown headquarters where the women pickets could go for at least hot coffee, for it soon was deep winter and bitter cold. While the National Women's Trade Union League was supposed to be financing our work, I knew that Mrs. Robins was going down into her own purse for many of these expenses. The headquarters proved a convenient place for the pickets to report and also for those who needed help.

One of my jobs was to go to the magistrate court every morning, because picket-line girls were being arrested every day. We had to be prepared with bail and also to hire an attorney where necessary and to follow the cases in court.

The courts were supposed to open at seven in the morning. They never did. However, we could not take any chance of being late for the hearings. At seven I was always there though it meant going without breakfast for I had to leave the settlement before breakfast was served.

The magistrate would go from one court to another, always due at the next within an hour. I had to follow him to each court. It was often ten o'clock or much later before I could return to the settlement for my breakfast, which would be waiting for me on a grill. After being out for two or three hours on a cold January morning, I would have a fine appetite!

A striker whom we knew only as Anna was brought in with other pickets one morning at one of the later hours of the court. Anna, who was always cheerful, smiled at the magistrate. He fined her for contempt, holding her for bail, charging her with laughing at him.

I hurried to telephone Mrs. Laurence Lewis, a well-known woman who belonged to one of the old families of Philadelphia. Mrs. Lewis had been our very good friend during the strike and had persuaded a group of young lawyers to volunteer their services in behalf of the girls brought into court.

When I told Mrs. Lewis I needed a bail that was quite high, she asked first whether I had had my breakfast. I said that I had not.

"You come right over to my home," said she, "and we can talk while you are having coffee. I will see about the bail!"

Mrs. Lewis lived in one of the lovely old houses on Pine Street, and inside there was a small table drawn up before a blazing log fire. On that table the loveliest breakfast was laid for me, including strawberries — in January!

While I ate, Mrs. Lewis telephoned to someone, returning in a moment to say she had secured the bail.

THE STRIKE continued all through January, and so did the daily arrest of the pickets. Even girls walking past the strike-bound shops were arrested and taken to jail.

The strikers wore small cardboard badges with the words, "We Strike for Justice." As I walked through town, crossing the square around the court house, the large sign, "JUSTICE," above the court house entrance seemed a mockery after my experience in the courts morning after morning.

Sometimes the girls were penalized with fines of five dollars and costs. But more often they faced sentences of "ten dollars or ten days in jail." With so many of our pickets being fined day after day, raising the money to pay these fines soon became a difficult job.

Also, when girls were arrested, it meant we had to get other girls to replace them on the picket line. Most of the arrests were made late in the afternoon, so that the girls could be put in jail overnight. They were being charged with "disorderly conduct." But these arrests, rather than discouraging the girls, as had been police intention, only made them more determined to picket and fight on. Also, when the facts became known, these arrests won public support for the girls. On the other hand, many of the newspapers supported the charges against the girls, who were mostly foreign-born, or of foreign-born parentage, with few friends in the community and known in their own neighborhoods disdainfully as "Strikers."

Since many of the girls were being charged with acts not committed, we decided to have as observers particularly well-known women of Philadelphia who would find out at first-hand what was really happening in the picket line and whose word would be taken in the courts. The officers of the Consumers League became interested in this and several dauntless women volunteered to aid us. Miss Frances Traveris Cochran, the daughter of one of the old and wealthy families of Philadelphia, came into our strike headquarters one afternoon to say that she wanted to go out with one of the pickets as an observer. That evening one of the strikers came and told me that Frances Cochran had been arrested. As everyone knew the young lady's reputation and status in the city, her arrest made quite a stir.

When this news reached the settlement house, Anna Young, a worker for the strikers, went to the police station to bail out Miss Cochran. The police sergeant, learning who the prisoner was, offered to release her at once. But Miss Cochran refused to leave unless the girl picket arrested with her was released also.

"We were both doing the same thing," said Miss Cochran. "We were walking up and down the street. Therefore we both should be treated alike."

Both were released. Miss Cochran continued to be an observer. She felt so strongly the injustice of these arrests that she bought a small house in order to have property in her own name to schedule for bail for girls arrested for picketing.

In the meantime word was given the police, "Be careful in all future arrests that no society ladies are picked up." After that, any unknown girl walking in the picket line was comparatively safe.

But not always. Martha Gruening, the daughter of a prominent physician, a New York girl who had been doing graduate work at Bryn Mawr College, exchanged her hat and coat one day with a picket-line girl and walked in the picket line with her. The two were promptly arrested and had to spend the night in Moyamensing Prison, the old city jail. When Miss Gruening, brought before the magistrate the next morning, gave her name and background and declared that she was not a striker, the magistrate was furious.

"I was at the factory only to see if arrests were made unjustly," replied Miss Gruening.

This made the magistrate more indignant than before.

"I charge you with inciting a riot and hold you for five hundred dollars bail!" he declared.

Then he charged: "It is the women of your class, not the actual strikers, who have stirred up all this strife. Had your kind kept out of this fight, it would have been over long ago!"

The girl arrested with Miss Gruening was held for two hundred dollars bail.

The arrest of Miss Cochran and then of Miss Gruening brought us much public support. Public meetings were held protesting the arrest of the strikers, and a delegation of prominent Philadelphia women visited the city officials to protest the "disorderly conduct" charges and other unjust procedures.

All during this time, in addition to my other work, I was visiting the homes of American-born girls who had worked at the factory and who had refused to go out on strike. The foreign-born girls were making the fight alone. The girls I visited were very bitter. They blamed the "foreigners" for existing conditions in the sewing industry, claiming that the foreign-born girls had lowered the working conditions. I tried to make them understand that it was because they were unorganized, with none to uphold standards, that these sweatshop conditions prevailed. They were difficult to convince at that time, however, and they informed me that their employers would not hire any "foreigners" again after the strike was over.

"True," I told them. "They will want to hire girls who will not stand up for their rights!"

The strike seemed to be becoming hopeless as time dragged on and January was nearly over. Mrs. Robins and I were due back in Chicago, but we couldn't leave because the "other side" would then accuse us of deserting the strikers.

One cold night as we sat around the fireplace at the settlement house, we were wondering what could be done. No strike settlement seemed in sight. I reminded the group that it is always darkest before the dawn. The very next day a settlement was proposed and negotiated. I helped in the negotiations, which gave the Philadelphia garment workers the identical arrangements we had achieved in our glove factory. The strikers hailed it as a great victory. They now would have a fifty-two-and-a-half-hour week. There would be no more charging for power, for machine straps, or for needles. The strikers would go back to work with wages adjusted. A board of arbitrators would be set up to settle other differences upon which the manufacturers and the union could not at once agree.

Everyone interested in the final negotiations was present, even the girls who had refused to join in the strike. Mrs. Robins and I both made speeches, and so did some of the other women who had helped us. Isadore Dornblum, the leader of the pickets, had been forbidden by the police to speak, but his speech was read by Max Kazimiercki, one of his co-workers.

When Mrs. Robins and I came onto the platform, and after each of us had spoken, there was wild cheering and hand-clapping lasting fully five minutes. We considered it a meeting long to be remembered.

The groups in the sewing industry now had some base to build upon. They built well, because since that time the Philadelphia locals have become well-established unions. The girls who had refused to strike finally joined the union, and when I visited Philadelphia in later years I found that every one of them had become a good union member.

Mrs. Robins and I arrived back in Chicago in time to attend our Sunday afternoon Women's Trade Union League meeting and to tell the story of the strike to our league women who had been following the strike's progress in the newspapers. We were welcomed with rousing acclaim. For the first time in my life I had missed Christmas at home, but I felt that I had been amply compensated.

10

Women Workers in the Breweries

EARLY in 1910 the need of exposing working conditions of the women in the Milwaukee breweries was brought to the attention of our Women's Trade Union League.

Mother Jones, the idol of the mine workers, who had gone through so many strikes with them, had pioneered in making a study of the breweries. While everything she reported was true, we feared that her report, since it came from just a single individual, might be considered exaggerated. Mrs. Robins appointed Emma Steghagen, Alice Henry, and me to make an investigation.

We spent much time going through the breweries, visiting the girls at their homes, and interviewing them about their working conditions. Here was an industry where the men were well organized but where we found women working full time in the winter months for an average of two-and-a-half to three dollars a week. The same rate was paid regardless of the length of time they had worked there.

The Brewery Workers' Union was concerned about these women and wanted them organized. But whenever one of the women showed any activity toward joining a union, the management discharged her.

There were comparatively few women working in the industry, perhaps four hundred. But we deplored the conditions under which they were forced to work, and in our report we strongly urged that all efforts be made to organize them. Our report was published in the national publication of the Brewery Workers' Union.

In the washing room, where bottles were washed, the women wore wooden shoes and stood on planks. But still with the splashing of water and the sweep of their wet skirts against their ankles, it was impossible for them to keep dry. Their hands were constantly in water. This damp atmosphere resulted in rheumatism for them and was the chief grievance of the women in this department.

The washers had to work at the pace of the conveyor which carried the bottles in front of them. They had to clip the wires and then finish off with tinfoil. Each bottle had to be inspected in front of glaring electric light bulbs, which was a great strain upon the eyes.

And all this for two-and-a-half to three dollars a week!

We made many trips to Milwaukee to assist in the organization work among these women. The forelady of one of the larger breweries tried to keep the girls from joining the union, and twenty-seven girls were discharged because they had joined. But we continued the work. Finally, when a strike was threatened, the brewers came to an agreement with the union. Improvements have now gradually changed processes and working conditions for the women in this industry. The employment of women in breweries has now fallen off considerably, but every woman working there now belongs to the union and receives equal pay with the men workers for equal work.

PROGRESS had been slow, but through its aid in helping women working in such industries as the meat-packing industry, the brewery industry, and the garment-making industry, the Women's Trade Union League had become an important movement within the A. F. of L.

Back in 1906 when Mary McDowell and I had gone to the Illinois State Federation of Labor convention at Streator, Illinois, we had been the only representatives of women in industry there. Later, at these conventions, a morning session was set aside for the Women's Trade Union League program. Mrs. Robins had presided on these occasions, but our delegation was still so small that we all sat on the platform. We had managed, however, to bring before the labor men the needs of women in industry. By 1913 they were saying that "Agnes Nestor, Elizabeth Maloney, and Emma Steghagen can stir up more enthusiasm when they have charge of a meeting than half a dozen men." Two years more, and the new officers of the A. F. of L. felt that the women delegates had so increased in attendance and had become so much a part of the conventions that there was no further need for separate sessions.

Meanwhile, because of the great amount of work which I felt needed to be done, I felt impelled to take up the pen again in a campaign to get more members for our Women's Trade Union League. The *Union Labor Advocate* published my paper urging every working woman to join a union.

WHY A WORKING GIRL SHOULD JOIN A UNION

Second paper by Miss Agnes Nestor, President Glove Operators' Union, No. 18, and Third Vice-President of the International Glove Workers' Union

Girls have entered the industrial world, so it is also necessary that they should enter the great Trade-Union movement. Yes, girls have entered the unions, although slow they have been to come to the decision; and they did not organize until forced into it by conditions.

But now that they are in the Trade Unions, they have found that they can do a great deal to uplift themselves as working girls. There is no reason why they should not have something to say as to what wages they should receive and under what conditions they should work. It is simply a business proposition. The old term used by the employers was that the manufacturer would run his own business, and he did not consider that we, the workers, form quite an important part of that business.

We all know that the wages of girls in general are far below what they ought to be, and still in view of this fact there seems to be a tendency to continue reducing them. Girls are working longer hours than they should, and the conditions under which they are working need many improvements. But how are these things to be remedied and reductions resisted. Only in one way, and that is through the united effort of the workers in their unions.

As individuals we can do little, that we all know. Imagine a girl going to a foreman to protest against working conditions—a cut in wages or some other grievance! Why! she simply would be told that if she did not like it, she knew what she could do, which would be, of course, quit. One girl the factory could lose. But if the same protest came from 300 or 400 girls, that would be a different matter, a matter to be considered; and I daresay demands would be more apt to be granted.

The Glove Workers have found that, as a rule, we cannot get our demands unless in a position to enforce them. Before we were organized, the question of asking for higher wages was not heard of among our girls. We did not dare think of such a thing. The one question which was repeated day after day was: Can we keep up the prices we are getting? As our work is all piece-work, that was very hard to do. Men do the same class of work that a great many of our girls do, and all receive the same price per piece. It was not until after we were organized that we were told that the work had been given to the girls in order to have it done more cheaply, and that it had been intended to pay us the old prices only until we had learned the work, to encourage us. But, happily for us, the Glove-Operators' Union came into existence just in time to save our old prices.

Girls should receive the same wages as men for the same work performed, and this is one of the strong principles we stand for. We do not want to crowd the men out of positions; we want to protect their wages as well as our own.

A Trade Union tends to educate the working girl. The girls gather at their regular meetings, discuss the many questions which arise, learn to conduct meetings, learn to debate and to vote intelligently on important matters, and to fill the various offices. After they have attended meetings and served on committees, the girls begin to feel as though they are waking up, and that there is a great deal to be learned through their organizations. The educational side of Trade-Unionism, if nothing else, should be a strong reason for a working girl's belonging to a union. And surely we need all the education we can get.

But there is still another side to Trade-Unionism—the social side. Life should not be all business and work; we want a little pleasure. There is no way in which we can all meet for a good, social time if not through organization. Many a poor girl is lonely in a new place to work; but when she joins her Trade Union the girls are all ready to help her and stand by to be her friends.

There are so many benefits to be derived from the Trade Unions that summing it all up we must acknowledge it a great movement for the working girl. The girl who belongs to a union surely has more in life to look forward to! The girls' unions are proving very successful, and we hope soon to have all women who are working join our ranks.

11

The League in Politics and Pulpit

"THE BALLOT is the power of effective protest in modern civilization," Mrs. Robins had declared in one of her Chicago speeches.

With characteristic enthusiasm and vision, she enlisted the interest of those around her, and I became a member of the delegation on the Suffrage Special going to Springfield for the Suffrage Session.

As arranged, the train stopped at various towns en route, and the various delegates spoke to groups at the stations. Because it was an industrial town, I was selected to speak at Joliet.

At Springfield I met Caroline Hunt, editor of the "Women's Section" of *La Follette's Weekly,* and she told me during one of the sessions that she could not work in the noisy hotel where she was staying. Fortunately, Mrs. Lee, at whose house I was a guest, had told me that I might bring in another friend. I extended the invitation to Caroline Hunt.

The George E. Lees were most hospitable. Mrs. Lee said that the only thing that justified their having a large house was taking care of folk like us. In the days of our fight for the Women's Ten-Hour-Day Law, this kindness had helped us to stretch our meager funds, and it was always most comforting after a discouraging day at the State House to go to our friends, the Lees, and talk things over.

The Lee home was a center for liberals, and there I met many interesting people. Vachel Lindsay was one of these. The Lees had encouraged him since his earliest writing days.

Willis J. Spaulding, Mrs. Lee's brother, was a crusader for good government in Springfield. City commissioner for thirty years or more, he fought for the right of the city to own its own electric plant. It was a fight which led all the way to the U. S. Supreme Court. He won, with Justice Holmes writing the decision. I asked Mr. Spaulding what this plant had meant to the people of Springfield.

"It brought within the reach of the common man," said he, "many comforts and advantages formerly enjoyed only by the well-to-do; and, incidentally, it blazed the trail for similar city-owned electric plants throughout the country."

During the years when we were going down to Springfield to promote bills dealing with the employment of women, we followed Willis J. Spaulding's struggles for the city-owned electric plant. We saw bill after bill brought into the legislature which would prohibit cities from owning electric plants; but always we saw, too, the labor group on hand to support Mr. Spaulding. It was what one might expect in Abraham Lincoln's old home city.

BACK IN THAT TIME, around 1910, there was a movement to invite labor representatives to take the pulpits in churches on what was known as Labor Sunday, the day before Labor Day. I had that experience on two occasions — first at Jenkin Lloyd Jones' Church at Lincoln Center in Chicago, and the next year at the Congregational Church of Winnetka. The newspapers described me as "a militant labor leader preaching to a millionaire congregation. One headline ran: "GIRL

LABOR LEADER OCCUPIES PULPIT." A reporter covering one of these occasions was heard to ask where "the Rev.
Nestor" was to speak.

The celebration of Labor Sunday was a good custom. It
brought a labor message direct to groups not usually reached.
In those days we did not talk about "public relations," but
many things were done in those days which might be included
under that phrase. Labor leaders occupying pulpits on Labor
Sunday was certainly one of these.

My Winnetka appearance was written up in the *Chicago
Record-Herald* like this:

In Factory Girl's Plea
Piecework Is Scored

Agnes Nestor of Glove Workers' Union
Urges Better Working Conditions
in Address at Winnetka Church

Better working conditions for the factory girl was the plea of
Miss Agnes Nestor of the Glove Workers' Union in the Congregational Church in Winnetka yesterday. The piece-work system
and the pace-maker were scored by Miss Nestor as being responsible for sapping the vitality of the woman worker and producing
a race of anaemic women, which she said would prove a real
menace to society unless laws are enacted to protect them.

"You are so far removed from the life of the factory girl that
you cannot understand the view she takes of life," said Miss
Nestor to her audience.

"The incessant, monotonous grind of the factory takes the
life and vitality out of her in three or four years. Where the
piece-work system prevails, a strong girl coming in from the
country thinks at first she can make big wages and she works at
top speed throughout the day. It takes her some time to realize

that she is not only killing herself but others in the same factory.

"If she turns out much above the average output of the others, the prices will be adjusted and she will find that her wages are reduced. She gradually gets into that frame of mind where she says, 'What's the use?' and becomes embittered and loses hope.

"The piece-work system ought to be abolished, and the trade unions are doing what they can to wipe it out. We have been too long unmindful of the needs of the working women. Though there has been a ten-hour law in force in Massachusetts for sixty years, it was only last year that we succeeded in getting one in Illinois, and then the manufacturers did their best to have it declared unconstitutional.

"In nearly every State the men workers have an eight-hour day. Surely if eight hours is long enough for a man to work it should be long enough for a woman. Employers, however, accept the eight-hour working day for men and think it is all right for their women to work ten or twelve hours a day. We must have legislation to protect the women workers from the unscrupulous employer, and public opinion has been slow to come to our aid."

When Miss Nestor finished speaking, one of the members of the congregation passed her a slip from the —————— Laundry stating that on account of the ten-hour law it would be necessary to work on Labor Day.

"That's just the way with some employers," said Miss Nestor. "They are prohibited from working their women more than ten hours a day, and because of that law they will deprive them of the holiday that is recognized the country over."

ANDREW FURUSETH

THAT FALL OF 1911, Mrs. Robins and I attended the A. F. of L. convention in Atlanta, Georgia. As a delegate from the International Glove Workers Union, I was an independent voter. There were certain voting alignments then, and as I was going into the meeting I passed delegates checking a roll call. The vote to come up that day was on the amalgamation of certain organizations. I asked the checkers how they had checked on me. One replied:

"We just didn't know how you would vote, so you are not checked."

I sat near Andrew Furuseth, president of the International Seamen's Union, and we voted alike on a certain issue. Furuseth said to me, "You will convert me to woman suffrage yet." He was opposed to women voting.

In spite of his queer ways, Furuseth was one of the most interesting figures at those early conventions. When the convention photograph was taken, he turned his back saying that he would not have his picture taken until the seamen were free. Mrs. Robins used to plead with him to change his mind, telling him how much it would mean to the workers.

Furuseth had a wonderful face, all the lines showing the hard life of the seaman. A tall, angular Norwegian, he had a sailor's gait as he swung into the hall, his head high. I used to think, "What a fine subject for a sculptor!"

Furuseth was photographed for the first time in 1915 when the Seamen's Bill passed. His picture appeared on the cover of *La Follette's Weekly*. The senior La Follette had been the sponsor of the Seamen's Bill.

Charles R. Crane engaged the noted sculptor, Ivan Mestrovic, to make a life-size bronze of Furuseth. Jo Davidson, the American sculptor, also made a bust of Furuseth. After Furuseth's death, the Mestrovic bust was presented to William Green, who placed it in the A. F. of L. Building. Jo Davidson presented his to the U. S. Department of Labor. When the Labor Building was dedicated, Frances Perkins, then Secretary of

Labor, placed it suitably in the building.

Andrew Furuseth lived a simple life, spending his last days at the Old National Hotel in Washington until friends moved him to a more comfortable place. He typified labor in its long struggle.

AFTER THE ATLANTA CONVENTION OF 1911, I returned home Thanksgiving week to find my dear mother very ill. A Grand Rapids friend, Margaret Mulligan, was our guest, and Mother rallied and went through the holidays in good spirits. But by the end of the week she became worse and died on the following Friday. Her illness was so short that at first we could not realize that she was gone from us. It seemed as though we could not go on living without her. This was the first break in our family. Everyone was very kind to us in our bereavement.

Arthur came home and stayed with us as long as his work would allow. We were happy to remember that that spring Mother had visited her old friends in Troy and Cohoes. That visit had brought her such joy that she never tired of talking of it.

Three years later, her brother Charles died, and that brought to an end the little Tribes Hill family.

12

Fifty Thousand Refuse to Sew

I WAS just settling down to accumulated desk work, when the Women's Trade Union League became involved in a strike in the Chicago men's clothing industry.

The strike began at the Hart, Schaffner and Marx Company and quickly spread to all the other clothing plants. It was a strike in another unorganized industry. Accumulated grievances had brought it on — wages reduced systematically a few cents at a time, sweatshop procedures, tyranny of foremen, unjust fines such as a sixty-cents fine imposed for a lost spool whether filled or empty.

The garment workers' union, the United Garment Workers of America, was not equipped to meet the needs of the strikers, so we of various organizations came forth to lend assistance. A joint committee was set up. It represented the United Garment Workers Union, the unorganized strikers, the Chicago Federation of Labor, the Women's Trade Union League.

The garment industry was located on the North and Northwest Sides of Chicago. The strikers met in convenient halls in these areas, the chief meeting place being Hod Carriers' Hall where Sidney Hillman had headquarters.

Our organization opened an office in the old Open Board of Trade Building at 275 South La Salle Street. The Open

Board of Trade Building was so called on account of the open balconies outside the offices and overlooking the large open space in the center of the building. In this open space the strikers congregated for their informal meetings.

Food and fuel had to be provided for the strikers and their families. From our office, commissaries for the distribution of food were organized. Corps of workers, mostly volunteers, gave valuable service all during the long strike. I was on the committee for the meal tickets and helped to work out a system whereby we distributed the tickets through the shop chairmen. Through arrangements with our financial committee, certain restaurants honored these meal tickets. Mrs. Robins was treasurer of our financial department, and she managed to find the necessary money by interesting many groups in the problem. Collections were taken at women's clubs, at suffrage organizations, at churches, at settlement houses. Unions assessed their members. Funds were solicited in shops.

Serving on the ticket committee brought me in personal contact with the striking shop leaders. They came by at the end of the day when their own meetings were over. By the time everyone had been taken care of, it was usually very late, so that all during the long strike of that winter of 1910-1911 I seldom went home to dinner, or, in fact, stopped for an evening meal. In addition to the distribution of meal tickets, there were a hundred other details to be taken care of. Shop chairmen would call asking for speakers for their meetings, and invariably each caller would demand "a good speaker." Cheerfully I would assure each caller that we would supply the speaker, even though I knew that I would probably have to fill in, because it was impossible to find enough speakers every day. Emmet Flood, an A. F. of L. organizer, and I became a regular team, travelling often from one meeting to another. If I did not know all the meeting halls in Chicago, I learned where they were during that strike.

A settlement offer which Mr. Thomas Rickert, president of the United Garment Workers Union, had secured back in November when the strike had first begun, was presented once more to the garment cutters. It was what we considered a good offer. But the garment cutters had voted it down when first it had been presented to them. They voted it down again.

Meanwhile the rumor of a compromise proposal spread around to the various halls, and excitement grew. Strikers began to flock to the headquarters in no mood to consider any settlement which did not give them all their demands. It became our difficult task to quiet them.

Another settlement offer came from the negotiating committee. It was printed in several languages and distributed to all the meeting halls. Time was given for its study, but this only resulted in an organized movement to defeat its acceptance. One provision in the settlement offer particularly bothered. It was that all employees would be taken back, *except those guilty of doing violence during the strike*. The delegates from the strikers argued that fake charges would be trumped up.

We tried to point out that an arbitration board had been set up as a protection against false accusations. But the strikers' delegates continued to be suspicious of the hated clause.

After a while a proposal came from the Mayor's Committee, and our Joint Strike Committee decided to send the strikers to their various meeting halls so that all groups could consider the new proposal simultaneously.

Soon we found that something was holding up the vote at a Northwest-Side meeting place. I went there and spent the whole afternoon trying to convince the delegates that they should vote on this new proposal. "Closed shop! We want closed shop!" they shouted back at me. Again I pleaded for a vote and finally got them to ballot.

The next morning Emmet Flood and I went to Hod Carriers' Hall where we expected the Big Fight. There was a large foreign-born element, mostly Polish, in the group meeting here, and it was difficult to make them understand that we were all working for their good. It made me feel more than ever the need for educating these people so deprived of it.

Our Joint Strike Committee was guarding the ballot box, and I was on the platform speaking to the delegates in the lower hall, when I heard a commotion upstairs. "It's all off! The Polish delegation is not going to vote!" someone came down announcing. The Poles had organized the fight against any settlement which did not include "closed shop."

John Fitzpatrick was talking to the delegates, when in came a strange procession. The Polish leader, a young clergyman from the Independent Polish Church, was being brought in on the shoulders of his group, all of whom were shouting, "No vote! No vote!" I learned later that this leader had made his delegates pledge, as he raised his cross, that they would not agree to any proposal which did not include "closed shop." Bedlam broke loose as the procession filed in, and the meeting had to be adjourned.

Bessie Abramovitz (later to become Mrs. Sidney Hillman) came to us saying, "Come over to my pants-makers' group on Halsted Street. They will listen to you. You can get a vote there all right!"

Mrs. Robins, John Fitzpatrick, and the rest of our group went to Halsted Street with the ballot box. We found old men, many of them with patriarchal long beards, seated patiently in the meeting hall waiting peacefully for our committee.

John Fitzpatrick advanced to the front of the hall and was

speaking to this attentive audience when a loud knocking was heard at the door. When the door was opened, in rushed the Polish delegation shouting, "No vote! No vote!"

Fitzpatrick stopped speaking and held up his hand for silence. "Just be quiet, brothers!" he pleaded. Then he said, "There will be no vote!"

I took the ballot box and our group marched from the hall. We conferred as we walked up Halsted Street. There seemed no use in trying any further to get the proposal accepted. We decided to report to the City Council Committee that the proposal sent in by the Mayor's Committee was defeated without a formal vote or balloting — but defeated!

Time dragged on. The strikers began asking when another proposal would be forthcoming. It was getting late into the winter, January. At the office we too began asking ourselves, How long will it last? How long can we keep the strikers and their families fed? How long will our funds hold out? From the beginning we had promised there would be no "hunger bargain." That we would avoid! The strikers, though uneasy, were standing solidly together. But the problem of feeding them all and their needy families was vexing our committee on La Salle Street.

SUNDAY AFTERNOON, January 11, had been set for a great mass meeting at Hod Carriers' Hall. The United Garment Workers Union decided to negotiate the settlement agreement which had been recommended by the Joint Strike Committee. At the mass meeting the terms of the agreement were to be explained to all the strikers and after a vote the strikers were supposed to return to work the following Monday morning.

Emmet Flood and the rest of our committee were on the

platform as the meeting began. I was the first speaker. The audience listened attentively. When I finished talking, there was applause from one part of the hall but strange silence in other sections. Emmet Flood had started to address the meeting, when suddenly the officials of the United Garment Workers Union came in. At once there broke out a horrible demonstration of dissatisfaction directed toward these officials who had been responsible for the negotiations. Emmet Flood could no longer be heard above the booing and jeering. Others of our committee rose to try to quell the disturbance, but each in turn was shouted down. Emmet Flood suggested to me that I try to see what I could do, since they had always listened when I spoke. But no one could now get a hearing. The meeting had turned into a riot. Someone called the police. When the police squad came, there was no further disturbance. As we left the hall, we gave instructions that everyone was to go back to work the next morning.

Thus ended the fourteen weeks' strike. Most of the strikers seemed happy to go back to work. But the "foreign" group, which had raised the disturbance at the last meeting, tried to argue that all the strikers were opposed to the settlement.

The settlement covered only the Hart, Schaffner and Marx shop, with about eight thousand workers. The other strikers, controlled by the "Association," held out until February 3. They were the "dissenters." They remained unorganized for many years.

The strikers went back, but even at the Hart, Schaffner and Marx shop all was not well. The question of wages was still to be arbitrated. There was quibbling over the language of the agreement. The company refused to recognize the union.

Arbitrators had been chosen, with Clarence Darrow representing the union and Carl Meyer the company. But there was no meeting of the strikers with the company, or with the foremen, through whom most of the difficulties in the shops arise. The "arbitration" bogged down.

Finally the company asked our office to send over Sidney Hillman, then president of the United Garment Workers of America, Chicago Local No. 39. The company was now seeking practical ways of dealing with the difficulties. At last the company was willing to recognize that the union was the proper medium through which to deal. "Hereafter," the head of the company said to Sidney Hillman, "when there is anything wrong, just come in and settle it with us." Gradually, more and more, the company's recognition of the union was gained. Some years later, Hart, Schaffner and Marx helped our Women's Trade Union League to settle a strike, urging recognition of union preferments, union-shop arbitration boards, committees on grievances, and adjustment and wage boards. In the intervening years, the Hart, Schaffner and Marx union agreements have become models for those of many other industries.

After this arbitration case, Clarence Darrow, who had a large law practice, found that he could not continue to serve with us. He selected William O. Thompson, his law partner, a man of considerable means, to take his place. Mr. Thompson became so interested in the work that he gave almost all his time to it. He remained a friend of the garment workers during all the rest of his life.

One day Mr. Thompson asked me to come to his office to meet with him and Sidney Hillman. When we were seated, he said to me:

"I want you to tell Sidney how you make agreements and negotiate them."

Mr. Thompson knew of my long experience in negotiating

agreements for the glove workers where I dealt with the largest employers in our industry. I began to relate our procedure and to give Sidney what advice I could.

Mr. Thompson then said: "Sidney, you ought to see a good deal of Agnes Nestor. She can help you."

It is amusing now to remember that I gave Sidney Hillman his first lesson in collective bargaining.

FOLLOWING THE BIG STRIKE, our Women's Trade Union League put in Bessie Abramovitz as an organizer for the United Garment Workers Union. Bessie had played a leading part throughout the strike. A happy element in her nature allowed her always to see the funny side of things, and she was a joy to work with. We became close friends and this friendship lasted throughout the years. I will always remember the day she came into my office with Sidney Hillman to announce to us that they were engaged. We were all happy about it. They left Chicago, and a few years later Bessie returned to be a special guest at a convention of the United Garment Workers Union. A dinner in her honor was arranged by the committee for the convention. She was queen of the evening, with her husband sitting beside her beaming with pride. Bessie said at that time that she had just revisited the various garment shops in Chicago and that the improvement in conditions was almost unbelievable. As one of the many examples of previous hardships, she mentioned that the girls in her department had used to take home from two to three hundred needles to thread at night, in order that this work might not delay them during the working day.

Mary Anderson was another organizer from the Women's Trade Union League who worked among the garment workers. She was a human dynamo, and under her guidance the garment workers' union organization grew steadily.

Following the strike, the number of grievances unsettled multiplied. One day, about a year after the strike, Mrs. Robins called our group together to meet with a representative of the U. S. Department of Labor to work out machinery for setting up a local Trade Board to handle many of these grievances. This board became a pattern for other similar set-ups throughout the clothing industry. Dr. James Mullenbach, the distinguished social worker and churchman, was selected chairman of this Trade Board, and the credit for working it out in practice belongs to him more than to anyone else. He had a broad human understanding of all groups involved. He was tolerant, thoughtful, and kindly in all his negotiations. He had a deep appreciation of the realities of life. I remember one time in later years he was invited into one of our glove centers to mediate a strike situation. When he met the committee of the strikers, the first thing he asked them, even before any discussion had begun, was, "Are you people eating?"

13

1913, Busy Year of
Failures and Successes

B EWARE of the Lady Agitator!" an editorial in a Berlin, Wisconsin, newspaper greeted my appearance in that small community where I had gone to organize glove workers. Accused of stirring up strife in a peaceful town, I knew that it would be useless to remain. I took the train for Grinnell, Iowa, feeling discouraged and expecting the same treatment.

I had put in a long-distance call to Mary McDowell asking her if she knew anyone in Grinnell who might be helpful. She told me to see Professor Edward A. Steiner at Grinnell College, that he was interested in the problems of the foreign-born, and that he had worked on one of our committees for the protection of immigrants.

Professor Steiner invited me to speak at the chapel services at the college.

This started me off with dignity, for, since I had been allowed to address the students, I would be considered safe and not a lady agitator.

I began my organization work in Grinnell, but all was not well. One day an employer, passing me on the street, stopped me with the warning that I would not get any of his workers to join a union. I did, however, get one good meeting with a large attendance. We planned a second meeting, but only a handful attended. They reported that the employers had called a meeting in their shop and had warned the workers that if they organized, the plant would be moved to another town.

In recent years our International Glove Workers Union did organize these glove workers and secured for them agreements with the company. A few years later the factory was moved to the South.

THE YEAR 1913 was full of organization work and defeats. Late in the fall of 1912, the National Women's Trade Union League had encouraged me to go into the field to do some special organization work among the Fulton County glove workers. The A. F. of L. offered to supply the necessary funds, for, since the disastrous strike of 1903-04, the Fulton County glove workers' unconcern about firm organization had been a source of anxiety to the A. F. of L.

I had been to Gloversville in 1911, at the invitation of Walter Rhode, an officer of the Gloversville Glove Workers' Union, at the time an independent union. Rhode thought it a good time to try to bring the Gloversville union back into the International Glove Workers Union. This we succeeded in doing.

But this Gloversville Glove Workers Union represented only a portion of the glove workers of the area. In Gloversville nationality grouping was very strong, as that had been one form of organization in the old International Table Cutters' Union. The English table-cutters still remained aloof; so I asked the A. F. of L. to send Israel Solon, one of our most persuasive organizers, to work with them. Solon got some members of each nationality elected as officers of the Gloversville union, and in this way succeeded in getting many of the

English table-cutters back into the International Glove Workers Union.

But to organize again the women glove workers of Fulton County proved a difficult task. They were still bitter with memories of the old strike of 1903. Some progress was made, but Fulton County remained a "trouble spot."

MEANWHILE, back in Chicago, politics was engrossing much of the energies of our National Women's Trade Union League. The year 1912, an election year, had seen the rise of a new national party, the Progressives, whose national convention was meeting in Chicago. Raymond Robins was heading a group at this convention, and he and his group were standing for a platform which included the eight-hour day for women workers, protection for working children, one day's rest in seven, a minimum wage and the elimination of night work for women — all of which proposals our National Women's Trade Union League had been working for for years.

I was asked to serve with Jane Addams as one of the two league delegates to this convention. But, while I agreed with the platform which was being proposed for the Progressive Party, I felt that that party's real interest lay in the fight against "bossism," the issue over which the Progressives had broken away from the Republican Party. I was not so sure the Progressives would protest against industrial conditions, or of what kind of a fight their candidate would make in behalf of women in industry. The Progressive candidate heading their Illinois state ticket had not voted for our Women's Ten-Hour Bill in the Illinois senate. I could not bring myself to join the Progressive Party, and I forfeited being a delegate to the convention. In my place, Mary Wilmarth was elected to serve with Jane Addams.

Though the Progressives lost the Presidential election, in the state of Illinois the party elected twenty-nine state congressmen. A senator of the party proceeded to introduce a bill for every plank of the party platform. One of these bills sought a minimum-wage law for employed women. Another sought an eight-hour-workday law for women. We of the Women's Trade Union League helped to draft these bills.

Barratt O'Hara had been elected Lieutenant Governor. Aggressive and fearless, though unknown politically, at the opening of the legislative session, O'Hara got a resolution passed creating what was called the Vice Commission for the study of the white-slave traffic in Illinois. O'Hara was made chairman of the commission. In the course of its work, the commission held hearings concerning the wages paid to employed women, and several employers were called in to testify. Most of these employers called in were from department stores and mail-order houses. They paid such low wages to the women workers, and O'Hara pointed this up so strongly, that the commission soon became known as "the O'Hara Commission sponsoring minimum wages for women."

With public interest thus aroused over the low wages paid to clerks, it seemed to us a good time to try to organize the retail clerks in Chicago's State Street stores. We held meetings at which we had as speakers such prominent Chicago women as Mrs. Joseph T. Bowen and Mrs. Medill McCormick. On one occasion, although she was ill Mrs. McCormick insisted upon making a scheduled speech. Just as she began speaking, she fainted; and this made the front pages of the Chicago newspapers. Mrs. McCormick was embarrassed over the incident, but she said that since the incident brought before the public the cause for which we were working, the embarrassment she had suffered could easily be borne.

It was the "spy" system which kept us from making any great headway in organizing the clerks. Spotters were sent to our meeting by the employers to find out what clerks were joining the unions. One of these spotters even tried to get herself elected secretary of one of the newly-formed unions so as the better to find out the names of the clerks who sought to belong. Clerks who joined the unions were fired by their employers, and, more serious still, black-listed on State Street. The organization of the clerks, we saw, would have to wait for a happier time.

IN 1913, our National Women's Trade Union League held its biennial convention in St. Louis, and, headed by Julia O'Connor of Boston, representatives of the Telephone Operators' Union, recently organized, attended the conventions for the first time. Despite setbacks in various fields, we were all full of youthful enthusiasm, and the future looked bright. At that convention Mrs. Robins recommended the formation of a training school for women organizers. Our league was ten years old. We had come a long way. It was time now to pass on some of what we had learned to other field workers and to give them a definite training for the work they would seek to do.

Meanwhile, in that year of 1913, there was work for us at Springfield, for it was a legislative year. Back to Springfield once more went Elizabeth Maloney, Mary Anderson and I, this time to work for the eight-hour-day bill and the minimum-wage bill for women.

It soon became evident that neither of these bills could be passed at this session. But worse still, we were called upon to fight a threat to our Ten-Hour-Day Law. This threat was in the form of the "Bailey Bill," which was an attempt to exempt women in the canneries from the protection of the ten-hour-day limitation. We went strenuously to work. If we could not strengthen our ten-hour law, we were determined that it should not be weakened. Despite all our efforts, in the last-minute confusion of the early hours of the morning of the last session, this bill was passed by the senate. We sat in the gallery sick at heart. But we were not through with the fight. Amy Walker and I worked up our case against the bill and went to see the Governor. We felt we had a good case. We presented it as best we knew how. In a few days the Governor wired us that he had vetoed the bill.

Though we had not gained any new ground in our struggle for the eight-hour day, that session of the legislature had not been a complete failure. At that session we had seen passed the Woman Suffrage Bill giving women the right to vote in municipal election. This meant women could vote for aldermen and judges. It was a right which women in one district exercised a little later on one occasion with a vengeance.

ALSO IN THAT YEAR OF 1913, Mr. A. A. McCormick, then president of the Cook County Board of Commissioners, asked the officers of our Women's Trade Union League to meet with him to discuss the conditions under which women were working at the Cook County Hospital. He said he had always been impressed at budget time to find men from the organized trades at the meetings, but that the women at the hospital had no one to speak for them. He appointed Anna E. Nicholes a member of the Cook County Civil Service Commission, and he appointed Mary Anderson and me members of a special commission to investigate the working conditions of the hospital's women employees. We were given free rein to go through the great institution interviewing the nurses, laundresses, janitresses, kitchen help, and all other women employed

there. Our report recommended many improvements in work-
ing conditions, increases in pay, and an eight-hour day. Mr.
McCormick approved our report and submitted it to the Cook
County Board of Commissioners and it was adopted.

We also organized the women workers in the hospital so
that at budget time they would have representatives to present
their needs.

The working conditions we found at the Cook County Hospital suggested that the working conditions at other state institutions would bear looking into. Many such institutions were
in small towns where young men and women found few employment opportunities open to them. Wages at such institutions were consequently pitifully low. One woman at Dunning,
after twenty-six years of work, had reached the top salary
bracket of thirty dollars a month! We found nurses who were
earning only thirty-five to forty dollars a month. The average
salary of women employees was twenty dollars a month.

The Illinois State Federation of Labor gave our Women's
Trade Union League two hundred dollars for organization
work among these employees. Using this fund, and assisted by
Emmet Flood, the great A. F. of L. organizer, we travelled
through the state organizing as we went. We secured for these
employees a minimum wage of thirty dollars a month, one day's
rest in seven, pay for time lost through illness due to duress
of employment, and finally an eight-hour day in all state institutions. It was the beginning of working standards in Illinois
state institutions.

At Marion, Illinois, I visited a union of glove workers and
learned that a little town near by called Anna had a glove
factory but no union organization. Anna was only fifty miles,
but it was a full day's travel — just one example of the difficulty
of organization work in 1913.

THE NEXT YEAR, 1914, saw a general strike in Gloversville and Johnstown. A series of mass meetings had been held with both the union and the non-union cutters voting for the strike. I made a trip there in the fall and found the two groups co-operating. An A. F. of L. organizer went in and remained all during the strike. He gained many members for our International Glove Workers Union. But the strike lasted into the winter months and ended once more in defeat for the Fulton County glove workers.

3-On a Broader Stage

AGNES NESTOR AT HER DESK IN WASHINGTON

14

The Vocational
Education Commission

BACK in 1908, I had been a member of a committee appointed by the A. F. of L. convention at Denver to prepare a report on industrial education, or "vocational" education, as it came to be called.

Our report, presented at the A. F. of L. Toronto convention of 1909 ran to 114 pages. In that report, we urged that the welfare of America depended upon the industrial training of its young workers. We recommended the establishment of industrial schools in connection with the public school system where pupils between the ages of fourteen and sixteen could be taught the principles of the trades and the necessary technical knowledge to enable them to follow a particular kind of work.

In regard to these schools, two things we particularly urged — that such industrial schools be set up as a public function, the cost to be a public cost; and that this industrial education be supplementary to, and not to the exclusion of, such liberal courses as might enable the student to formulate an intelligent understanding of his duties as a citizen and as might give him a background for the enjoyment of life. Heads, we urged, must be educated as well as hands.

Our report was introduced by Senator Carroll Smalley Page

of Vermont in the Senate of the 62nd Congress and thereby made a public document.

Seven years later, by 1914, industrial, or vocational education had become a stormy issue in Chicago, as well as over most of the nation. The need for industrial education was generally admitted. But over what form these new schools should take there was bitter controversy.

In Chicago, one group headed by Ella Flagg Young, then superintendent of Chicago's public schools, and Edwin G. Cooley, a former superintendent, favored what is called the Dual System, a separating of academic and vocational training. This was the plan then in force in Germany. Edwin G. Cooley had been sent to Germany by the Chicago Commercial Club to study this system, and he had come back completely won over to the German plan. It was a system considered "more practical." In favor of it were chiefly the business and industrial owner groups.

But to the student being trained as a worker, such a school tended to deny all opportunity for cultural development. Such a school tended to place the student being trained as a worker into a separate "class." It was the opposite of what we had been so long struggling for. We of the labor group, we of the Women's Trade Union League, were strongly opposed to it. What we desired was a Unit System, a combination of vocational and liberal education which might give the worker-to-be vocational training without denying him cultural background.

William J. Bogan, then principal of Lane Technical High School, and later superintendent of the public schools of Chicago, was leading our fight. Our Women's Trade Union League brought William J. Bogan and Ella Flagg Young to the stage of Chicago's Orchestra Hall in a big debate, in order that the whole issue might be aired.

I remember my first meeting with Mrs. Young. Our National Women's Trade Union League had passed a resolution at its convention to ask our schools to include in their curriculum a course in collective bargaining, so that boys and girls upon entering industry might have some knowledge of this procedure. In pursuance of this matter I went to see Mrs. Young.

I had a feeling of awe concerning her as I entered her office. Because I felt that she was such a busy person, I sat on the edge of my chair expecting to leave as soon as my brief mission was over. To my surprise, she seemed in no hurry and said that she would like very much to talk over some of her plans with me. We had a very interesting talk. She did recommend our resolution to the board of education. But, unfortunately, Mrs. Young thought our resolution referred to the cooperative movement — collective "buying," instead of to the labor movement — collective "bargaining." Evidently our terms were not familiar to her, as she had no previous familiarity with labor.

At the Illinois State Federation of Labor convention that year, a committee was formed to formulate and recommend a "feasible plan for vocational education." Victor A. Olander was chairman of the committee, and Matthew Woll was secretary. The three women members were Mrs. Robins, Mrs. Young and I. We reported to the next convention with six major recommendations. We, of course, declared against the Dual System.

Our first recommendation was for compulsory school attendance of all children between the ages of seven and sixteen. Up to 1914 not more than a third of the children who entered the public schools completed the elementary grades, and not half of them completed the sixth grade. "One-half of the children leave school before they acquire the knowledge to read a newspaper intelligently," our report pointed out. It was not until 1945 that such a law as we recommended was enacted, although agitation for it had persisted through the intervening years.

BESIDES WORKING for the welfare of youth, we were vitally concerned over the problems at the other end of the life cycle — the comfort of the aged. Employers at that time were not in favor of old-age pensions. At a special hearing held by the Labor Relations Commission, a representative from a large department store said that if the workers would refrain from the use of liquor and tobacco they would be able to save enough to take care of themselves in old age. One of the members of the commission told him that he was presenting a novel theory of old-age pensions.

Whenever the Illinois Legislature had pension bills up for consideration I was in Springfield; and I sat in the gallery of the house sick at heart as at session after session I saw such a pitifully small group voting for old-age pensions. It was not until after the matter had become a live issue, following the Townsend Movement and the Social Security Act, that we were able to see the Illinois Legislature pass an old-age pension bill. Then such a bill was passed without a dissenting vote. No one dared vote against it then.

IN THAT YEAR OF 1914, two very important positions beckoned to me. Mrs. Robins was president of the Women's Trade Union League of Chicago, and also president of the national organization. In order to devote all her time to the national organization, she desired to be relieved of responsibility for the local chapter. Following her resignation, I was elected president of the Women's Trade Union League of Chicago.

The other position which beckoned to me in that crowded year offered to me the opportunity to do, in behalf of vocational education, some definite work on a wide scale.

By an act of Congress, President Wilson had been directed to appoint a commission to study the subject of Federal aid for vocational education and to make recommendations to Congress in regard to the matter. When one day in February of 1914, Richard Finnegan, editor of the *Chicago Journal,* telephoned me that it had just come over the wire that I had been appointed to serve on this commission, I simply could not believe his news. So many very prominent people all over the country were wanting representation on this commission that my own appointment to it by the President of the United States seemed utterly unbelieveable. On my way home from my office that evening, I was amazed to see on all the newsstands I passed the *Chicago Journal* with a large picture of me and a long article by a noted newspaper writer. In big letters across the newspaper I read:

Chicago Girl, Champion of Labor Now Tackles Labor's Biggest Problem

Little Agnes Nestor Appointed by President Wilson on National Commission to Investigate and Report on Vocational Education

By Mary Synon

Agnes Nestor ... stands today under the blazing limelight of an international calcium as the representative of union labor on the firing lines.

For President Wilson's appointment of the Chicago girl, President of the Glove Workers' Union, as a member of the commission to investigate and report on vocational education places on her shoulders the Atlean burden of the labor world's most important and immediate problem, the question of the future of the children of the country who will have to earn their bread by the work of their hands.

If you should meet Agnes Nestor without happening to know what she had already done, you might think, at first glance, that here were small shoulders for the great load that has been set on them. She weighs not more than 90 pounds. She has a little girl's quick upward look, a little girl's instinctive friendliness. But anyone who knows how Agnes Nestor has fought for the principles in which she believes, how she pitted her wits against some of the greatest lawyers in Illinois, winning from them a greater measure of success than anyone before her ever won, knows that Agnes Nestor is not only the biggest little woman in Chicago, but one of the ablest, gamest, quickest, most loyal and honest labor leaders in the United States.

When the President of the Glove Workers' Union takes her place on the committee with United States Senators Hoke Smith of Georgia and C. S. Page of Vermont; with Representatives D. M. Hughes of Georgia and F. D. Fess of Ohio; with John A. Lapp, legislative librarian, of Indianapolis; with C. H. Winslow of the Department of Labor, and Miss Florence Marshall, principal of the Manhattan Trade School for Girls, of New York, she will be the only representative of organized labor in that body, with the opportunity to present the beliefs of her people and the obligation of doing her utmost to present them clearly, graphically and convincingly.

MORAL VICTORY AT SPRINGFIELD DECISIVE

That she will be able to do it is the certainty of all those who saw her work for the fifty-four-hour-week at Springfield. Although she was successful only in securing a sixty-hour bill, the victory was, from a moral standpoint, decisively hers. And the men who opposed her conceded, with some little amusement, watching the little-girl stride of their victor, that Agnes Nestor could command her own figure of payment if she were working for money.

She isn't working for money. Nor is she working for glory. She's working for the women who work. And when she begins to talk of them, of their problems, of their needs, of their ways of life, of their opportunities or lack of them, of their character and courage, Agnes Nestor isn't a little girl at all. She's an earnest, serious woman, prematurely aged by her responsibilities, whose whole heart is in the cause of the women who labor, whose whole soul is in their fight against a world of injustice and indifference.

The way in which she received the news of her appointment to one of the most important commissions of this administration, a place of honor whose value can be better estimated in the future than now, is characteristic of the woman. Her first surprise over—for, although she knew that she had been mentioned for the place, she had not expected the choice to fall on her—she considered the news a moment without speech.

"It's a great honor," someone said to her.

She looked upward.

"It's a great duty," she said, "and a great opportunity."

Then she puckered her brows.

"Who else is on that committee?" she asked.

She scanned the list thoughtfully, her gray eyes contemplative and her mouth tightening a little. It was the look that many legislators at Springfield have come to know, a scanning of the field before the battle . . .

When she talks of herself, her opinions, her work even, she shows a diffidence that one seldom finds among leaders. But when she talks of the women who work, especially the women of Chicago's laboring world, she is a prophetess leading her people, voicing their plans, crying their demands.

"Oh, we need so much," she said, clenching her hands in her intensity of emotion. "We need justice, and right, and understanding. If we have the understanding, I think the rest will come. But we've been so misrepresented, so maligned.

"People think that the women are selfishly working, each for her own interests. They aren't. Why, when we were working for the fifty-four-hour-week bill, some of the women who helped us most were the women who already had the eight-hour-day rule in their trades, and who couldn't be helped at all by any state enactment. But they wanted to help the others who were begging justice.

"Then the waitresses, who were included in the law, dropped out when they found out that their inclusion might affect the constitutionality of the bill. Isn't that standing by each other? Isn't that the spirit of co-operation in women? And it's the women who work who have that spirit."

No one knows that better than Agnes Nestor. She has risen from the labor ranks, by dogged determination, by a lightning-quick brain, by a great glow of belief in the rightness of her cause. It is the same flame of faith that she is taking to the work that the President of the United States has imposed upon her.

"It is such a great, big question," she said, "this question of vocational education. It is a problem to the educators, but it's life to the working men and women. Their children have to be trained for earning their livings, but trade schools have so often exploited the workingman for the capitalist that is it any wonder that we are afraid of them?

"The boys and girls who go to school now, though, are wasting years at studies they'll never use when they might be learning the rudiments of a trade at which they could work when they have finished their course. But vocational education should go hand in hand with cultural education. If you take away from the boys and girls who'll have to work at labor, the opportunity to broaden their minds by other studies, you're doing them an injustice that you can never repair, and you're striking at the roots of freedom. I don't know very much about the theories of psychological pedagogy, but I do know that."

VERY SOON THE COMMISSION was called to Washington for its first meeting. On this Commission on National Aid to Vocational Education, there were nine appointees. There was Senator Hoke Smith, who was chairman. There were Representatives Simeon Davidson Fess and Dudley M. Hughes. And there was Senator Carroll S. Page who back in 1912 had introduced our A. F. of L. *Report on Industrial Education* in the Senate of the 62nd Congress.

Serving with these Senators and Representatives were two women, Florence Marshall and I. There was also John A. Lapp, Dr. Charles A. Prosser, secretary of the National Society for Promotion of Industrial Education, and Charles H. Winslow, who had edited our 14-page 1912 A. F. of L. report.

We began work at once. The bill which had created the commission provided that the report be ready by the first of June. Those against the idea of Federal aid to vocational education had used as one of their arguments against the bill that the commission would ask for extended time and increased appropriations. We wanted the report ready on schedule.

"Look out for Senator Hoke Smith!" I had been warned on leaving Chicago for Washington. I was prepared to be wary. But as I worked with him through the next few months, I grew to admire Senator Smith more and more. He was big-hearted and considerate in his views. We all worked with him well.

Miss Florence Marshall and I foresaw difficulties when we found out that some of the men wished to give girls more domestic science than opportunity to learn trades. We knew that most of the girls would have to become wage earners as well as homemakers. We, too, loved the home; but the girls needed also training which would equip them to earn a living.

Strange it is how small incidents stand out in memory. One member of the commission strode across the room one day, saying with great feeling:

"I cannot face the country unless we do something for the girls!"

He meant unless we gave them lots of domestic science. He was entirely forgetting that Miss Marshall and I, the two women members of the commission, were not afraid to face the country, and we had other ideas. We felt that if domestic science were allowed the greater appropriation, it would be too easy to push all the girls into that field and not give them the technical training they were likely to find themselves in need of.

We finished our report on schedule, and we even turned back some of the appropriation!

Meeting with Senators and Representatives every day proved a very interesting experience and gave me a deeper insight into the procedures of Congress. Senator Hoke Smith introduced the bill for vocational education in the Senate, and Representative Hughes introduced it in the House. They were the two Democratic members of the commission. Bills for Federal aid for vocational education had been before Congress at several previous sessions, but no agreement had ever been reached on any of them. Senator Page had introduced some of these earlier bills, and he took a certain pride in having his name connected with this kind of legislation. He would have liked to have introduced our bill, but he deferred to political prerogative in the matter. The Morrill Act, the first Federal-aid-for-education bill, had been introduced in 1862 by a Vermont Senator. The bill had been signed by Lincoln. So Senator Page of Vermont's pride in this direction was justified.

The bill which grew out of the work of our commission was passed by Congress and became known as the Smith-Hughes Act. Other Federal grants for vocational education have been added since, but the bill which grew out of our work made possible the vocational education departments in the schools throughout the country.

Just Before World War I

I HAD JUST ARRIVED in Washington, D. C., in the spring of 1914 to begin work on the Vocational Education Commission when I was given a message to call the office of the National Woman's Party. I called and was invited to attend a reception. This National Woman's Party was then a new organization, the militant wing of the suffrage movement. It was pressing for the passage of the Woman Suffrage Amendment.

It happened that I had to return to Chicago on business the next day, so I had to make it understood that I was in Washington to do a particular piece of work in a short time and could commit myself to no other business. A few years later our Women's Trade Union League had to oppose this National Woman's Party on a very important issue.

In Washington, when I had settled down to work on the Vocational Education Commission, I did join in a suffrage parade one Saturday afternoon at the request of Mrs. Laurence Lewis, my friend of the Philadelphia shirtwaist-strike days. It was five years later, in 1919, that the Suffrage Amendment was finally passed by Congress and ratified by the states as the Nineteenth Amendment.

We were working on the Vocational Education Commission

during the spring of 1914 when the strike of the Ludlow County, Colorado, miners against the Colorado Fuel and Iron Company aroused the nation. That strike had resulted in bloodshed. John Lawson, the miners' leader, had been jailed. Wives, even children of the miners had been killed. A congressional investigation into the matter was in progress, and we saw the miners' delegates and their women and children who had come to Washington to protest the lawlessness which had been perpetrated in the mining regions of "Bloody Ludlow."

It was also while I was in Washington working on the Vocational Education Commission that the Federal Commission on Industrial Relations, with Senator Frank P. Walsh as chairman, was holding hearings before going out to other cities of the country. It was an historic time in the world of labor. The Federal Government was becoming concerned over the relationships between industry and labor, and this Commission on Industrial Relations had been directed to inquire into the "extent and results of 'Collective Bargaining.'" This commission had been appointed by President Wilson under an act of Congress of 1912, and I have reached the conclusion in my own research into the use of the term that President Wilson, or his economists drafting this legislation, must have coined that phrase since used so generally and now an official term in legislation dealing with labor relations.

That summer when this Commission on Industrial Relations held hearings in Chicago, I was among the various representatives in the field of industrial relations called upon to testify. I was elated to learn afterwards that, next to John Fitzpatrick, I had the greatest number of pages of testimony.

On my way to the hearings one day, I met Victor Olander of the Seamen's Union. Mr. Olander had just been elected secretary of the Illinois State Federation of Labor, the office in which he served so well for so many years.

"Miss Nestor," said Mr. Olander, "I was asked several months ago to endorse you for the Vocational Education Commission. Now I shall have the pleasure of going over to see you perform!"

While I was on the stand at that particular hearing, Senator Walsh, with very subtle questioning, revealed to the group that I had left school at a very early age and that I had made my way from an ordinary working girl up to membership on the Commission on Vocational Education. I saw Mr. Olander again after the hearing, and his comment was characteristic:

"I do not know whether this man Walsh ever committed a sin in his life," he said, "but if he has, I am willing to forgive him because of the way he handled you on the witness stand."

Victor Olander had not met Senator Walsh at that time, but later they became good friends and close associates, serving together on the War Labor Board during World War I.

The Commission on Industrial Relations submitted its final report to the 64th Congress, August 23, 1915. That report was a strange document. Chairman Frank P. Walsh and three labor members of the commission, John B. Lennon, James O'Connell, and Austin G. Garretson, signed one set of recommendations as their report. Mrs. Boardman Harrison and Professor John R. Commons, representing the public, signed another. And a third report came from the employers' representatives, Richard H. Ashton, Harris Weinstock, and S. Thurston Ballard.

Then Weinstock presented a separate report of his own, dissenting on the recommendation concerning immigration as prepared by Professor Commons. And after the section signed by the three employers' representatives, there was appended a further supplementary statement by S. Thurston Ballard.

The report signed by Mrs. Harrison and Professor Commons,

called "The Commons' Report," recommended a Federal fund for social welfare to be supported by an inheritance tax and administered by a "Commission on Industrial Relations" aided by "an Advisory Council composed of representatives of employers and employees." All this, of course, was before there was a Federal inheritance tax.

The commission recommended Federal employment agencies and the mediation of industrial disputes. Boycotts, both primary and secondary, were endorsed; also the principle of collective bargaining, and the application of the British Disputes Act, according to which workers were to have absolute freedom in organizing.

The various reports contains many proposals. The commission had held hearings in fourteen industrial centers during 154 days, had heard 740 witnesses, of whom 230 were affiliated with employers, 245 with labor, and 265 with neither group. The testimony filled four volumes, amounting to four thousand pages. All of this should have resulted in some legislative action; but perhaps the very airing of so many views may itself have been of great value.

I should like to put on record this interesting sentence from the report of the employers' representatives:

"We say frankly," the report stated, "that if we were wage earners, we would be unionists; and as unionists, we would feel the keen responsibility of giving the same attention to our trade union as to our civic duties."

It is worthy of note that the Walsh group recommended legislation which, by forbidding the discharge of persons for trade-union membership, would protect the workers' right to strike.

This group asked that the Federal Trade Commission consider as unfair *the exploitation of labor through long working hours, low wages, unsafe or unsanitary conditions; or through the refusal of employers to meet and deal with the authorized representatives of employees; and that the Secretary of Labor be authorized and directed to prosecute such action before the Trade Commission, either on its own volition or upon the request of any organization or individual.*

These recommendations became the kernel of the later labor laws — the N. R. A., the National Labor Relations Act, the Fair Labor Standards Act. But nearly twenty years had to pass before much of this desired legislation could be enacted. The Clayton Anti-Trust Law, hailed as "Labor's Magna Charta," however, had been passed in 1914, limiting the use of injunctions in labor disputes and asking for statutory distinction between property rights and human rights in industrial disputes. This Clayton Act was a legal declaration that the labor of a human being is not a commodity or article of another, the opposite of which is the essence of slavery. Samuel Gompers considered this the greatest declaration of human freedom enacted by authority since the Magna Charta and the Declaration of Independence.

IT CONTINUED to be a busy time, what with commissions, strikes, and our attempts to put through legislation in relief of the women workers.

I returned from Washington in the late spring of 1914 in time to see the climax of the waitresses' strike which had been going on in Chicago since January.

I was entirely in sympathy with the group of waitresses who had struck in protest of these grievances: that a dollar a day was deducted from their pay for laundry (aprons, etc.), that they were forced to make payments to the bus boys, and that they were forced to pay for food which the customers refused and sent back to the kitchen.

The girls who did picket duty in behalf of this strike were arrested, forced into patrol wagons, and taken to the police stations, where bonds were required. Injunctions and court cases followed, requiring the services of a lawyer and making the strike expensive. But if the employer thought he was discouraging the girls and breaking their spirits by these tactics, he was mistaken. All this made the girls only more determined to persist in their protests.

Carrie Alexander and Elizabeth Maloney were directing the strike, and we of the Women's Trade Union League brought in public support. Mrs. Medill McCormick and other prominent women went on the picket line to observe what was happening. Emma Steghagen, secretary of the Women's Trade Union League, and Florence Sherwood from our staff, picketed during their lunch hours, or replaced other pickets when these were arrested.

In those days the police were brutal in handling pickets. Also, our pickets had hired thugs to contend with. Professor Charles E. Merriam from the University of Chicago and an alderman in the city council, one day asked Mrs. Robins about the strike.

"Why don't you go stand in front of the place and see?" said she.

Professor Merriam went to see firsthand what was happening. He was soon told by a "thug," as Mr. Merriam called him, to "move on."

"By what authority do you ask me to move on?" asked Mr. Merriam.

"By the authority of the law," was the reply.

"You don't look like a policeman," said Mr. Merriam. "You haven't any star."

The man then threw back his coat to show his star.

Whereupon Mr. Merriam threw back his own coat to show his own star.

Ellen Gates Starr of Hull House, who, with Jane Addams, had founded that famous settlement, picketed one day and was arrested. Miss Starr came from an old American family; her ancestors had fought in the Revolution. She was a cousin of Eliza Ellen Starr, a noted writer, artist, and lecturer. But the police did not recognize her and took her to the police station with the other arrested pickets. She was formally charged and brought to trial. Harold L. Ickes came to defend her. The jury acquitted her, and this was a great victory for the strikers, for it called public attention to the unjust arrests which were being made.

Newspapers reported a meeting of businessmen from the State Street stores, wholesale houses, packing plants and mail-order houses, at which meeting a resolution had been adopted demanding that Jane Addams take a hands-off attitude and "withdraw Ellen Gates Starr from further participation in this conspiracy!"

In those hectic days the newspaper men and women were our good friends. William L. Chenery, now a well-known publisher, was then with the *Post*. He was a frequent visitor to our office, lectured and wrote for our publication, and his column, "Guide Post," was an outlet for much liberal news.

Mary Synon, a writer on the *Journal* and noted in the fields of journalism and education, was always interested in our work after she had done the assignment on my appointment to the National Vocational Education Commission.

Carl Sandburg was a reporter on the *Day Book,* a six-by-nine-inch daily paper in book form which the publisher, N. D. Cochran, was experimenting with, using no advertising so that he could be free to present any news. The *Day Book* carried daily stories and special feature articles on the strike.

Carl Sandburg would make daily visits to our office, and I used to say to him that whenever he had space to fill he could interview me about conditions in some place he wanted to expose. One day I gave him an interview about girls working in the telephone exchanges. The next morning I had a visit from the "welfare worker" for the Telephone Company. He explained how fine their working conditions were and invited me to come over and go through their exchanges.

WHILE THE WAITRESSES' STRIKE was still going on, we became concerned in another strike which involved only about fifty women, but which nevertheless was a very important affair to us.

A Chicago broom factory was introducing women to the heavy work of broommaking, work formerly done by men, at about half the wages they had paid the men. These women were recent arrivals from foreign countries, a few from Russia and the rest from Lithuania. This broom factory was notorious for using convict labor before the state had prohibited that by legislation. Now they resorted to using foreign-born women, to whom the pitiful wage paid them seemed large in comparison with what they had been accustomed to receive in their own countries — until they tried to live on it!

They complained not only about the low wage, but also about the difficult labor of operating the heavy machines, about the painful labor of tying the rough broom corn with strong wire which bit into the hands. They were being paid $3.51 for sewing 103 brooms, while other shops were paying $8.92 for the same labor. A woman tying 36 dozen whisk brooms earned $3.40, as against $7.20 in other shops. The union wanted to organize these women as they had those of all the other broom factories in the area. When one woman was discharged for attending a union meeting, it started a revolt and the strike followed.

We had a Northwest-Side headquarters in the vicinity of the factory. We turned it over to these women for their strike center and organized a committee to assist them. I was treasurer of the fund we collected for their strike benefits, which amounted to $4.00 each per week. That may seem a small sum; it was more than they had been earning! We organized classes in English for them, for only two of the whole number could speak English, the forelady and one other.

A large wholesale house in the city had been taking most of the output of this broom factory. A committee from our Women's Trade Union League — Mary McDowell, Mary Anderson, and I — visited the officials of this wholesale house to ask them to use their influence to secure a settlement for these women. The next day each of us was served with injunctions naming us, our Women's Trade Union League, the Broom and Whisk Makers Union, and William Boyer, its president, all in the usual form covering sixty typewritten lines restraining us from the usual activities in a strike.

We had to agree that things had come to a sorry pass when one could not visit a businessman to discuss a strike situation without being served with an injunction. But they had failed to put in the injunction any clause to restrain us from paying strike benefits and collecting funds for the strikers!

No settlement was reached in the strike. But the women concerned secured other more suitable work where they could earn more money, and they didn't have to go back to that broom factory. Not long after the strike, the factory closed.

These early strikes bore fruit in time. In 1918, when women were replacing men during the war period, the Broom and

Whisk Makers Union could report a hundred-percent organization among the women workers in this industry. Many of these women had learned their trade prior to the 1914 strike. They were working in union shops under good working conditions and were earning from twenty to thirty dollars a week.

The waitresses' union, too, grew into a strong organization. Elizabeth Maloney was a great inspiration to the girls. She placed a picture of the Sistine Madonna in the union headquarters, saying to the girls: "This is woman on her highest plane. You can see here what woman can be and from this example learn to respect yourselves accordingly."

That picture of the Madonna must have guided those courageous girls through those early years.

THE SUMMER OF 1915 saw us besieged with strikes of a wide variety. One was that of the Pullman-car cleaners, who were working a ten-hour day for $1.35 a day, and a seven-day week with every third Sunday off.

There was also a strike at the Argo Starch plant, with about two hundred girls involved. There was another strike at the International Harvester Company's three plants, with some seven hundred girls concerned. Their protest was against a speed-up system.

The Argo Starch plant workers and the Pullman-car cleaners lost their strikes, even though they had the assistance of Frank P. Walsh, chairman of the Industrial Relations Committee, and, in the case of the Pullman-car cleaners, Federal mediators.

But in the garment industry, meanwhile, two strikes won important concessions, and it was Mr. Schaffner of Hart, Schaffner and Marx who came to our aid in one of these and helped in formulating the agreements. In the felt-goods industry the girls returned to work after ten days, having secured a minimum wage of $8.00 a week for a nine-hour day in one plant, and an increase in pay and reduction of working hours in another.

The Herzog strike won improved arrangements for dressmakers and glove workers. In connection with this strike I remember an amusing incident concerning Clarence Darrow. When we were negotiating the agreement, there were present, besides the arbitrators and myself, two lawyers, Clarence Darrow representing the workers, and Mr. Sonnenschein representing the employer. We of the above group sat at a table in the middle of the room, while union representatives and workers sat about in groups behind us. We were trying to settle a price dispute concerning piecework rates for sewing in sleeves, when Mr. Darrow, who had a deep sense of humor, leaned across the table and said to Mr. Sonnenschein:

"Do you know anything about sewing in sleeves?"

With a twinkle in his eyes, Mr. Sonnenschein replied:

"No, do you?"

Everyone laughed; it sounded so ridiculous for two high-priced lawyers to be talking about sewing in sleeves.

That ended the session for that day, and the dispute was left to people who did understand how to sew in sleeves.

———

That fall, when the International Glove Workers Union held its convention in Chicago, I was elected president. Since Elisabeth Christman was now secretary-treasurer of the organization, this meant that we now had two women heading our International Glove Workers Union.

———

WE CONTINUED to have trouble in the field of education in Chicago.

In September of 1915, the Chicago Board of Education adopted the so-called Loeb Rule, which denied to teachers the right to belong to a trade-union organization.

This Loeb Rule was worded to aim at the Chicago Teachers Federation, although there were two other teachers' organizations affiliated with the labor movement at the time — the Federation of Women High School Teachers, and the Federation of Men Teachers. The ruling was directed against Margaret Haley and Catherine Goggin, two former teachers who had withdrawn from the public school system to devote full time to the Chicago Teachers Federation. The ruling was that no teacher could belong to a trade-union organization having on its staff officers not on the teaching staff of the Chicago public schools.

Following the passage of the ruling, the fearless leader Catherine Goggin was struck and killed by a truck. Public honors were accorded her, the city council allowing her body to lie in state in the council chambers.

Catherine Goggin's death, however, did not lessen the fight made upon her organization. In June, sixty-eight teachers, active members and officers of the Chicago Teachers Federation, were dismissed from the school system by the refusal of the board to renew their contracts, although they had been recommended for re-election by the superintendent of schools. One must know something of the early activities of Miss Goggin and Miss Haley to understand why this fight was made on them and their organization. Back in 1907, the teachers in the public schools of Chicago had failed to receive a long-promised fifty-dollars-a-year raise "because of lack of funds." The Chicago Teachers Federation investigated and found that certain corporations were not paying taxes on their capital stock and franchises. Catherine Goggin brought suit against these corporations — with the result that a large sum was paid into the public treasury and increased taxes continued to be received each year.

In 1913, when the board of education had attempted to change the pension laws in order to take the control of the pension fund from the teachers, who were the contributors to it, Miss Goggin and Miss Haley had successfully fought this injustice. Later they had helped also to defeat the Dual System for vocational education.

Miss Goggin and Miss Haley had, moreover, investigated the matter of the leases for the land which had been given by the Federal Government for the maintenance of a public school system, and they had succeeded in having the ten-year revaluation clause in these ninety-nine-year leases maintained.

The Chicago Teachers Federation had thus become a powerful champion of the interest of the public schools and the children of Chicago. After Miss Goggin's death, Miss Haley continued the fight against the Loeb Rule, and she had the organized labor movement behind her.

The Chicago Teachers Federation had the record of being the first teachers' organization to affiliate with the labor movement. But Chicago's Loeb Rule remained in force for many years, and finally, in 1917, after fifteen years in the labor movement, the Chicago Teachers Federation had to withdraw from all labor affiliations, including our Women's Trade Union League. Frances Harden, secretary of the Chicago Teachers Federation, had even to resign from the office of secretary of our Women's Trade Union League. In later years the several other teachers' unions, A. F. of L. affiliates, merged into one union, but the Chicago Teachers Federation remained apart.

Margaret Haley, however, never formally retired from her work. She went to California in the thirties. But after some years she returned to Chicago, where she died in January of 1937 at the age of 77. She is remembered as one of the most brilliant, able, and resourceful leaders of her time.

BETWEEN THE TIMES that I was assisting strikers in that summer of 1915, I went as a delegate to the National Women's Trade Union League convention in New York City.

World War I was going on in Europe, and most of our delegates wanted the United States to stay out of that war. The International Congress of Working Women had just met at The Hague, with women from both the neutral and the war-stricken countries attending. Jane Addams had presided. Leonora O'Reilly, a pioneer in the Women's Trade Union League and a forceful peace advocate, had been our delegate.

Reflecting our peace sentiments, the convention passed a resolution directed to the President and to the Honorable William Jennings Bryan, who had just retired from the office of Secretary of State in President Wilson's Cabinet. Our resolution asked the President and the Congress to place an embargo upon the exportation of arms, war equipment, and war supplies, and to forbid the manufacture of arms and munitions for private profit.

Since our Chicago delegation was returning through Washington, D. C., we were directed to present the resolution to the President and other officials. Our National Women's Trade League officers wired the President for an appointment. A reply came from Mr. Joseph Tumulty, the President's secretary, regretting that the President could not see us and suggesting that the resolution be transmitted to the President through him. Mr. Tumulty asked us to come to see him at four o'clock the afternoon of our arrival in Washington.

In Washington, we decided to telephone Williams Jennings Bryan, hoping that he would approve our resolution. The telephone for the Bryan home was not listed in the directory. I spoke to the telephone operator, explaining our mission. She was interested and said very softly:

"If I give you the number, will you forget where you got it?"

"Of course," I agreed. I reached Mrs. Bryan, and she made a five-thirty appointment for us. That suited us fine.

We went on to the White House, and as soon as Mr. Tumulty met our delegation, I began to present our resolution. But he interrupted me, saying:

"So you want to see the President?"

Of course we wanted to. I reminded him of his telegram which had directed that the President could not see us.

"Wait a minute," said he, and he called Pat McKenna, the Doorkeeper for the President. "Pat, bring the President's engagement book," he directed. Pat obliged very willingly. Mr. Tumulty consulted the book, then asked, "How about nine o'clock tomorrow morning?"

Nothing could have suited us better. We left the White House walking on air. Tomorrow we were going to meet President Wilson!

We went next to meet the Secretary of Labor, William B. Wilson, and his Assistant Secretary, Louis F. Post, an old friend from Chicago.

After our visit with Mr. Post, we went to keep our appointment at the Bryan home. The house had once been pointed out to me, a large house on a corner. I thought I remembered it, but I was not sure. A woman with a parasol was coming along the street; I decided to inquire of her. Luck seemed to be pursuing us that day, for the woman was Mrs. Post. She was delighted to see us, and she offered to accompany us to the Bryans, whom she knew very well.

Mr. and Mrs. Bryan received us in their large living room. Mr. Bryan stood beside a table as I presented the resolution to him. But there was no formality. He read the resolution and discussed it with us. He told us he did not agree with it.

He did not hurry, but took time to define his opinions.

As we were leaving, I could not resist telling him that he had been one of the first persons to influence me to think deeply about national conditions, and that I had followed closely his speeches through his early campaigns. He laughed and said:

"Then perhaps I have done more good in the world than I had supposed."

When we had got away from the house, Mrs. Post said she hoped we realized that we had had an intimate and very unusual conference with Mr. Bryan, that he could not and did not give that much time to everyone who came. She said also that the picture of me standing at the table discussing our resolution with Mr. Bryan was a memory she liked to recall.

The next morning we were at the White House for our appointment. Mr. Tumulty met us in the reception room and said:

"When I made that appointment yesterday, I had forgot that the President was not coming to his office this morning." Then, seeing our deep disappointment, he smiled as he added, "But he has come over especially to meet your delegation."

Then he ushered us into the presence of our great President Wilson, who greeted each one of us and received our resolution in a formal but gracious manner. It was the crowning glory of our visit to Washington. In our delegation we had garment workers, including Mary Haney, later our secretary; Elisabeth Christman, our fellow glove worker; Agnes Burns, a teacher, daughter of a miner from southern Illinois; Julia Pugh, a grocery clerk from Springfield; and my sister Mary. It was a day long to be remembered. We left with the "Affairs of State" dropped from our shoulders and ready to begin our holiday with a trip to Mount Vernon.

16

Our Fight During the War

SAY! These working girls down here in Springfield are living in luxury! Didn't you see them eating strawberries when I can't afford to eat them!"

That was one of the arguments used against Elizabeth Maloney and myself by a downstate senator when we were in Springfield fighting once more for the women's eight-hour bill.

For a while it looked as though we might get our bill passed. In the senate it was being introduced by Kent E. Keller, later a U. S. Congressman. In the house it was being introduced by Medill McCormick, later U. S. Senator from Illinois. Hearings were being held both downstate and in Chicago. Since employers' representatives were packing the hearings, the best we could do was to talk for the benefit of the women workers who had been brought in by these representatives to testify against the bill. We succeeded in winning some of these women over; one of them even testified for our bill.

The morning after one of the hearings, the senator who had criticized our eating strawberries came to me embarrassed and apologetic. He admired me, he said; but, said he, some of the things Elizabeth Maloney had said about him had provoked him. I smiled and asked:

"Is that why you told the people in your town that we were

eating strawberries in the middle of winter?"

He seemed a bit confused.

"I do not blame you," I added quietly. "Working women have no right to eat strawberries." And I walked away.

That was the end of his criticism.

Our eight-hour bill was killed in the house by having its enacting clause struck out, a practice manipulated to kill bills on their second reading.

In the senate the bill died in a sub-committee. The chairman of that committee kept it from being reported out even after we had presented a petition signed by the majority of the committee's members. The chairman induced one member to take his name off the petition. The bill was changed to a nine-hour-day, fifty-four-hour-week bill. Our minimum-wage bill for women also was killed.

By an irony of fate, the senator responsible for killing our eight-hour bill decided to run for a judgship the first year that women had the right to vote in municipal elections. We printed a hundred thousand leaflets exposing how this senator had ruthlessly killed our bill and asking the women voters to defeat him. It was a lively campaign. He lost.

His office was in the same building in Chicago where our Women's Trade Union League also had an office. The morning after the election, in he stormed berating us for defeating him. He got our *deepest* sympathy.

OUR EIGHT-HOUR-DAY BILL was up before the Illinois Legislature again in 1917. With Carter J. Allen, an old friend, sponsoring the bill in the house, William Sneed, a miner from southern Illinois, sponsoring it in the senate, and with Frank O. Lowden, an advocate for shorter hours for women, the Governor, we had every reason to be hopeful.

Then suddenly the picture changed. War was declared on April 6, and those who wanted to oppose our eight-hour bill could use the emergency of war as a reason why no labor-limitation legislation should be passed. The house committee chairman told his committee that the Secretary of War in a message to several states was opposing the eight-hour legislation in the interest of war.

Newton D. Baker was then Secretary of War, and we felt sure that he had not intended his message to defeat our bill. We knew his policy in regard to industrial standards. But merely knowing this was not enough. We needed evidence. We had to work fast, for the Illinois Legislature was recessing for the week end, and in a few days — on the following Tuesday — the committee's report would be made to the house on our bill. We knew that report would not be favorable.

From Chicago I sent a telegram to the Secretary of War, advising him that his message was being used to defeat our bill, and asking him to clarify his position. By Monday we had received no reply, and we were to leave for Springfield that evening. In desperation, I called Mr. Baker long distance, expecting to get to talk only to his second or third assistant. But, to my surprise, I found myself talking to Mr. Baker himself. Of course he had not intended his message to defeat our bill, said he. I asked him if he would state his position in a telegram which we could present to the Illinois Legislature the next morning. The telegram came through without delay, and we were fortified with it for our coming battle at Springfield.

In the house that next day, the house committee chairman presented his report, backing it, he said, with a request from the Secretary of War.

Representative Patrick W. Gallagher, an old member of the house, an able man and a good lawyer, had a minority report ready. Then he announced that perhaps the members of the house would like to hear the latest word from the Secretary of War. He proceeded to read Mr. Baker's telegram. It was a blow that floored our opposition. In the house our bill passed.

But our success was only half a success. Though the Governor sent a special message to both house and senate and tried working over the bill to silence certain oppositions to it, our bill was killed in the senate.

Something, however, was accomplished. Senator Morton D. Hull (later a U. S. Congressman), one of those who had helped in the passage of the ten-hour law, introduced a bill to create a commission, called the Illinois Industrial Survey, to investigate the matter of "hours-work for women and its effect on their health." This bill was passed.

ONCE OUR COUNTRY had been plunged into war, our Women's Trade Union League shelved its peace aims temporarily and plunged into war activity.

Women were being mobilized, not only for factory but also for volunteer work. Under the Council of National Defense, national committees were being set up to deal with labor relations during the war. On these committees organized labor was well represented — but not women laborers.

The National Women's Trade Union League, headed by Mrs. Robins, was determined that the trade-union women in our country should have ample opportunity to do their part in the war effort. We knew about the English women and the important part they had been playing in their country's struggle. We decided to make ourselves heard.

Samuel Gompers was chairman of the labor group on the Council of National Defense. We wired Mr. Gompers, the President, the Secretary of Labor, and the Secretary of War, asking that the trade-union women be given representation on that committee. Our efforts brought about the formation of a Committee on Women in Industry, with Mrs. J. Borden Harriman as chairman. All of our group who had signed the wire to the President were named members of the committee. Mr. Gompers advised us that we were members of his committee also.

I and the other members of our group made frequent trips to Washington to serve on this Women in Industry Committee. Meanwhile, Mrs. Robins had been appointed chairman of the Women in Industry Committee of the Illinois State Council of Defense and was getting that work organized throughout the state.

On the national scene, the Council of National Defense had appointed a "Woman's Committee" about which we knew little and had not concerned ourselves. One night I received a long telegram from William B. Wilson, the Secretary of State, advising me that the Secretary of War had appointed me a member of this committee also. Then I received a telegram from Dr. Anna Howard Shaw, chairman of the committee, welcoming me to the group and asking that I come to Washington as soon as possible to meet with them.

The make-up of this Woman's Committee was interesting. When the Council of National Defense had decided to set up the committee, it had selected as members such leading suffragists and clubwomen as Dr. Anna Howard Shaw, Mrs. Carrie Chapman Catt, Mrs. Antoinette Funk, and Mrs. Stanley McCormick.

Then, to balance this group, the council had selected some noted anti-suffragists to serve with them, such as Ida Tarbell, the noted writer, and Mrs. Joseph R. Lamar.

It was quite an experience to see this group working together.

Dr. Anna Howard Shaw would storm about "men running everything." (Often this Woman's Committee did seem like a fifth wheel and not to fit into the regular machinery of the Council of National Defense.) Mrs. Lamar would gently remind Dr. Shaw that this was still a man's world, that we had a man for President, men for Governors of our states, and so on.

But Dr. Shaw was most generous in her praise of these fine women of the committee, and I often heard her say, "Well, as long as they selected anti-suffragists, I am glad they selected two such splendid women," meaning of course Mrs. Lamar and Miss Tarbell.

Miss Tarbell, reporting on a letter given her to write, would say modestly, "I have it ready now for Dr. Shaw to put the punch in it." Dr. Shaw did have a particularly forceful touch whether writing or speaking. Before I worked with her, I had been a little prejudiced against her, I having heard that she was quite domineering. But this prejudice soon left me and I grew to love this fighter for woman's rights.

As I continued to work with this Woman's Committee, they learned to know me and to accept me, and we worked together very well. Mrs. Lamar became my very good friend, as did Ida Tarbell and Mrs. McCormick. But that day when I first received the wire from Dr. Shaw welcoming me to the committee, I was sure that this group, of whom I knew only one, Mrs. Antoinette Funk of Illinois, was eager to meet me so that they could look me over. I learned later that they had been recommending another trade-union woman for the position and that I had been appointed without their advice.

Soon after I had met the group, I was appointed chairman of the committee's Women in Industry Division. Early in June of that year I was obliged to leave Washington for a few days to attend the National Women's Trade Union League convention in Kansas City. Meanwhile, the Woman's Committee continued to hold daily meetings. Minutes of these meetings were mailed to absent members of the committee, but in Kansas City I was so busy at the convention that I had no time to read these minutes until I was seated on the train headed back for Washington. To my amazement I read in the minutes that the committee had voted to select an executive chairman of my division for me. It was not so much that I was dissatisfied with the woman who had been selected; it was the manner in which the selection had been made — without at all consulting me, the division's general chairman.

When I arrived back in Washington, I called a member of the committee and told her how I felt about the matter, adding, "If that appointment stands, I shall resign and the country will know why!"

I knew full well that the country was not at all concerned about my office on that committee. But I felt keenly my responsibility. I knew I had to take a stand if I intended to represent properly the working women whom I had been chosen to represent.

The next morning when the committee met, the motion for the appointment of that executive chairman was rescinded, and a motion was carried to ask me to appoint my own executive chairman.

MY FATHER had been ill for more than a year. In late June he took a turn for the worse, and I came home and stayed to be with him. Arthur came home, too, so we were all with Father when he died early in July. We felt very lonely.

Owen had been rejected by the Army, he having recently undergone a major operation which had left him much underweight. He received a permanent physical disability status, but when after six months he had regained his health, he enlisted in the Navy. Mary, who had remained home during our father's illness, returned to work. In order to do her part in the war effort, she went this time into the U. S. Employment Service. When the war ended she was transferred to the Illinois Free Employment Service, where she remained through the years.

I did not go back to Washington until late in the summer. My old friend, Mrs. James A. Field, with whom I had worked in the Women's Trade Union League in Chicago, came to Washington about this time to join her husband who was working with the U. S. Shipping Board. At once I engaged her as my executive chairman for the Women in Industry Division of the Woman's Committee. It was an excellent arrangement. She understood our work and I could well trust it to her. Meanwhile, I had to divide my time in order to take care of my Chicago work, which also was heavy.

A MAJOR NATIONAL EMPHASIS against long working hours for women began during World War I, and I know that this was due to the influence of the trade-union women who served on the various defense committees. Mrs. Field and I held national and regional conferences, bringing together women from various states. The keynote of our conferences was "the achievement of industrial standards for working women." It was now a measure to help the war effort as well as the women. When Great Britain had first entered the war, so great was her need for munitions, that women had worked unlimited hours a day. But this long working day had only resulted in reduced production. A Royal Commission appointed to examine into the matter had recommended a shorter working day as a measure to increase overall production. We, on our part, recommended that America profit by the experience of the British. The War Department finally issued a set of working standards for men and women — an eight-hour day, a six-day week, and other provisions. It was our committee which pressed for these standards.

Meanwhile, our Women's Trade Union League felt this was the time to ask for a Federal eight-hour-day law for women as a war measure. Mary Anderson and I were sent as a committee to President Wilson. We met with the President on an historic day; he had just come from an appearance before Congress, where he had presented his famous Fourteen Points as our war aims. He met with us in one of the smaller rooms of the White House. We sat across from him near his desk. Our meeting seemed much less formal than when we had been received in his stately office. Two years before, when the Adamson Law in regard to the railroads had been before Congress, he had publicly taken his stand in favor of the eight-hour working day. As we talked, we found him helping to make a case for the eight-hour working day in the interest of production. He, too, knew that where there is fatigue there is inefficiency.

But soon any chance of Federal legislation of the kind we desired seemed to disappear. In April of that year, 1918, in the famous *Hammer* v. *Dagenhart* case, the U. S. Supreme Court declared unconstitutional the Federal child labor law. This decision was not reversed till 1940. Meanwhile, the Federal Government was denied the right to legislate limitations upon hours of work.

DURING THE SECOND YEAR of the war, trade-union activity was vastly stimulated when the National War Labor

Board declared for the right of workers to organize and to bargain collectively through chosen representatives. This all-important right, the board declared, "shall not be denied, abridged, or interfered with by the employer in any manner." The same right was accorded the employers, although they had never needed an order from any board to allow them this right.

The National War Labor Board had been set up to govern industrial relations between employers and workers in war industries for the duration of the war. The members of the board had been appointed by the Secretary of Labor in March of 1918. On the board were two groups, one nominated by the A. F. of L., and the other by the National Industrial Board. Each group had its own chairman. Frank P. Walsh headed the group representing the workers, and former President William H. Taft that representing the employers. The labor members of the board were Frank J. Hayes, W. L. Hutchison, William H. Johnson, T. A. Rickert, and my old friend of the Seamen's Union, Victor A. Olander.

Meanwhile, in Chicago we had a wide variety of organizing campaigns underway. We worked on the "council plan" in the big industries covering several kinds of occupations. This meant that we had a delegate body representing all the trades involved and all contributing funds and workers toward the campaign. It was an effective way of organizing.

I was attending the electrical and the department store councils, while my friend, Mary Haney, was working with the stockyards council. This stockyards campaign had almost resulted in a strike in 1917. The strike had been avoided only through the work of a special mediation board set up by the President, who declared the stockyards essential to the war effort. But the difficulties in the stockyards remained unsettled. In 1918, the

National War Labor Board decreed that there should be no strikes or lockouts during the war. The six points remaining unsettled in the stockyards disputes were to be settled by an arbitrator. One day while all this was going on I met John Fitzpatrick, who said to me:

"Agnes, we have just submitted your name as arbitrator in the stockyards matter."

I thought he was joking, as he often did. But in all serious-ness he added:

"And they will have to give us a darn good reason why if they don't accept you!"

Both sides to the disputes had submitted many candidates for the position of arbitrator. All were rejected. The grounds on which I was rejected fascinated me. The report stated that I had made a speech during the shirtwaist-makers' strike of 1909 which indicated that I had a bias against organized labor!

Judge Samuel Alschuler was finally agreed upon as arbitrator. The hearings began in February of 1918 and continued for a month on the six points under dispute. The six demands the workers contended for seem mild now: an eight-hour working day, to be completed in so far as possible within nine consecu-tive hours; twenty minutes of paid lunch time where plants operated three shifts; one dollar a day increase over amounts paid December 31, 1917, for the same classification for the ten-hour day; a piecework price raise equal to the hourly raise allowed elsewhere; the same wage rates for male and female employees doing the same class of work; and no change in the guaranteed work time in effect as of November 30, 1917.

I supported all these demands, with particular emphasis on the "equal pay for equal work." Our Women's Trade Union League had been working for that for many years.

On March 30, 1918, the administrator made his awards.

Comments on the case ran through a dozen pages. Decisions favorable to the workers were given on all six points. We hailed it a great victory.

EARLY IN 1918, the Council of National Defense directed the Secretary of Labor to appoint an Advisory Council of seven members — two representatives of labor, two of employers, and three from the public — to work out a War Labor Administration Bureau.

The women were concerned about having a woman on this council, and a host of likely candidates for the position were being recommended to the Secretary of Labor. One morning Mrs. Field and I visited the Secretary's office to ask him to approve a program we wanted to set up. We saw the Secretary, and then to my surprise he asked me if I would serve on the new Advisory Council as representative of women. In no way prepared for the offer of such a position, I told him I would need a little time to think it over.

In the building we met the Assistant Secretary of Labor, our Chicago friend, Louis F. Post. Was I going to accept the appointment? He wanted to know. He had known the Secretary was going to offer me the position. He insisted that I accept it.

Amy Field was equally insistent.

I accepted the appointment that day. Then I went to the Children's Bureau to see its chief, Julia Lathrop, on another matter, and she showed me a wire asking her to press for the appointment of a certain woman to the Advisory Council. "But I have just accepted that appointment," I said meekly.

Julia was delighted.

From there I went to the Woman's Committee, where a telegram urging the appointment of still another candidate for the position had just come in. Again I had to break the news. Nothing seemed to please the committee more than that one of its members had received the position.

I realized something of the full importance of the appointment when that evening I had dinner with a newspaperwoman who told me that the story of my appointment had been cabled, the release sent abroad as well as throughout our own country. Miss Tarbell of the Woman's Committee told me later that she had more requests for my photograph than for that of any other member of the Woman's Committee, because I had been appointed to represent on the Advisory Council all women.

The work of the Advisory Council began very soon, with Governor John Linn of Illinois as chairman, L. C. Marshall, economist, as secretary, and I in the "public group" representing women. John B. Lennon and John J. Casey represented labor. Wardell Catchings and A. R. Landon represented employers.

Government recognition of labor had now come a long way. The request for labor representation in the Cabinet had begun as early as 1869, but it had not been until 1903 that labor had secured even the Bureau of Labor in the then newly-formed Department of Commerce and Labor, then the newest and smallest of the Departments. An act of Congress signed by President William Howard Taft on his last day in office, March 4, 1913, had finally created a Department of Labor with Cabinet status. Now, within this Department, a special War Labor Administration Bureau had been deemed necessary. Our Advisory Council met day after day for two months working out the plan for this new bureau and reporting our progress from time to time to William B. Wilson, the Secretary of Labor.

President Wilson, Newton D. Baker, Secretary of War, and Josephus Daniels, Secretary of the Navy, all turned to Mr. Wilson as the authority on all labor matters. Mr. Wilson was

respected and beloved by everyone. He was a real labor states-
man. He had gained a wide experience as secretary-treasurer
of the United Mine Workers Union; he had been a leader in
the general organized labor movement; he had served in Congress; and all this experience had qualified him superbly for his
new post. He gave our Advisory Council free rein. He gave
no orders as to what should be done. He blocked us with no
interference. And he was always ready to give us his wise
counsel.

In late March we made our report. We had recommended
several "Divisions" for the new War Labor Administration
Bureau, each "Division" to handle a certain work for which
there was a great need. Several groups, headed by the officers
of the National Women's Trade Union League, had for some
time been interested in seeing established a Woman in Industry
Service. This was one of the "Divisions" we of the Advisory
Council were recommending, and the case for the need for this
Woman in Industry Service it became my task to prepare.

Our Advisory Council recommended an expanded U. S. Employment Service. It recommended, too, that legislation be
enacted authorizing the Secretary of Labor to provide houses
for war needs. It recommended that a "Conference Board" be
set up, and out of this recommendation grew the National War
Labor Board. Our recommendations were accepted by the
Secretary of Labor, and soon the War Labor Administration
Bureau was set up and operating.

After the end of World War I, one service set up as a part
of the War Labor Administration Bureau was made by statute
into a permanent bureau. This was the Woman in Industry
Service. John J. Casey, who had served with us on the Advisory
Council, was elected to Congress and sponsored the bill which
effected this. Later (1920) this Woman in Industry Service

became the Women's Bureau. Mary van Kleeck became the first director of this Woman in Industry Service and of the Women's Bureau. Mary Anderson served as her assistant, succeeded her as director, and filled that post with a distinguished record for twenty-five years. The Bureau has served the working woman well.

17

American Labor Mission to Europe

E ARLY IN 1918, while the war was still in progress, and at the time when there was a tremendous enthusiasm over the idea of union and co-operation between the common people of Europe and America, it had been planned to send an unusual "American Mission to Europe."

The mission was to consist of about twenty representatives of labor, journalism, banking, and other interests. Its purpose was to observe and report on war conditions in Europe. Its purpose was to demonstrate our goodwill and readiness to help the war-stricken peoples of Europe. Its purpose was mutual education and the cultivation of international fellow-feeling.

Of the group composing this mission, nine had been selected from organized labor. Seven of these were men: James Wilson of the Pattern Workers' Union, the chairman of the group; William Johnson, president of the Machinists' Union; George Berry, president of the Printing Pressmen's International; William Short, president of the Washington State Federation of Labor; Chester Wright of the Typographical International; John P. Frey, an executive officer of the Moulders' International; and Martin F. Ryan.

The two women members of this labor group were Melinda Scott, an organizer for the A. F. of L., and I.

At the beginning of the year, Mr. Samuel Gompers had written me that I had been appointed a member of this group. Then, one day while I was finishing up my work on the Advisory Council, I received word that the group was to sail on a certain day. I went to Chicago to talk over the proposed trip with my sister Mary, my brother Owen, and my Chicago friends. They all seemed alarmed at the idea of my venturing across the submarine-infested Atlantic. There was no air travel in those days, and with frightful frequency German submarines were attacking our ships running with food and troops to the war zones. They advised me not to attempt the dangerous voyage.

I went back to Washington undecided. But after talking with Mr. Gompers, I realized it was my duty to make the trip. Home to Chicago I went once more to make preparations for the voyage. Soon I wired Mr. Gompers I was ready to go.

Mary and Owen and a group of my Chicago friends were at the station to see me off. Mary had tears in her eyes. She was sure that she would never see me again. Owen, who had come in from Great Lakes Naval Training Station, gave me as his parting words, "I'll see you 'over there!' " He was expecting to go to sea any day.

Back again in Washington, I received my passports in record time, got my credentials from the A. F. of L., had another conference with Mr. Gompers, and I was ready to sail.

Our ship moved out from the port of New York after dark. At once we were ordered to our cabins, and a sentinel was posted outside each door. Boat muster was held each day of the voyage, and we were given instructions as to what to do should "anything unusual" happen. As we reached the danger zone, that part of the ocean where most of the German submarines lay in wait, we became truly frightened. I prayed as I had never prayed before. I felt that if I ever saw land again, I would never again want to venture upon a limitless ocean whose depths held enemy U-boats.

We moved safely through the danger zone until we had only one more night at sea. We were told not to undress that night, but to be ready for any emergency. We were awakened in the middle of the night by the sound of a depth bomb exploding. Colonel O. S. Shirill, in command of the ship, met us as we assembled on deck ready to go to our lifeboats. He assured us our ship had not been hit. A torpedo intended for our ship had missed by about eight feet and passed on to explode against the side of another ship in the convoy. The torpedoed ship, crippled but not sunk, was proceeding on to port. We exchanged messages with the warship guarding our convoy and sweeping the sea for mines. That next day even the troops on board our ship were allowed to be at ease all day. We docked that night at Liverpool but did not go ashore. The next day I sent a cablegram to Mary, "Ship reported arrived safely."

In Britain we were the guests of the British Information Service. Their courtesy to us was unsurpassed. They sent as our host a party headed by Captain Stephens Saunders and Commander Guy Standing, the British actor who was so well known in America at that time.

London was having frequent air raids, and we had had an anxious voyage. Our hosts decided to take us to Birmingham, in the northern part of the country, for a rest over the week end.

At Birmingham we were taken to see the manufacturing of tanks and aeroplanes. Women were working here side-by-side with men, doing work unknown to them before the war. We were taken to the fields where the tanks were tested, and we had the novel experience of riding in one. We saw these tanks push down trees as easily as though crushing weeds. We saw them climbing hills and crossing trenches on a terrain constructed to resemble that of France where they were to be used.

We were then taken for a visit to the model town of Port Sunlight and brought back again to Birmingham to spend the night. We were ready to retire after a strenuous day, when we heard a terrific noise overhead. Birmingham was experiencing an air raid, its first in two years. My reaction, after my recent terror at sea, was that I was not going to worry about what was happening overhead so long as I had the secure feeling of being on land!

On Monday we went to London to begin the official duties of our mission. We went first to the American Embassy where we were received by the U. S. Ambassador, Walter H. Page, and by Admiral Sims of our Navy. Part of our morning was set aside for callers. My first visitor was Charlie Wheeler, the London Correspondent for the *Chicago Tribune,* whom I had known very well since those early days of our work in Springfield. Even the newspapermen were glad to see people from home. He cabled the interview to Chicago.

Margaret Bondfield and Mary Macarthur, the two outstanding British labor women, came next to see us. They were old friends whom I had met back in 1908 when they had visited America. They had visited our Industrial Exhibit of those days.

That noon we got our official welcome from the British Government. It was held in the Harcourt Rooms of the House of Commons. Mr. G. N. Barnes, M.P., labor representative in the British War Cabinet, was our host. We met some famous men, some of whom we already knew of, such as Lord Bryce, A. J. Balfour, Secretary of State for Foreign Affairs, and Winston Churchill. Mr. Churchill told us that two-and-a-half million men and women were engaged in war work, and that nine-tenths of the British shells were made by women. He praised the workers, who, since the beginning of the war, he said had lost less than one day out of a thousand through strikes.

At that luncheon we soon learned about British formalities. All the speeches were in the form of toasts (as they were, too, at the dinners given for us). The speakers for our party were Mr. Wilson, our chairman, and Edwin T. Meredith of Des Moines, who represented the farm group. At the close of the program, Mr. Meredith, in contrast to the formal toasts, rose in his breezy way and offered a toast to the British Navy. Everyone, of course, raised his glass in response. But as this was not on the formal program, it may have surprised or even shocked some of our British friends. They were being introduced to the spontaneity of a Midwestern American who would not stand on ceremony when he felt moved by the occasion to offer a toast.

Our own newspapermen were very informal, too. One picture of the entire party was taken on the plaza outside the House of Commons after the luncheon. Melinda Scott and I were seated one on either side of our host, and Mr. Barnes and the other dignitaries were grouped around us. The picture was used by the *Chicago Evening Post* with the heading: "Our Little Agnes in Swell Company." Indeed I was in swell company that day!

Afterwards we learned that a special rule had had to be made to allow the women of our party to be entertained in the Harcourt Rooms where we had enjoyed the luncheon. An integral part of the mission, we had had to be admitted with the men.

The next day we went to Brighton with a group of labor leaders including Arthur Henderson, G. N. Barnes, and Mary Macarthur. We were met by His Worship, the Lord Mayor of Brighton.

Brighton, once a fashionable resort, had been turned into a

rehabilitation center for injured soldiers. The famous Royal Pavilion had been made into a military hospital. Built by George IV about 1787, the extravagance of this Royal Pavilion and its fittings had been proverbial, as shown in Lord Byron's lines in *Don Juan:* "Shut up — not the king but the Pavilion, Or else 'twill cost us another million." Deserted for many years, the Pavilion was finally purchased by the city of Brighton and made a "peoples" Pavilion, the room where royalty once dined becoming a concert hall. Turned into a hospital during the war, East Indian soldiers were quartered there. Because the Pavilion was decorated in Hindu style, it was thought that these men would feel somewhat at home among the surroundings.

On visiting another hospital, at Roehampton, we were thrilled by their advanced work of rehabilitation. In that spring of 1918 they were fitting splendidly-constructed artificial limbs to disabled soldiers and teaching them their use. This hospital, sponsored by Queen Mary and called Queen Mary's Convalescent Hospital, was a pioneer orthopedic military hospital.

One week end we spent as the guests of Mrs. Henry Marsh, an American, in the famous old Warwick Castle whose long history dates back to the days of Alfred the Great. Our rooms were reached through long corridors and up winding staircases whose walls were covered with antique armor and weapons. The walls of the sleeping-rooms were covered with brocaded red satin or other rich material. The bedspreads were gold cloth and the canopies were equally fine. I was in a dreamy rapture, living in the splendor of it all. It was too grand even to describe a little of it! I was living in the novels of Walter Scott as I often stood gazing entranced out the castle windows at the view of the Avon. I was looking out on Shakespeare's

"Our Little Agnes in Swell Company"
(Reproduced from an old newsprint)

beautiful countryside. When as a girl sitting at my glove-machine, I had dreamed dreams of splendor, but never had my imagination dared go so far as to dream that I one day might sleep in a castle!

At the close of the week end, we were tendered a reception in the Great Hall of the castle where the Lord Mayor of the village welcomed. It was a very formal affair. In this hall stood the mace of the "Kingmaker," the helmet of Cromwell, and the ancient punch bowl which, whenever an heir came into possession, was filled with one hundred gallons of punch.

WE WERE IN ENGLAND at the most critical time of the war. The terrific Battle of Flanders was in progress; there was the gravest anxiety and the bitterest losses since the dark days of 1914. In a town of 5,000, we saw 300 widows as a result of one week's action. In another town we visited, there was a solid block of mourning as the result of one naval battle.

The British were meeting this crisis with the same calmness and determined confidence with which they met all the other strains of war. They showed the weariness four years of war had wrought. But this weariness did not mean that they were giving up; it rather accented their determination to win. Almost every family we met had lost at least one relative at the front. But they bore their grief silently. We met labor men who had lost their sons, but no word of sorrow came from them.

Throughout our stay we were on war-time rations, which was only fair, and which did not bother us too much. We had our meat-ration cards to use in the hotels, but we found little use for them. We attended so many affairs where meat was not served, and often we had delicious salmon from Scotland that more than made up for the absence of meat.

What I minded most was the lack of heat. We could have

wood for our fireplaces once a day. I chose the evening for my fire, but it was hard to get up in a cold room and to eat one's breakfast there. Breakfast was always served in one's room.

ONE IMPORTANT PURPOSE of our mission was to confer with the British labor representatives. They entertained us at receptions, teas, and dinners, and when much of that was over we sat in all-day conferences.

Among the British labor leaders, Arthur Henderson, secretary of the British Labor Party, was the outstanding figure. He had come to the fore in the British labor circles and was the center of interest among the American liberals after the publication of that well-written document, the *British Labor Party's Program*. An iron-molder by trade, a trade-union leader, he had become a member of the first British War Cabinet.

It was a time of great dreams among the common peoples of Europe. The Blackpool Convention of the British Labor Congress had met in 1917 and adopted a resolution which provided for the calling of a conference of representatives of the workers of the war countries to discuss peace terms. In February of 1918, an Inter-Allied Labor and Socialist Conference had been held in London with representatives of the trade-union and Socialist movements of Great Britain, France, Belgium, Italy, Servia, Bosnia, Herzegovina, Roumania, and South Africa present. This conference had adopted a memorandum of war aims which was accepted by those present as a guide for the workers in the represented nations.

One section of this memorandum provided for the calling of an "International Congress of Labor and Socialist Organizations" for the purpose of removing misunderstandings and obstacles standing in the way of world peace. Such a conference was to be held in a neutral country under the auspices of an impartial committee and was to seat representatives of the Central Powers. As an essential condition all organizations desiring to be represented would be called upon to state in precise terms, through a public declaration, their conformity with the principles of "No annexation or punative indemnities," and "The right of all peoples to self-determination."

Further, the memorandum asked that such a conference "Provide an opportunity for the delegates from the respective countries now in a state of war to make a full and frank statement of their position on these questions and their future intentions, and to endeavor by mutual agreement to arrange a program of action for a speedy and democratic peace."

Our mission, of course, had no authority to negotiate with, or sanction the actions taken by, the labor movements in any of the Allied countries. We had been authorized only to state the war aims and policies adopted by the A. F. of L., to confer with labor representatives of the Allied nations, and then to bring home to our labor movement an accurate report on the Allies' aims and policies.

We felt that when the conditions of the "Inter-Allied Labor and Socialist Conference" had been accepted by the labor and Socialist representatives of the Central Powers, everything would have advanced a long way. Meanwhile, we discussed with the labor representatives from the Allied countries many of the existing conditions which we believed could be adequately dealt with through the re-establishment of an effective International Federation of Labor.

During our weeks in Great Britain, we traveled about the country speaking and observing firsthand their war activities. The British labor women, headed by Margaret Bondfield and Mary Macarthur, entertained our labor women members of the mission in London, giving us the opportunity to meet the women representing the various unions.

One of the most interesting entertainments given us by the Ministry of Information, under whose auspices we were visiting the country, was a luncheon for our party to meet the Press of the world. The luncheon was held in historic Whitehall Palace where Cromwell once held Parliament, and where, through one of its windows, Charles I stepped to his execution. It was the first meal served in the old banquet room in the nearly two hundred and seventy years since then. We were given the menus of that last meal, and they tried to carry on the traditions of the place even to the toastmaster.

At the luncheon, one long table was set the length of the room, with a speaker's table for four at the head. The toasts were to His Majesty the King, to the President of the United States, to the American guests, and to the Press of the world. Edward Price Bell, London correspondent of the *Chicago Daily News,* James Wilson of our labor group, Sir Campbell Stuart, and Harry E. Brittain all responded.

Before each toast, a pompous man in tail-coat and white gloves and looking very solemn, placed himself behind the speaker and called out the speaker's name in a loud voice. This was the toastmaster, a professional functionary for very formal occasions, a custom dating back to the time of the Stuarts. In Stuart times it was the custom to drop a piece of toast in the wine before drinking. The toast was thought to improve the flavor of the wine. Thus the origin of the phrase, "to toast."

We spent a week in Scotland, stopping first at Gretna Green, the romantic run-away-marriage place just inside the Scottish border. It had been converted into a munitions-making center. We held a meeting there and spent the night.

We made a trip up the Clyde as guests of the British Navy, stopping at the shipyards where some of our members addressed the workers. But our two great meetings were at St.

Andrew's Hall at Glasgow, where I was one of the speakers, and at Usher Hall in Edinburgh. At the Usher Hall meeting the stage was so crowded it seemed like a mass meeting.

A week in Scotland, and we received our "marching orders" to proceed to France.

FRANCE IN 1918

IN FRANCE, at Le Havre, we were welcomed by the Mayor of Le Havre and representatives of the French War Department. We were received, also, by the officers of the Belgium Government, whose temporary "Capital on French Soil" was a short distance from Le Havre.

There to welcome us, too, were U. S. Ambassador and Mrs. Brand Whitlock. They were from the Middle West, Springfield, Illinois, and we felt at home together.

During that day and on our trip to Paris we were accompanied by Mme. Henri Carton de Wiart, wife of the Minister of Justice, the ranking member of the French Cabinet.

Our way to Paris lay through Rouen in Normandy where Joan of Arc was burned at the stake. That Easter, as a result of the Big Offensive, a hundred thousand men, women, and children, packed into cars, driven from their villages and homes, had passed through Rouen on their way to Amiens.

It was late in the evening when we arrived in Paris. We were received in warm French fashion. Our reception started at the station, where the Minister of Labor gave us the official welcome. Crowded into the room were French Government officials and representatives from the French labor and Socialist organizations. They escorted us to our hotel, where we had a conference with the labor officials about plans during our stay. A long schedule had been worked out for us, but our time being shorter than had been expected, changes were having to be made.

We were received by American Ambassador Sharp, by Marshal Joffre, the hero of the Marne, by President Poincare, by Premier Clemenceau, by the presidents of the Senate and the Chamber of Deputies. Also present were such celebrities as Anton Dubost and Paul Deschanel.

The next day, M. Pichon, the Minister of Foreign Affairs, gave us a luncheon. It was followed by a reception at the Town Hall given by the Paris Municipality and another reception at the Chamber of Deputies, where we heard the bill to ration meat being debated.

In the Chamber of Deputies it was announced that there would be an adjournment in honor of the American Mission, and at this pronouncement there awoke a great demonstration with everyone cheering and waving to us. We were told it was the first time in its history that the Chamber had adjourned in honor of visitors. We felt honored indeed!

That afternoon, in addition to other affairs, there was a special reception given by Miss Valentine Thompson for the women members of our mission to allow us to meet the French *Feministes* of Paris. But not only did we meet the leaders of the French suffrage movement, but we met also the young leaders of the new movement of working women who had organized into trade unions in the past two years. One of these latter young women touched the audience deeply in telling of the hard struggle her group had undergone to obtain wage enough to live on. Her group was not unpatriotic, she said, but human necessity had forced them to strike. There was present also Madame Duchene who had made the fight for "Equal pay for equal work" in France.

The French women, like their English sisters, were doing

their share of war work. We visited one large factory near Paris where six thousand women were making artillery shells.

The shelling of Paris by long-range guns had occurred before our arrival, and here and there we saw signs of the destruction the falling shells had wrecked. Sandbags were piled around the monuments, and the stained glass was being removed from the windows of the churches. Signs of another kind of destruction were even more evident. Everywhere we saw women in mourning. Black — black — black was all we saw on women young and old. Almost every woman was wearing it. In this they differed from the English, who did not wear it. With the French it was a tradition.

Sunday was our day with the French labor movement. That morning a delegation of the labor leaders called to escort us to their headquarters to meet the officials of the various unions and to see their large assembly hall. A luncheon was arranged for us by the *Confederation General du Travail* and the Socialist Party, which had been working together. I sat next to Albert Thomas, the Socialist leader who later became Secretary of the International Labor Office under the League of Nations. He spoke English. I told him how much I regretted not knowing the French language, and he said that we should all know each other's languages because such knowledge would become very important after the war.

The luncheon began at one. I had hoped to be able to leave by five to visit Grace Gassette, an old Chicago friend. But at five the speeches were still going on. The translations took up so much of the time.

Late as it was, however, when the luncheon was over I did go to see Miss Gassette. She was then a famous artist. In 1914 in Chicago she had painted my portrait, to be included in a collection of portraits of people whom she admired for their particular work. Shortly after her Chicago exhibit in 1914, the war had broken out in Europe. Miss Gassette had returned to France, had given up painting, and had devoted her time to making ingenious surgical appliances for injured soldiers. Her knowledge of anatomy and her skill in the arts had enabled her to contrive devices that allowed many an injured soldier to use an otherwise useless limb. In recognition of her work, the French Government had given her its highest decorations.

The next day I had a delightful surprise when an old school chum and long-time friend from Grand Rapids, Jennie Daniels Carpenter, called on me. She was in France doing work for the Red Cross.

Our Labor Mission spent the day in conference with the French labor leaders discussing the same issues we had discussed with the labor leaders in London. Then, early the next day we started out for the war zone, traveling in military cars under military orders, and carrying gas masks.

We rode through village after village, some of them only a block long with a row of white stone houses built up to the street. They looked as though they had stood there for ages. From the doorways and windows there looked out at us women and old men and sad-faced children. Soon they would be evacuated, as the enemy approached this territory. We could comprehend their sadness at the prospect of having to leave their homes. Most of them were peasants who had never been outside their village. These homes were sacred to them and full of centuries-old traditions and family lore.

Whenever we stopped, these people looked at us in wonder and fear. But as soon as they would learn that we were Americans, their fear would turn to joy. They loved the American soldiers and seemed never to tire of watching the American troops go by. But they urged us not to hesitate long in their villages; they feared the presence of our military cars would invite bombing.

As we rode farther, we came to villages which had been completely destroyed. Not a soul was left in them. I was still haunted by the faces of those sad-faced children in the windows of those other villages, children whose only memories of childhood would be of tragedy, of terror in the night, of the death of loved ones, of being driven from their homes and perhaps separated from their familes. The picture would often come up to me again as later during World War II, within the lifetime of these sad-faced children I had seen waving to me from their windows, war again scarred its terrible way across this beautiful countryside.

We could hear the sounds of battle as we sped through the Vosges. This cannonading had been an everyday horror to these people.

Late that afternoon we halted at the little town of Domremy, the home of Joan of Arc. Built in the fourteenth century, the house where she was born in 1411 still stands, a large stone house with very few windows. Why so few windows? I asked. There was a tax on windows in the days when the house was built, I was told, so people built houses with as few windows as possible.

We went in and saw the room where Joan of Arc was born. To me it was a holy shrine. Outside the house I walked among the trees where she had heard the "Voices" directing her crusade to save France. We visited the little church where she had worshipped. It was a Joan of Arc pilgrimage for me, and to complete it, our next stop was to be Rheims.

Not far from Domremy we met our first American troops returning from their first battle. Our long convoy passing their camps attracted their attention, and when the boys saw the

American flags flying and American women in the cars they
ran down to the road waving and shouting. This was in the
region of the Marne where the terrible battles were fought.

Near Rheims, a French officer entered our car and our convoy
was rearranged. Only two cars were allowed to proceed at a
time. Then a wait of ten minutes and two more cars, and so on.
Upon entering Rheims there was the danger of bombs.

At the gates of Rheims we looked out over a sad sight.
Spread out before us was a mass of ruins, a city of rubble with
here and there a broken wall left standing. Of a former population of sixty thousand, no one was left. Those who had not
died in the bombardments had been evacuated.

We drove toward the cathedral to find ourselves in full view
of the German observation post! The French captain in our
car pointed to a shattered building across the way which had
been one of the city's finest. He said he had had dinner there
only a month before.

Copies of a proclamation from the German commandant
appeared on walls and buildings. The writing was in French;
the translation read:

NOTICE TO THE POPULATION

In order efficiently to insure the safety of our troops
and the tranquility of the population of Rheims, the
persons mentioned have been seized as hostages by
the Commander of the German Army. These hostages
will be shot if there is the least disorder. On the other
hand, if the town remains perfectly calm and quiet,
these hostages and inhabitants will be placed under
the protection of the German Army.

THE GENERAL COMMANDING
Rheims, 12, September, 1914

As we entered the venerable Cathedral of Rheims we were saddened at the sight of so much destruction. Two hundred years had been required for the building of the cathedral. It had stood for centuries. Here Clovis had been baptized. Here the kings of France had been anointed. Here, in 1429, Joan of Arc had stood beside her king, Charles VII, and watched him solemnly crowned. Now the venerable old building was a shambles. We felt bitter indeed toward the vandals who had destroyed this landmark of history.

We had hardly begun to look around when we were hurried away. A German aeroplane was overhead.

A short journey took us to the military headquarters of General H. J. E. Gouraud, commander of the Fourth Army and the hero of the Dardanelles campaign. He had been the man behind the movement which had barred the advance of the Germans into the Champagne, the country we were now visiting. He had brought the enemy to a halt and driven him back on a wide front. American troops had been in that counter-offensive.

General Gouraud greeted us warmly, and one felt that knowing this kindly officer it was easy to understand why he was so beloved by his men. Fighting for him was a way of showing their affection for him. He had lost an arm in battle a year before. It could have been saved, he knew, by long medical treatment. But that would have taken him too long from active combat. He ordered the arm amputated! General Gouraud praised highly our American Red Cross and other relief agencies we had sent to France. The climax of our evening in the French camp came with our drinking of toasts to Rheims in champagne in the heart of the Champagne country.

We rested overnight and were ready to leave the next day

to visit another famous battleground. I had dreamed all that night of Joan of Arc.

VERDUN

WE DROVE to Verdun at night. It was pouring rain. No lights were allowed on the cars. To light our way we had only the distant flash of guns. We arrived several hours late. We were tired, cold and hungry. But when we met the men who were in their fourth year of war, we forgot our little discomforts.

Here at Verdun, for six months of 1916, the French had repulsed all the German attacks. Their firm resistance and retaliating offensive had made them the marvel of the world.

First we were led through a long tunnel, one of the galleries, as they were called, to the citadel. We walked what seemed an interminable distance through this underground fort from which the holding of Verdun was directed. At the end of the long passageway was an attractive room arranged as a banquet hall and with its walls covered with the flags of the Allies. French officers were our hosts, and, true to French custom, we were served a delicious meal. Afterwards a soldier collected the menu cards. On them there was an artistic sketch of the fort at the top and the menu typed in below. I tried to make the soldier understand that I would like to keep mine as a souvenir of the visit. But he said something in French very politely and took mine along with the others. Later he returned the cards, each with the autographs of the French officers in command of the citadel. It was another of the thoughtful touches we found so often during our visit in France.

The men of our party were put up at the citadel, but we women had to go to a near-by hospital to spend the night. Our driver started off in the wrong direction and got lost. We drove

Snapshots taken by Agnes Nestor at Verdun. (1) An underground shelter. (2) Bomb damage to a building. (3) A damaged cathedral.

for hours on the dark roads before we reached the hospital. It was 1:30 in the morning as we groped our way up a little hill in the pouring rain to our destination. Our hostess, Mlle. Yoland de Bayes, a beautiful young Frenchwoman, had established the hospital early in the war with a contribution of a million francs. But not only did she give her money; she also gave herself along with it. There were four thousand beds in her hospital and her devotion to her work was endless. The summer before our visit, she herself had been severely wounded and for weeks had been near death.

An American captain in charge of the engineering work of that section welcomed us too. It was he who told us of the wonderful devotion of Mlle. de Bayes, speaking of her as of another Joan of Arc.

The next morning we drove back to Verdun to join our party. We were taken through the fort. We saw the huge bakeries where, even during the bombardment, five hundred thousand loaves of bread were baked in a day. We visited the little chapel and happened to go in while High Mass was being celebrated. We realized then the core of French courage. Faith had bridged over the agony of war.

General Hirschauer presided over the noonday "banquet" given in our honor. The general not only autographed our menu cards but also presented each of us with a bronze medal which had just been struck in commemoration of "the living and the dead" who had held the fort during the long bombardment. On one side of the medal were the famous words, "They shall not pass." On the other side was the figure of Joan of Arc with her sword.

General Hirschauer gave us also a medal for Mr. Samuel Gompers inscribed to him with the date, May 8, 1918. Upon our return to the States, our chairman presented the medal to

Mr. Gompers on behalf of General Hirschauer at the next A. F. of L. convention.

After the banquet we climbed upon the old fortification of the city of Verdun. This fortification had been built in the seventeenth century. Other parts of the fortifications were built in 1880, but there was one part which dated back to Roman days. The officers knew every inch of the place, for they had lived here all during the bombardment. We heard how the city had been stormed with fire during the long seige, and we marveled how even the broken walls could have been left standing. In some places were only piles of rubble with no signs of former habitation.

We saw the ruins of the Hotel de Ville, a private dwelling before the Revolution but afterwards the Town Hall. The American flag had been raised over this building when the United States had entered the war. The building had been gutted by German bombs. We went through the ruins of the Bishop's Palace where one could see remains of the artistic decorations. We walked through the banquet hall where the Germans had planned to feast in celebration of their entry into Verdun on their way to Paris.

Next we visited the ruins of the St. Louis Cathedral. The floor had been cleaned and fragments of the shattered stained-glass windows were piled high on a table. We were allowed to take pieces as souvenirs.

Then we went to the Church of the Good Shepherd, a small church which had been destroyed by a single shell. There was a mass of fallen plaster, broken statues, twisted candlesticks, and, on the altar, a water-soaked Missal. In the midst of all this desecration the statue of Joan of Arc stood unharmed, although everything around her shrine had been shattered. The French officers told us that the statues of her had remained unharmed wherever they had stood. They maintained that this was a symbol, because all through the country the universal prayer was "Joan of Arc save France!"

From Verdun we were to go to the American Army Headquarters. As we started on our journey, we saw cars with a group of American officers approaching. They had been sent by General John J. Pershing to be our escort. We rode on to a tiny village where a regiment of American boys had been waiting for us. They met us in true American style — with a brass band. Of all the receptions we had throughout our journey, this one pleased us the most. The boys were lined all around the public square, but as we left our cars the Colonel ordered them to break ranks so that they could visit with us.

They seemed to be so happy to see American women! They were the Massachusetts and Connecticut regiments just returned from a big battle. They told us of their fighting and of how eager they were to get back and finish it up so we should have no occasion at home to be ashamed of them. They were full of enthusiasm, so different from the weary French veterans of the fourth year of war. The contrast was inevitable.

About eight o'clock that evening we reached the American Army Headquarters and met General Pershing in his temporary home. His entire staff was there to meet us, including General McAndrews.

Junius Woods, war correspondent for the *Chicago Daily News,* I found had left a message for me. I had known him well, back in the days when he covered legislative proceedings at Springfield. He had expected to meet and travel with us. But he had been sent up to the front that morning. Newspapermen were as anxious to see someone from home as the soldier boys were.

When I returned home to the States I learned that James

Connors, a Chicago boy and the son of old friends of mine, was General Pershing's chauffeur. James had heard that we were at General Pershing's headquarters, but Army regulations had prevented his asking to see me.

Another soldier, Frankie Brinkman, son of our old-time Grand Rapids neighbor who used to lend us her sheets for our stage curtains, was fighting "somewhere in France," his mother had told me. I wrote to Frankie, and he wrote to his mother about hearing from me. It was his last letter; he was killed in action the following week.

The American officers wanted to show us the bases they had built and the other work our troops had done since their arrival. We had already seen what they had done in the way of great docks and supply houses. And we did see some of the bases and some of the railroads they had built. But we could stay at the headquarters only one day and could not see all that they wanted to show us.

I was particularly interested in visiting the lofts where carrier pigeons were bred and trained. It was remarkable how quickly they could be trained. Two-and-a-half months and they were ready for service. They could fly five to six hundred miles in a day, and it was estimated that ninety-seven per cent of their messages were delivered.

I was interested not only in seeing how the war was being fought in France, but also in observing the reactions of the French people to the Americans. The warm feeling between the French peasants and our soldiers was shown in many ways. Often we would see an American soldier coming down the road with a French child by the hand or helping one of the older French women to carry a bucket of water. I was told about a group of American officers who, wanting to learn French and also to get away from camp during their furlough, had rented a

room in a French peasant's house. The woman of the house
was at the end of her resources. But when the Americans
offered to pay rent and board, she seemed distressed. She could
not take money from them, said she. They insisted upon paying
her. To satisfy them she took the money; then she sent it to
the Allied War Relief. Parisians also opened their homes to
the American soldiers, although they were most exclusive,
inviting only personal friends as guests at their table or to stay
with them.

During our last days in the war zone, we stopped for lunch
at Dijon, the university town. From there we took the train
for Paris. As a reminder of our visit to France, the French
Government presented us with an album of mounted photographs of the special events of our travels. The pictures taken
at Verdun, however, did not include the American Army Headquarters, because its location had to be kept secret. Even in our
report to the A. F. of L. convention the following month, we
referred to it as an "unnamed place" and to our meeting with
General Pershing as "somewhere in France."

French and British labor leaders had accompanied us through
the war zone, and a French delegation waited on us the evening
we were leaving Paris. The warm hospitality of the French
made it seem we had been with them a long time. It had been
only three days. But during that brief while, a close bond had
been established between us and a better understanding of one
another.

IRELAND, 1918

UPON OUR RETURN TO ENGLAND, we again met with
the British labor representatives to give them our impressions
of the French labor and Socialist leaders. We pointed out the

need for a closer and more continuous communication with the French trade-union movement.

In both Great Britain and France we had found that President Wilson was regarded as the hope of the democratic world. His clearly and definitely stated war aims inspired a great confidence. His ideals had won the support of every labor group. They looked to him for leadership.

Our time was now running short. We divided our party to cover various speaking engagements in England. I had an interesting trip to Sunderland to speak before the shipyard workers there. Back in London once more, we were given a reception by Premier Lloyd George in his Cabinet Room. A few days later, we were received at Buckingham Palace by Their Majesties King George V, Queen Mary, and Princess Mary. After the formalities of the reception, the Queen and Princess Mary visited with the women and the King with the men. Our party formed a group at the close of the audience, and the King addressed to us a short speech. "I trust," said he, referring to the women of our group, "that you may be able to give a satisfactory report on the manner in which British women have come forward to replace men in the industries during the war and how efficiently they are carrying on the work entrusted to them.

"Between Great Britain and America," said he, "science is daily increasing the power of rapid transportation and thus facilitating exchange of visits and strengthening of ties of mutual understanding, confidence, and good-fellowship. Please God may ever henceforth unite us."

Little did we then imagine that within the lifetime of most of us on that mission there would be another world war and that transportation would be so highly developed that high-powered passenger planes would be carrying our war missions, our important military officers, and even our President to far places of the world.

A NUMBER OF US wanted to visit Ireland. This was during the most troublous times in that country. Dublin newspapers had asserted that the British would not allow our Labor Mission to see Ireland because we might then learn the truth about conditions there. A woman who represented the American press in London was so disturbed by this statement that she called the British Information Office to point out that it would be a mistake for us not to go to Ireland. A short trip was arranged.

I had received a communication from a member of the United Irish League Organization for Scotland who had written me as follows:

"There exists a censorship over all news between Ireland, Great Britain, and America. The news usually sent your country about Ireland is generally against the democratic views of the majority of Ireland's people and opposed to the opinions of 83 out of the 101 men returned to represent Ireland in the British House of Commons.

"We Irish Nationalists thoroughly believe in the Allied policy in the war, and the chief difficulty now in obtaining Irish recruits LIES IN BRITAIN'S FAILURE TO PUT IRISH SELF-GOVERNMENT INTO OPERATION.

"I deem it necessary, in order to prevent your deputation's being hoodwinked by tactics of keeping it out of Ireland, to place this statement before you.

"Mr. Joseph Devlin, M.P., has publicly offered, if the British Government puts in operation a satisfactory measure of Home Rule, to join the Army as a private and lead into it young Ireland in the fight against German militarism.

"The people of Ireland fear no inquiry into the case or into their present position in reference to conscription. Archbishops, priests, Members of Parliament, and the people are absolutely united on the subject. Had Britain put in force Home Rule she might have obtained thousands of additional men as the free-will offering of a race that never required conscription to battle for a just cause."

The communication was signed: "Your faithfully, J. O'Derrick, United Irish League Organizer for Scotland."

After such a message, I was of course anxious to get to Ireland.

I had also a personal reason for wanting to see Ireland. I had long hoped that I might some day be able to visit my father's birthplace in Galway. My pulse quickened as our ship touched the shores of Ireland, the country of song and story, and, best of all, the land of my ancestors.

We docked at Larne harbor and hurried to Belfast to visit the York Street flax-spinning mills. It was Saturday, the mills closed at noon, and we barely had time to see the weaving rooms. The women of the mills did not look like those in the munitions plants. These mill workers, most of them old women, had spent the greater part of their lives weaving. They were still at their jobs, but now instead of weaving fancy patterns for fine table linen and dainty handkerchiefs, they were weaving heavy linen for aeroplanes.

We lunched with the Lord Mayor of Belfast and his officials in a magnificent white marble municipal building which, so they proudly told us, had cost the city not a penny. It had been built, they said, out of the profits of the municipal gas.

After luncheon, we visited the technical institute at Belfast. The institute had the reputation of being one of the greatest of its kind. We squeezed these visits into four hours, and then we were on our way to Dublin.

We arrived in Dublin at an exciting time. The Sinn Feiners had been arrested that morning, charged with complicity in a German plot. The *Dublin Morning Irish Independent* claimed that there was an ugly significance in this choice of time for the issuance of the anti-Sinn Fein proclamation, that it had been deliberately planned to coincide with the arrival of the American Labor Mission in Ireland.

Everyone was tense. It was certainly the most critical time since the Easter Monday Rebellion two years before. All seemed quiet, but one wondered what would happen next. I met Charlie Wheeler again, covering the news in Ireland. He wanted me to hear all the shades of opinion rife at the time and to meet some of the Sinn Feiners.

That evening our party was taken to the Abbey Theatre to see the Irish Players in *The Suburban Grove*. After the first act, we visited the Green Room and met the players — Fred O'Donovan, Arthur Shields, Maureen Delaney, Irene Kelly, Eric Gorman, and Louis O'Connor. We had been fascinated by their acting; it was interesting to see them also in their own environment.

When we returned to the hotel, I received a call from Charlie Wheeler inviting me to meet a group of Sinn Feiners assembled in one of the hotel's large parlors. Charlie Wheeler presented me, telling them that I was "all right" and reminding me that I must understand all sides of the Irish question because when I got back to Halsted Street in Chicago the people there would want to know all about it. The men in the group assured me it was not of political matters that they wanted to talk to me, but of social and economic conditions. They told me about the poverty of Ireland and the hardships of the women and children. Economic as well as political conditions were responsible for the Irish fight for self-determination, said they. If I would understand the Irish nationalist feeling, Wheeler told me, I should read Mrs. Green's book, *Irish Nationality*. I jotted down the title of the book and the name of its author.

We met John Dillon, and when in the conversation the name of Mr. Shortt, the new Home Secretary, was mentioned, Mr. Dillon said Mr. Shortt was a decent sort of fellow; that it was not the man himself they were objecting to but the way the man had been appointed; that the Irish wanted to choose their own officials, not to have them selected by the British.

We met also Mr. Devlin, the famous leader of the Nationalist Party, and John Redmond, who represented the Home Rulers who were very much to the "right" just then. We met also Sir Horace Plunkett, the father of the Irish Agricultural Organization to guide the Co-op Movement.

I met Mr. Dillon again later at the Mansion House with Mr. Lawrence O'Neill, the Lord Mayor of Dublin. Mr. Dillon, then young and fiery, talked with much feeling at that meeting. The Irish, said he, had been very eager to enlist at the beginning of the war, would then had furnished a hundred thousand men; but too many "incidents" had since broken their spirit. The Irish had wanted a distinct uniform or insignia, such as the Canadians and Australians wore, so as to designate their nationality. This had been denied them. They had asked for Irish officers to lead them, and this also had been denied.

Dillon explained that before the Easter Rebellion the Sinn Feiners had consisted of only a small group of idealists, but that after the manner in which the leaders of this group had been dealt with by the British Government, the movement had grown by leaps and bounds. He pointed out that after a similar rebellion in South Africa, the rebels had been treated with leniency.

We were not able to meet the Sinn Feiners, because they were in jail. But a deputation of women Sinn Feiners called on our women members, providing us with their literature, and stating that their objective was an Irish Republic.

Sunday afternoon we met the new Home Secretary, Mr. Shortt, and the Lord Lieutenant, Mr. French, at Lord and Lady Decies' castle, Lixlip on the Liffy, a picturesque palace which dates back to the days of King John. We were guests at a garden party.

The next day Lord Decies gave us an official luncheon to have us meet the officials of Dublin and the leaders of all the parties.

The afternoon was left free for callers. The Irish labor women came to see us, while the men of our party met the labor men. The Irish women, too, were making munitions, in factories located in Dublin, Cork, Waterford, Wexford, and Galway. These were national factories under the direction of the Ministry of Munitions. It was only during the last year of the war, however, after the women workers were organized, that they had been taken under the provisions of the Munitions Act. The Irish Rebellion, they said, had hastened the growth of trade unions among the women.

We met Miss Louise Bennett, whose Irish Women Workers' Union represented five thousand women workers, and Miss Mary Donovan of the Irish Locals of the National Federation of Women Workers. The headquarters of this latter federation was in London. These two national unions had been successful not only in improving the working conditions of the munitions workers but also of the tailoresses and laundresses as well. Before the union had been formed, the laundry workers, who started work at the age of fourteen, had received only five shillings a week. After the formation of the union, this rate had been increased to fourteen shillings, six pence, and the total working week had been reduced to fifty hours.

As we talked, an older woman who up till then had been sitting quietly by, turned to me and said:

"Miss Nestor, I have brought you one of my books and some pamphlets I thought you might like to have."

I looked at the book. It was *Irish Nationality,* the book Charlie Wheeler had recommended that I read.

"Why, are you Mrs. Green?" I asked.

"Yes," replied she very modestly.

I told her that her book had been recommended to me and how pleased and grateful I was for her gift. I asked her to inscribe the book for me. "To our Welcome Irish Visitor, Agnes Nestor, from Alice Stopford Green," she wrote in the book for me. The book has remained one of my prized possessions.

Widow of the noted Irish historian, John Richard Green, Mrs. Green was also in her own right a historian of distinction. Her book, *Irish Nationality,* widely read by the English working people, had been influential in turning the sentiment of English labor towards the Irish cause. Later she was appointed by William T. Cosgrave, President of the Irish Free State, to a seat in the Irish Senate. She had been born in Ireland, the daughter of an Irish dean, but she did not live in Ireland permanently until after the truce of 1921.

I WAS INTERESTED IN FINDING, if possible, some of my father's Irish relatives. On the committee for a society entitled, "Back to the Land and Evicted Tenant's Association," I had found listed the name of a J. J. Nestor. I wrote to the association, asking about this J. J. Nestor, giving such information as I had concerning my father's Irish family, and inquiring if this J. J. Nestor might be a relative of mine. In reply I received the following letter which I believe expresses some of the feelings behind the Sinn Fein Rebellion:

1 ANNESLEY PLACE
DUBLIN, 3/6/1918

DEAR MISS NESTOR,

In reply to yours of the 22nd inst. from Liverpool, I regret indeed that myself and friend, Mr. John Nestor, I dare say your relative, were disappointed at not seeing you.

I dare say your grandmother, father, and other members of the family were the victims of landlordism, who were evicted and had no other alternative but to leave their own homeland to make room for the rancher's cattle as thousands are still unhappily compelled to do from year to year. This is the accursed system which with maladministration and misgovernment has reduced our population from nine millions to less than four millions during the last half century. Thus the flower of the countryside, gallant Irish blood and sterling Irish brains, were cast adrift, and in all parts of the world to which they went proved their worth and their genius, aspiring to and gaining as by right, the very highest places, though denied by English law any place in their own country. These were of the people whose properties England confiscated and divided among Cromwell's brutal soldiery, among Elizabeth and James' settlers...so that for foreign landlords they became hewers of wood and drawers of water in their own native land.

Later came the evictions when the harrassed people were unable to pay the exorbitant rents. They left Ireland in tears and anger, longing for the day of reckoning against England and her cruel and crushing laws.

Time and distance have made many among our far-flung race forget their wrongs. But we here in Ireland, sprung from the remnant driven to the hills, the bogs, and to Connacht, have had it handed down, have learned from father to son that here and there where no homestead now exists such and such a noble family once lived, and where now nought but the sullen grazier holds sway was once a fertile and contented countryside. It is the victims of all this oppression that our Association represents. There are many thousands of evicted tenants in Ireland at present seeking to be put back on the land, and the maladministration of the law is such that it has taken sixteen years to plant about 3,000 of the 11,000.

The graves have closed over many and who can say how many more may go at the lethargic rate that highly-paid Government officials work. Not the least consideration has been shown to all this misery. In addition there are thousands of landless young people anxious to be put on the land. For these our Association has made repeated appeal for legislation to divide up the large ranches (thousands of ranches under cattle). These ranches should be divided up among those young people who have no way to a home but by the emigrant ship.

This in brief is the uphill fight we are making against the throned forces of misrule...

Faithfully yours,

THOM. M. O'KEEFFE

The time schedule of the American Labor Mission did not allow me to attempt a side journey to Stradbally, the place of my father's birth, to see if what Thomas O'Keeffe said seemed true. But a few years later, on another European trip, I found myself delayed for a week in England while we waited for the ship to take us back to America. I used that week to go to Ireland and fulfill my long-cherished dream. When I got to Ireland I found that the railway guidebook made no mention of a "Stradbally." But I remembered that my father had often mentioned a place called "Clarinbridge," and for that place the guidebook said, "See Oranmore."

At Oranmore I dismounted from the train to find only an open road before me. There was no station, and no one was in sight. I started walking down the road and soon came to a small village where I inquired in a co-operative store how far it might be to Stradbally. The young woman clerk replied that it was about three miles.

When I asked how I might get to Stradbally, the young woman replied that I would have to walk. An old lady who was listening said, "Wait a minute." Whereupon she went out to talk to her husband who was at work near by building a road. She returned after a while to say that her husband would hitch up his trap and drive me over.

While the trap was being hitched, I asked the clerk if she knew anything of Stradbally and anything of a family by the name of Nestor living there. Stradbally, she told me, was a village of only seven families, but among these there was a Thomas Nestor, she said. This gave me great hope. Thomas was the name also of my own father. If there were so few families living in the village, I felt sure that this Thomas Nestor of Stradbally must be connected with my father's family.

In Stradbally we found without difficulty the home of Thomas Nestor. It was a primitive hut with thatched roof, mud floor, and a large open hearth where the meals were cooked. The door to the hut, a friendly sort of door, was divided so that the top half could be opened separately.

I was received at the hut by Mrs. Thomas Nestor and her daughter Bridget. Thomas Nestor was off at Galway that day, so nothing could be learned from him. Bridget, the daughter, was of course too young to be able to give me much information of the kind I sought. Nor did Mrs. Nestor's knowledge of Stradbally and its people reach back very far. "I have lived here only forty years," she explained, "and I know nothing about the family."

However, she did tell me that a few years prior to my visit, she and her husband had received a letter from Australia inquiring about heirs of a Nestor who had died there. "Never were any heirs found," she said, and apparently her mind had ceased to wonder about the matter.

But my mind did not. This piece of information seemed to fit in with what I had heard my father say of his family's history. His father had had two brothers. One of these had remained in Ireland— and this brother was probably the ancestor of the Nestors I was visiting in the hut in Stradbally. My father's father, of course, had migrated to Baltimore and had died there. The third brother, too, had come to America, had journeyed on to California, and had never been heard from again. California was then one of the "taking off" places for Australia. That following the death of a man named Nestor in Australia, an inquiry should be directed to so distant and so obscure a little place as Stradbally in Ireland seemed almost obvious proof to me that the Australian Nestor was an uncle, or a descendant of an uncle, of my father. This bit of information made me feel more certain that I was in my father's childhood village.

Soon conversation with Mrs. Nestor uncovered another bit of welcome information. Mrs. Nestor had had a neighbor who had died about three years before. This neighbor, an old, old woman, had used to tell a story, Mrs. Nestor told me, about a "Julia Mullen taking her geese down to the stream." "Julia Mullen" had been the maiden name of my father's mother.

I went with Bridget for a walk about the village, and Bridget pointed out to me a pile of stones, the only things remaining of the house where Julia Mullen had lived, the house which might have been my father's childhood home. We were walking about in a dying village, where, as families moved away, the old homes crumbled and fell into ruins. I was more convinced than ever before that life in Galway "was so hard that those who lived in that rugged country meet life with more fortitude than those who come from parts where life is easier." I felt satisfied over my little pilgrimage. The only sad part was that my father had not lived to know that I had visited his old home.

OUR AMERICAN LABOR MISSION returned to London from Ireland to find that we had but little time before sailing for home. Sir Guy Standing accompanied our party to Liverpool. As he said, he had been in the party which had met us, had been with us during our stay, and would be the last to see us off. That was not the last time I saw him, however. He came to our country after the war, and I saw him play in Chicago and met his daughter who was an actress in the same company.

We sailed for home on the "Aquatania," the beautiful liner which had been converted into a transport ship. Despite the fears we had had on the voyage from America, we left Liverpool without any feelings of apprehension. There was still danger. But we had been so close to danger "over there," that the ocean voyage seemed safe.

We landed at New York and went at once to Washington to meet with Samuel Gompers and Frank Morrison, who escorted us then to the White House. President Wilson was anxious to hear at firsthand about our trip. We told him how the workers in Great Britain and France regarded him as the hope of the world and were solidly back of him in the war aims he had outlined in his Fourteen Points. The President said that he had anounced those Fourteen Points early so as to make it clear to all what we were fighting for and to force other countries to state their own aims. We sat in a circle in the small Oval Room for our talk. It was an intimate meeting and an impressive and fitting end for our American Labor Mission. Some of us would meet again in June, at the A. F. of L. convention in St. Paul, Minnesota, to make our official report to that organization.

WHEN WE HAD FIRST reached England on our mission, we had bought up the English newspapers to read what they were saying about us. Seeing this, one of our hosts had advised:

"Do not trouble to buy these journals. We will send you all the cuttings."

When we had been about to leave England for home, as a souvenir of our visit, the British Ministry of Information had presented to each member of our mission a collection of photographs taken of us during our travels. Then, sure enough, upon our return to the United States, each member of our party received from England a handsome album containing every press notice we had been favored with, all beautifully mounted, a keepsake forever cherished in memory of the courtesies, kindness, and generosity accorded our mission in the midst of war, an example of gallant and great-hearted English hospitality.

18

We Seek Again the Eight-Hour Law

IT SEEMED HARD to get back to work after all my adventures in Europe. But there was much work to be done.

There were numerous speaking engagements to tell about my trip. One such engagement I especially cherished. I was asked to speak for the benefit of a day nursery on Chicago's Halsted Street. This was a settlement run by the Catholic Daughters of Charity. The program was under the auspices of De Paul University. A cement playground was badly needed at the nursery. With tickets selling for twenty-five cents, three hundred dollars was raised. It is pleasant to know that the children playing on that playground today are doing so as a result of my European trip.

Meanwhile we were going through the aftermath of the garment-workers' strike. Our Women's Trade Union League was anxiously involved, too, in the educational program affecting Chicago's schools. And we were getting ready also to make another strenuous effort at Springfield in behalf of our women's eight-hour bill.

In June of 1917, Governor Lowden, at the direction of the Illinois State Legislature, had appointed an Illinois Industrial Survey Commission "to make a complete survey of all industries in Illinois in which women are engaged as workers, with special reference to the hours of labor for women in such industries, the effect of such hours of labor upon the health of women workers, and to make a report to the Governor not later than December 1."

Appointed to this commission by Governor Lowden were three physicians — Dr. James B. Herrick, Dr. George W. Webster, and Dr. Solomon Strouse. Two employers were appointed — Milton S. Florsheim and P. C. Withers. As representatives of the working women, the Governor appointed to the commission Elizabeth Maloney and me, Agnes Nestor.

Our commission set up its staff and proceeded to make its studies. We found that the health of the women worker degenerated with accumulated fatigue. We found that industrial output lessened as human fatigue increased. We found plants where total production had been increased by a reduction of working hours!

Dr. Strouse was from an employer's family. But as we took a recess at our last meeting, he came to me and said: "I am going to vote with you people today." What he had observed had thoroughly persuaded him. He and Dr. Webster had become outspoken proponents of the eight-hour day.

When our commission was ready to draw up its recommendations, however, Elizabeth Maloney and I and the three physicians had to draw up a majority report recommending the eight-hour day. The two employers presented their own report of four pages, taking exception to our recommendations. They offered no facts, just protests — as for instance: "Inasmuch as the Saturday afternoon holiday largely obtains and the recommendations of the majority report would result in a forty-four-hour week, which is little more than a seven-hour day, we venture to say that should such a measure be enacted into a law, the women whose efforts would be so restricted and whose means of livelihood would be so injuriously affected, would be the first to complain."

Despite this minority exception to our commission's report, we who were proposing the eight-hour bill went to the 1919 session of the Illinois Legislature filled with optimism. World War I was over, and the urgency of war work could not be used as an excuse for an overlong working day for women. We had much new evidence that an eight-hour day was an efficient working schedule for both employer and employee. And in both the house and the senate we had strong leaders backing our bill.

Introduced in the senate by Richard J. Barr, our bill was passed by that body, despite a barrage of opposition. Then the fight turned to the house.

On the day the bill was set for a vote in the house, we found the house lobby filled with women workers from a hosiery plant in Kankakee. The hosiery company had shut down its plant, had chartered a train, and had brought all its women employees to Springfield. For these employees it seemed a holiday and a delightful trip. Most of these girls did not know what the bill was about, except that they had been told that if the bill passed they would all lose their jobs. "You cannot blame us for taking this trip," some of them tried to excuse themselves.

Such opposition proved too great; our bill went down to defeat. On my return to Chicago, I missed my father doubly. Always before at such times as this he had been awaiting me, no matter what the hour, to hear the account of what had happened at Springfield. I would tell him of our latest defeat, and he, never discouraged, would say:

"Aggie, keep at it! You will get it through yet!"

19

International Congress
of Working Women

IN THAT PERIOD just after World War I, we were
living in a time of great dreams — dreams of co-operation between the working peoples of the world, dreams of
dignity and plenty for all, dreams of lasting international peace.

The war the Allies had co-operated to win had given us a
taste of international brotherhood. With a little more understanding, many felt, perhaps we might all join together to
win the world-wide battle against ignorance and poverty. Those
of us who were working in the labor movements were stirred
by great hopes.

In 1919, the Versailles Treaty had created the I.L.O., the
International Labor Organization, under the auspices of the
League of Nations. Inspired by this movement, Mrs. Robins
saw the chance to organize an International Federation of
Working Women, an organization to work on an international
scale for higher working standards for working women, just
as our Women's Trade Union League had been working for
these higher standards on a local and national scale.

Then a strange thing happened. The I.L.O. had been invited
to hold its first meeting of October, 1919, in Washington, D. C.
But between the time of the invitation and the time set for
the meeting, our Senate voted against the United States joining

the League of Nations, of which the I.L.O., of course, was a part. Thus our Government found itself in the awkward position of being host to an international organization to which it could not belong. Somehow, however, William B. Wilson, then Secretary of State, managed to carry the program through.

Meanwhile, our projected International Federation of Working Women had scheduled the meeting of its first International Congress to coincide with the I.L.O. meeting in Washington, and delegations of representatives and advisors from various countries of the world had made arrangements to attend the meeting and with high hopes in their hearts.

We met in Washington, and Mrs. Robins was elected the first president of our international organization. Maud Swartz was elected our national representative on the international council. There were delegates from Argentina, Belgium, Canada, Czecho-Slovakia, France, Great Britain, India, Italy, Norway, Poland, Sweden, and the United States. There were delegates from Cuba, Denmark, The Netherlands, Serbia, Spain, Switzerland, and Japan. All had voting power.

Now we learned the difficulties of being a group speaking many languages and needing interpreters. But as we began to know each other it became easy to work together.

Few could stir an audience as could Mrs. Robins, with her animated face, her flashing eyes, her power to deliver a speech. She could inspire one to greater effort in any cause she sponsored, and this she did in this first International Congress of Working Women.

Our organization recommended to the I.L.O. the establishment of an eight-hour workday and a forty-four-hour work-week for working women, with a weekly rest period of at least one-and-a-half uninterrupted days, and with a minimum rest period of a half-hour in each eight-hour shift.

We made recommendations concerning child labor, night work, maternity insurance, protection in hazardous occupations, and concerning many other matters which affect working women.

And to be the more certain that women would be represented in the various national delegations to the I.L.O. in the future, we asked that the number of delegates from each government be increased from one to two, and that this extra delegate be a woman.

The second meeting of the International Congress of Working Women was held in Geneva, Switzerland, in October of 1921, and Mrs. Robins was re-elected president. The third and last meeting of this ambitious organization convened in the summer of 1923 in Vienna. Our National Women's Trade Union League sent a large delegation. There was Mrs. Robins and her sister, Mary E. Dreier; there was Maud Swartz, Elisabeth Christman, Rose Schneiderman, and Mary Anderson; there was Pauline Newman, Frieda S. Miller, Agnes Johnson and I. At the convention our delegation made an impressive group.

The countries represented at this convention were Belgium, Cuba, France, Great Britain, Italy, Sweden, and the United States. There were fraternal delegates from Argentina, Chile, China and Japan. The meetings were held at the lovely Town Hall of Hietzing. Schönbrunn Castle was the headquarters for the delegates though not all stayed there.

Our delegation stayed at the Park Hotel, which had once been a grand place. But royalty having disappeared from the castle, the hotel was fighting a desperate battle for existence. We had lovely, comfortable rooms, and they were inexpensive because so many services connected with them had been discontinued. The telephone was in use only for the office. There was no elevator, we were on the third floor, and everywhere we went we had to climb or descend stairs.

Mrs. Robins did not wish to serve again as president of the organization. Mlle. Burniaux of Belgium was elected to that office. Maud Swartz and I were made members of the Commission on Constitution. It was becoming fast apparent that there were forces working to change the nature of the organization. The British delegates came determined to have the organization taken over and made a part of the International Federation of Trade Unions. Our International Federation of Working Women would thus have become an organization made up of delegates from various national trade unions and composed of men as well as women. Women, thus, would have only a minor representation. It was a matter over which our organization was being split, and the reason why, the next year, our National Women's Trade Union League decided to withdraw from this International Federation of Working Women which it had been so instrumental in initiating.

Meanwhile, also, the first flush of international fellow-feeling which had swept America and the European world directly after World War I, was now being displaced by an intense new wave of nationalism which we could see already at work in Europe. The work the original International Federation of Working Women had proposed for itself would have to wait for another era and a new organizing force.

From the convention in Vienna, we went by boat to Germany. We landed at Bremen and were met by Lillie Brummerhof of Chicago. It was good indeed to have a friend meet us on a foreign shore. She spent the day with us, and we had coffee at her sister's that afternoon before leaving for Berlin.

We were in Berlin when the German mark dropped from one million for a dollar to five million for a dollar. It was quoted at five million for a dollar, but we never got that much on our exchange. We did get as high as three-and-a-half million, and on our last day in Berlin one of the girls got four-and-a-half million. We felt like accountants dealing thus in millions and trying continually to figure what it meant in our money. We dared exchange only enough money to carry us through for one day, for the difference in exchange value from day to day could often mean a great loss. We had to get out our largest bags to carry around our German marks. It made us sick at heart to see the poor of Berlin counting this paper money fresh from the presses and to hear them say, in utter bewilderment:

"But it doesn't mean anything!"

From Berlin we went to Nuremberg, arriving late in the evening to find the streets filled with young people, all singing, all preparing for the next day's celebration of "Youth's Day." We were awakened that next morning to the sound of singing, and as our hotel was just across from the station, we could see the young men and women coming into the city by the thousands, peasant boys and girls, some from the mountains, and all singing as they marched through the square. The processions kept up all morning, until the city was filled with the participants. That afternoon there was a great parade in which all the trade unionists took part. It took over two hours for the parade to pass, and all along the way there were shouts of "Long live the Republic!" and "Hurray for Freedom!" and then great cheers.

This group represented the Socialists and the Republicans, the more radical elements in the country. They had come from all parts of Germany and some from other countries as well. There was to be a celebration held by the military and reactionary groups the coming September, and this present celebration was in protest of the coming one.

We left Nuremberg that evening about eight o'clock, because

trouble was expected in the town. The hotel had already taken the precaution of not serving guests on their balconies and the heavy curtains in the diningrooms had been drawn. The red flags were in evidence every place one looked about the quaint old city, the oldest in Germany, a city kept quaint by a prohibition against the erection of any structure not in keeping with the style of the ancient buildings.

Everywhere in Germany one heard the sad stories of the struggles of the poor. They had no potatoes when we were there. We were told the farmers had refused to plant because they felt their crops would be taken for reparations.

From Germany we took a ten-day trip through Italy, stopping at Venice, Florence, Rome, and Naples. Then to Paris for a few days and from there to London to meet our boat for home.

4-We
Continue
the Fight

MARGARET DREIER ROBINS

ELIZABETH MALONEY

ELISABETH CHRISTMAN

JANE ADDAMS

20

Another Try for the Eight-Hour Law

ELIZABETH MALONEY was ill all through the year of 1921. I had been ill myself the year before when an attack of influenza had left me so weak that I had had to take a vacation in the mountains of Colorado to recuperate. But Elizabeth's condition did not seem to improve. I began making weekly visits to her early in the spring, continued through the summer and into the fall, only to see her slowly slipping away. One day when I was there she was in a coma, and that evening her mother called me to say that Elizabeth was gone.

Elizabeth had been a gallant fighter. Through the years we had worked together and there had developed between us a close bond of friendship. I loved her. I missed her.

Elizabeth had made all her funeral plans and had asked me to see that they were carried out. I went to her home early the next morning. The first tribute to arrive was a beautiful spray of roses. The card with them read: "From John Glenn, Secretary, Illinois Manufacturers' Association." Mr. Glenn had been her opponent in many a tough legislative battle, but he had always respected her as a fair fighter. Elizabeth left me a legacy, one of the nicest I ever received. During her long illness, she realized how much care one could need. Knowing that my own mother was gone, one day to her mother she said: "If Agnes should ever be taken sick, who will take care of her?" She asked Mrs. Maloney to promise that should I become ill she would take care of me.

Mrs. Maloney in telling of this quoted her own reply: "I will! I will!" But Elizabeth's dear mother did not live to carry out this promise. She herself was stricken with a heart ailment the next year and I attended her funeral, riding with the family, feeling that I was filling Elizabeth's place, as Elizabeth would have wanted me to.

Besides Elizabeth, I lost two other friends during this period. The sudden death in June of 1920 of Henry N. Greenbaum, general manager of the Eisendrath Glove Company, was a blow that left the whole plant grief-stricken. A kindly man, considerate and patient, his sterling qualities had helped us over many a difficult hurdle. "Peaceful Henry" was a name he had well earned.

The same year as Elizabeth, Mr. Eisendrath died. Mr. Eisendrath had been a man easily excited but wonderful to deal with. He would have all the members of his firm, including his young son Robert, sit in at our conferences. As he said, they could thus learn what he had to meet and make it easier to get acceptance from his side. Whenever members of his firm complained about the time taken for negotiating wage agreements, Mr. Eisendrath would remind them that time was required for all the other things in connection with their business, that wage agreements and labor relations were an important part of the business, and that a few weeks every two years could certainly be given to these problems. It was an attitude more employers should consider.

Mr. Eisendrath was always remembering that he and we were all human, not merely employer and employees. One time he was telling me about some of his pictures and he said: "Some day when you are not president and I am not president, maybe you will come and see them." That time never came, for we were both officials to the time of his death.

THE 1923 SESSION of the Illinois Legislature found our group once again at Springfield urging the passage of the eight-hour bill. For the first time since we had begun the fight back in 1909 Elizabeth Maloney was not there with us. But her spirit was, for none who had known her would ever forget her earnestness and courage.

There was also an injunction-limitation bill up before the legislature. We were told that only one labor bill could pass and that we could decide which one we wanted. We would not agree that only one labor bill should pass. However, the injunction-limitation bill was the only one that did pass at that session.

21

The "Equal Rights" Amendment

IN THE MID-1920'S we were faced with a new threat to all our labor laws for women, and this from a new source — from a group of women!

The National Woman's Party was an organization quite vocal and articulate because it contained many prominent women writers and clubwomen. In an effort to remove all legal inequalities in all states between men and women, it was sponsoring what it termed an "Equal Rights Amendment" to the Constitution. The proposed amendment was phrased: "Men and women shall have equal rights in the United States and every place subject to its jurisdiction." Noble-sounding on the face of it, this proposed amendment to the Constitution could, we saw, wreck all labor laws for women.

When this amendment was proposed in 1922, a hurried conference was called in Washington, D. C., by our Women's Trade Union League, and a representative group of working women from various sections of the country met to consider what we saw as a grave danger to all our hard-won labor legislation. As we saw it, if this amendment were to be passed, it would nullify all separate laws for women and at one stroke wipe out all the gains of a century of heartbreaking effort.

We sought and received legal advice on the matter from

William H. Holly, later a judge in the Federal courts; from Harold L. Ickes, then one of our Chicago advisers, and from Edgar L. Bancroft, a notable Constitution authority who was particularly interested because he had defended our amended Illinois ten-hour bill for women.

At the beginning of the movement, the sponsors of the proposed amendment, with the slogan, "Equal rights with equal pay," had seemed to meet our views concerning protective labor laws for women. On our part, we had got passed bills limiting the working hours for women on the grounds of protection of health of the mothers and potential mothers of the race. It was on this ground that the Supreme Court had declared that the police power of the various states could be invoked for women's protection. Our fight with the Woman's Party came out into the open when the Women's Bureau of the U. S. Department of Labor held the Women's Industrial Conference in Washington, D. C., in January of 1923. The Woman's Party insisted upon being heard, and a debate was arranged. The matter also became an international issue with the Woman's Party trying to get endorsements for its proposed amendment even from such organizations as the I. L. O. We had to be constantly on the alert.

The issue finally flared up in the Illinois Legislature. A Woman's Party delegation came from Washington to Springfield, Illinois, determined to put through a state bill similar to the proposed national amendment. A senator was inveigled into introducing the bill, and a few other senators stood by him on the measure.

A large group of partisans of the measure then descended on us. Senator Richard J. Barr, a veteran member, had a good time questioning them. "We have a law in Illinois against women working in the mines," said he. "Do you want that law repealed?

"We have an eight-hour-day bill for women before us," said he. "Do you want to defeat that?"

One of the members of the Washington group tried to show how much they were interested in helping working women by relating how well she treated her maid.

"So you are lucky enough to have a maid!" exclaimed Senator Barr.

The appearance of the "Equal Rights" group in the Illinois Legislature did them more harm than good. Their bill was defeated, and that was the last of their proposals in our state.

Though both the organized labor movement, the trade-union women, and most other national women's organizations continued their opposition to the proposed amendment, the fight continued, and eventually the proposed amendment became a national political issue with the Woman's Party getting it into party platforms. When for the first time it came to a vote on the floor of the Senate toward the end of the 79th Congress, it was defeated, failing to receive the required two-thirds majority. But it continued still to be an issue.

22

Milady's Raiment
and Court Injunctions

IN 1924, another bitter struggle had to be undertaken in behalf of the women workers in the Chicago ladies' garment trade. There was much wrong in the industry. The average wage, when prorated over a year, was $5.69 a week. There was a piecework problem and other bad conditions. But for many reasons this women's clothing industry had been a most difficult one to unionize.

Back in 1914, Rose Schneiderman had come from New York determined to organize "from scratch." She had come immediately to our Women's Trade Union League office to get a list of all the Chicago dress shops. She had begun at once to distribute handbills and to talk to the workers. But little could she accomplish.

The next year, Fannia Cohn had come from New York to try what she could do. It was at the time of the strike in the glove shop at the Herzog plant which manufactured all kinds of women's wear. Fannia was president of the Wrapper, Kimona and Housedress Workers' Local 41 of New York. She was a valiant fighter, and soon hers had become a well-known name in Chicago union organization work. But she was up against bitter opponents. In August of that year, some of the glove workers at the Herzog plant attended a meeting of the glove-workers' local and were promptly discharged from the plant. A strike at once ensued when two hundred and fifty glove workers walked out in protest. Seven hundred other employees took no part in the strike. But police arrested not only the picketing glove workers but also many of the non-strikers who were on their way to work. Among those arrested was Fannia Cohn. Little was gained through the strike. The bad conditions and the old grievances remained.

It was in 1917 that a most disastrous strike had occurred in the industry. In that year, there had been called at the old Empire Theatre on the West Side a great mass meeting to inaugurate a major campaign for the unionization of the dressmakers. Since all efforts prior to this time had resulted in no permanent organization, we were greatly pleased when we saw so large a turnout at the theatre. It was filled to capacity.

I spoke at the meeting, as a representative of the Women's Trade Union League, and I helped in the formulation of the demands which started off the campaign. These demands were very modest. The workers merely asked for a fifteen per cent increase in the pay schedule and a standard forty-hour week with a Saturday half-holiday. They did not even ask for a closed shop, but merely that their members be given job preference and an equal division of the piecework. They asked for an impartial investigation of working conditions and for arbitration of any disputes.

After the theatre mass meeting, I helped to organize a Citizen's Committee to investigate conditions in the industry. This committee was made up of Mrs. James A. Field, Professor F. S. Diebler from Northwestern University, and Professors Edith Abbott and H. A. Millis from the University of Chicago. The committee began its study.

Meanwhile, the workers' demands had initiated a strike.

Those demands, couched in mild, temperate letters, had been sent to each of the members of the association of dress manufacturers. Two thousand workers were seeking redress of grievances. Their letters were all ignored, and they were charged with "fomenting unrest and violence." The manufacturers called for the police and the courts to break the strike.

The police and the courts responded with great eagerness. Judge Jesse Baldwin issued sweeping injunctions against the strikers, against pickets, against the officials of the unions, against anyone who dared or seemed to offer help to the strikers. One injunction placed Benjamin Schlesinger, president of the International Ladies' Garment Workers' Union, under a bond of two thousand dollars "to keep the peace." In passing sentence, the judge said, "Mr. Schlesinger, I find nothing in the testimony that you have violated the injunction, but you have *not* told the strikers *not* to violate the injunction."

Steve C. Sumner, pioneer member and officer of the Milk Drivers' Union, made a speech to the strikers in their own hall. He was charged with encouraging them to picket, and upon this charge he was sentenced to seventy days in the county jail. He served most of the sentence.

Women pickets received jail sentences for from fifteen to thirty days on a variety of charges. A chairlady of a committee was charged with telling the strikers to picket; another "for calling a non-union worker 'insulting' names." Both were put under bond while the cases were being appealed.

Injunctions were issued prohibiting the strikers from picketing, prohibiting anyone from talking to or trying to persuade anyone working in the plant not to work there, or trying to persuade anyone who had worked there to join the strikers.

Secretary Wilson of the U. S. Department of Labor sent a representative to Chicago to try to arbitrate the strike. The effort met with failure.

On the 22nd of April, 1917, the strike was called off — after ten weeks. The striking workers had lost, and the defeat almost wrecked the struggling union. Only a few members remained. Julius Hockman came from New York in December of the next year and found the dressmakers' local union completely disheartened. He managed to revive the struggling union to a degree, and the fight continued. Then that December one of the largest of the dress companies signed a two-year contract with the union and became a union shop. It heartened us all to see that some progress was being made. But in the industry as a whole, the grievous working conditions persisted.

Six years passed. Then in 1924 came the industry's hardest fight. Once again a bitter strike was on.

In previous strikes we had had to contend with the brutality of the police, with arbitrary court injunctions, and with costly court costs and fines. But with Mayor William E. Dever in office we felt we had someone in authority who would make every effort to be fair. The mayor directed his commissioner of public welfare, Mary E. McDowell, to call a conference of the employers and a committee of the employees. But the employers would not attend the conference.

Meanwhile, the employers had replied to the strike with court injunctions and special police from the office of the district attorney. So sweeping were the injunctions they were able to obtain that almost anything one might do would bring one under contempt proceedings, and the wordings of the injunctions became more drastic as the strike proceeded. Not only did these injunctions name certain labor officials and organizations, but also "unknown members" were covered. Picketing was forbidden, but not only around the shops; it was forbidden along all the routes used by employees going to and from work; it was forbidden "at or near" their homes. It was forbidden to watch the employer's place of business. It was forbidden in any manner to seek to persuade an employee not to work. Small wonder that under these injunctions during that bitter strike there were twelve hundred arrests and fines amounting to $20,950.00! There were jail sentences, too.

A Citizen's Committee had been organized to investigate the industry and the conditions under which the strike was being carried on. Heading this committee was Father Siedenburg, head of the Department of Sociology at Loyola University. Professor H. A. Millis from the University of Chicago agreed to serve as he had served on the similar committee in 1917. Clubwomen were represented by Mrs. B. Frank Brown, and the Chicago Federation of Churches by the Rev. Norman B. Barr.

In March the committee presented its report to the mayor, emphasizing that the court injunctions interpreted literally were violations of constitutional rights, provocative of contempt of law, and the cause of unnecessary arrests; that almost all the arrests could be traced to the arbitrary action of the plain-clothes men and especially the private detectives; that the union officials and a majority of the smaller manufacturers were willing to arbitrate, but that the large manufacturers conducting open shops, or shops from which union members were excluded, refused to confer.

In its recommendations to the mayor, the committee suggested that there should be a special force of patrolmen to serve in strike situations; that this special force be instructed and empowered to enforce the law as against pickets, guards, private detectives, or others who transgress it; and that no policing be permitted except by officers in full uniform. The committee had discovered that the manufacturers were even paying thugs to initiate trouble so that excuses could be had for intimidating the strikers by arrests.

A clue to what was happening could be had from the circumstances of the twelve hundred arrests. One hundred men from the city police department had been detailed to police the strike area, and they had made 10% of the arrests. The other 90% had been made by fourteen men from the district attorney's office.

After a conflict of eighteen weeks, the strike was called off. The union had lost. The large manufacturers in the industry boasted that the industry would never be unionized. The women in the Chicago ladies' garment industry once again had been crushed — and mainly by one weapon, Court Injunction!

And this Court Injunction, what was it? Originally intended to protect property from irreparable damage, it had been twisted into a weapon to be used against strikers where damage to real property was non-existent. By this injunction certain acts, such as picketing, which was legal, could be made illegal by a writ from a judge. Acting in defiance of this court order subjected one to contempt of court and a fine or jail sentence. The same judge who issued the injunction, heard the case for contempt and sentenced the arrested party. He sat as lawmaker, judge, and jury. It was what Governor Altgeld correctly branded "judge-made law."

Twisted thus to be used as a weapon with which to break strikes, contempt cases arising out of the procedure were usually dropped once a strike was over. But not so in the 1924 strike in the Chicago ladies' garment industry. The manufacturers and Judge Sullivan who had issued the injunctions wished to see the strikers punished. Judge Sullivan talked about "this violence (meaning strikes and picketing) must be stopped."

For "contempt of court" thirty-odd young women among the strikers had been sentenced to from five to sixty days in jail. The union of course had appealed the cases. The cases were fought and continued for two years, while our appeals were carried to the Illinois Supreme Court. Then, in 1926, after two years of litigation, the Illinois Supreme Court upheld the sentences. This meant the girls, two years after the strike, would be sent to jail. Jane Addams had once before offered to organize a committee of prominent Chicago women to protest the sentences. I had told her then that we had appealed the cases, but that should the courts finally uphold the sentences we might need her help. I called Miss Addams to go ahead with her committee. She, Mary McDowell, Mrs. Harold Ickes, and Amelia Sears were among those who went before Judge Sullivan to plead with him to remit the sentences. But Judge Sullivan would not relent and claimed the matter "out of his hands."

Meanwhile, some of the young women involved had married and left the trade. One had a young baby she had to wean before serving her sentence. Another asked to have her sentence advanced a week so that she could serve it before going to Bryn Mawr College, where she had a scholarship to attend the Summer School for Working Women. Still another, to serve a thirty-day sentence in jail, had to come back from Colorado where she was being treated for tuberculosis. Some of the women had young children and babies, and these had to be boarded out while their mothers sat in jail.

Saturday afternoon, June 1, was the time set for the girls to be committed. We assembled at the headquarters of the union, the girls who were to serve their sentences, many of their relatives, officers and members of the union, and many friends. We marched in procession to the office of the sheriff of Cook County to have the papers signed for the girls' admission to jail. Then from that office we marched to the Near-North Side to the county jail and assembled to bid them good-bye.

At the top of the steps leading to the doorway of the jail the official stood and called out the names of the girls who had been sentenced. At each name we cheered and gave the girls flowers to make their entrance into the jail seem a triumph instead of a punishment. But I shall never forget the sight of those brave girls walking up those steps to enter the jail. As they reached the doorway, they would turn to wave good-bye to us before the grim doorway swallowed them.

Once inside the jail, the girls received the same treatment as the other prisoners — except they did not have to scrub floors, because they refused to! For this they were denied sugar in their coffee! Each day the union sent one good meal in to them from a near-by restaurant. The union also paid the girls' full salaries to them for all the time served in jail and paid also for the care of the babies and young children which had to be boarded out.

Having exhausted every means of keeping the girls from jail, once they had been jailed, we turned to the problem of getting them out as soon as possible. Our delegation went to see Governor Small shortly after the girls had begun serving their sentences. We had been advised that once the serving of the sentences had begun, then Governor Small could pardon the girls. We called not only on Governor Small but also on Attorney General Oscar Carlstrom.

Towards the end of August we received a word from Attorney General Carlstrom. "Authorities," said he, "do not warrant us advising the Governor that a pardon could be clearly legal." In other words, Judge Sullivan could make laws from which there was no appeal!

This reply came a little late; already most of the girls had finished serving the sentences.

But all this did not discourage the workers in the ladies' garment industry of Chicago. Rather, it hardened their will for justice. The fight, they felt, would continue. Only next time they intended to be better prepared.

In fact, work had never relaxed. Mollie Friedman had come from New York in 1925 to assist the dressmakers in building up their union which the 1924 strike had all but wrecked. Mollie came to see me and said that she would like to begin by building up good public relations regarding the union. I took her around to the newspapers and they offered their co-opera-tion. Mollie began her organization work in one of the larger plants.

However, the Chicago dress manufacturers were hostile, insisting on open shops and the "yellow-dog" contract. But after a long struggle, the union was able to negotiate for closed shops, a 40-hour week, unemployment insurance, and collective bargaining. Some time later, when Mollie Friedman had to return East, she asked me to take over her work and to meet with the head of a certain firm in the women's dress trade. When I met him, the head of the firm said: "You do not know us, Miss Nestor; but we know you." He proceeded to tell me that he had received a call from the Illinois Manufacturers' Association inviting him to attend the hearing of the proposed women's eight-hour bill at Springfield. "A dangerous piece of legislation," he called the bill.

I said that certain firms which had tried out the eight-hour day had found that it worked to the advantage of both em-ployer and employees, and that the eight-hour day was coming so he had better try it himself. He did not go to the hearings at Springfield; and after hearing our arguments for the eight-hour day, one of his associates ventured to say: "I believe what those girls are saying is good. Let us go back and try it."

We had been defeated in our effort to secure the eight-hour law, but gradually we were persuading some firms to put the eight-hour day into practice, at least as a trial measure.

I continued the organization work Mollie Friedman had delegated to me. It was just another job outside my own work and I was used to taking on extra responsibilities. I attended all the union's meetings. It was at those meetings that grievances were handed in. In a newly organized shop there are many matters to be adjusted, because both sides, the workers and the employers, are suffering growing pains. Then the next day after a meeting I would go to the plant and hand in the grievances, which I had written up for the company, and the company would proceed to investigate the matters. I would return for a report, calling in the foremen as well as the girls to state their complaints. I felt, however, that this was a futile method of handling the matters. I suggested to the company and to the union that grievances submitted at the union meetings be referred first to their shop committee for adjustment and then taken up with the foreman in charge. If no settlement had been thus achieved, then I would meet with the company officials. This seemed a more practical manner of handling the difficulties which arose, as it allowed those who best understood the issues involved to settle in most cases their own disputes.

ANOTHER WOMEN'S TRADE we found hard to organize in Chicago was the millinery industry.

Back in 1909, the Straw and Felt Hat Workers' Union had been chartered directly by the A. F. of L. It was a small organization headed by Marion McShea. Marion came to me to ask advice about how to proceed in dealing with the manufacturers. She had been put in the job without experience. I suggested that she draw up an agreement for the industry and present this to the employers. We worked out the agreement and Marion went with it to all the employers. The results were amazing. Most of the employers thought that she had their shops already organized. Most of them signed the agreement, and before long Marion McShea had the whole industry unionized and under union-shop agreements. It was easy then to get members for the union when they knew the agreements had already been signed.

Later, Marion met with difficulties when the cap makers tried to enter the millinery trade to do the operators' work and the milliners protested. A strike resulted, and Marion's fine organization dissolved. From then on, organizing the milliners was a long, slow job.

The United Hatters, Cap and Millinery Workers' Union sent Melinda Scott from the East to get things started. (Melinda had accompanied me on the American Labor Mission to Europe.) Max Zaritsky, the president of the union, came to Chicago with Melinda to lend what aid he could.

Melinda found not even a nucleus of an organization to work from. She worked out of our Women's Trade Union League office until an office could be found for her. We had leaflets printed announcing a first meeting of the millinery union; but only a very few girls responded.

One girl, very able and attractive, came to the front in the work, and when Melinda had to return to the East, this girl seemed the logical person to leave in charge of the union. There was a special reason, however, behind this girl's willingness to work in the new union; she was a Communist. But she promised not to let this enter into her union work, and we gave her the job of continuing the organization of the milliners. Her promise was not kept. The time came when she got her orders from the Communist Party and tried to indoctrinate the milliners. When this was discovered, she was obliged to leave the plant where she had a job, and, as far as we knew, she left the city.

Max Zaritsky then sent Carolyn Wolfe from New York to take up the work. Mary Haney, our Women's Trade Union League organizer, and I went out with Carolyn several times a night all one long winter to talk to the girls as they came out of the millinery shops and to give them leaflets which told about the millinery workers' union which we wanted them to join. It was a hard struggle to get them to join. Many of those old-time millinery workers would agree that they needed a union, but they would say, finally: "You cannot organize milliners. You just cannot get them all to join."

Carolyn's work progressed, but she met with stiff opposition from the employers in the form of the "yellow-dog" contract. This "yellow-dog" contract, which those employers who wished to conduct a non-union shop asked their employees to sign, constituted the employee's agreement to help the employer to conduct a non-union shop, not to recognize or have any dealings with any labor union, and not to communicate with any union officers, agents, or members. Almost twenty years afterwards, it is hard to believe that a proposal of this kind was ever presented to any group of workers. Yet it was one of the common practices in those days and it persisted until the Federal Government passed laws guaranteeing workers the right to organize and to deal with employers through agents of their own choosing.

In 1929 one shop forced the issue of having all its employees sign "yellow-dog" contracts, and a strike ensued. Mr. Zaritsky held a conference with the attorney for the Millinery Employers' Association. Besides those of the struck plant, representatives were present from six other plants. The attorney stated that he was having the discussion taken down by a court reporter so as to have a formal record of the meeting. He stated that because of the attitude of the local union officials during the previous two months, he could see no hope for the future of the millinery trade. He stated that the employers wished to deal only with the employees directly as individuals.

Mr. Zaritsky made a fine statement setting forth the employees' position that peace in the industry could be upheld only through arbitration machinery. It was a cold, formal meeting, with the employers' attorney asserting that the employees' views taken in the stenographic report would be transmitted to the employers. There was no chance to talk matters out and reach an understanding. It seemed as though the representatives of the employers had come determined not to reach any understanding.

The decision of the employers, after they had read the transcript of the meeting, was to be given the following Saturday. But before that date nine hundred millinery workers were locked out of twenty-eight shops because they refused to sign the individual "yellow-dog" contracts. By this time the workers in the struck plant had been out on strike for five weeks.

The officials of the struck plant had gone to Judge Dennis E. Sullivan to obtain an injunction and the usual drastic measures against picketing. But the union's attorney had insisted that the case be transferred to Judge John A. Fitch, and this judge had granted only the limited injunction in conformity with the 1923 Illinois law. This injunction permitted peaceful picketing.

As late as January 25 of the following year, 1930, the millinery manufacturers tried again for a full injunction. This time they applied to Judge William J. Lindsey. But Judge Lindsey refused to issue such an injunction; the allegations against the millinery workers were insufficient to warrant such an injunction, said he. The police, said he, could easily take care of anything that might occur and a new injunction was uncalled for.

Meanwhile, already the depression had begun. Also, it was bitter winter. The milliners had a strike and a lockout with little chance of winning their fight. But the employers could not cripple the strike with injunctions this time. The employees did go back to work; but they did not go back under "yellow-dog" contracts. They remained free to keep their union memberships and to build up their union.

23

Our Fight During the Depression

RETURNING HOME from a National Women's Trade Union League convention one day in the spring of 1929, I found awaiting me a very inspiring letter.

The letter was from my good friend Father Frederic Siedenburg. Father Siedenburg was then dean of the School of Sociology at Loyola University.

On behalf of the Loyola University Board of Trustees, Father Siedenburg advised me, it was his privilege and pleasure to inform me, that on account of my outstanding work as a citizen and a pioneer for industrial betterment, at a recent meeting of the board I had been voted the honorary degree of LL.D., Doctor of Laws.

The degree was conferred at the commencement exercises the following June 12. It was an impressive ceremony. As I walked in the processional with Father Siedenburg, wearing my cap and gown, a glove worker without higher education, I could hardly believe that all this honor was being conferred upon me. I had read of distinguished citizens being awarded honorary degrees. But never before had I heard of such a degree being given a labor representative. I felt it an honor not only to me but also to the cause I represented.

The citation ran as follows:

AGNES NESTOR IN CAP AND GOWN

CANDIDATE FOR THE DEGREE OF
DOCTOR OF LAWS: AGNES NESTOR

At the beginning of the 20th century, a Chicago factory girl without higher education, position, or prestige, organized her fellow workers to better their working conditions. In a few years she was President of the Women's Trade Union League of Chicago. Then her labors became national and she was appointed by two Presidents of the United States to commissions of industrial betterment. During the World War she was a member of the Council of National Defense and the only woman on the Advisory Council to the Secretary of Labor. Later she was sent as America's Labor Representative to conferences in Great Britain, France, and Austria. At present she is Director of the National Women's Trade Union League of America, a member of the World's Fair Commission and of a score of other social and civic societies.

This life consecration to the well-being of the laboring women of the world has ever been animated by the highest Christian ideals...

PRESENTED BY DEAN FREDERIC SIEDENBURG, S. J.

A FEW MONTHS LATER, October, 1929, and we were at the beginning of the worst depression in the history of the country. Soon so many people were out of work and had found their savings used up, that the needs of many were acute. By the fall of 1930 it had become evident that organized assistance to those in distress would have to be maintained. Governor Emmerson of Illinois appointed a Commission on Unemployment and Relief. Most of the fifty members of the commission were businessmen. But among the fifty there were five representatives of labor. And of this five, one was a woman. I was the woman.

We began our work at once, organizing committees and launching a drive for five million dollars to carry the unemployed of Chicago through the winter. At the time this seemed a large amount. We little imagined that unemployment would continue for years and would spread until at its peak in March, 1932, the need for the unemployed of Cook County would be seven million dollars a month!

There was at that time no unemployment insurance system. As savings of individuals and families were exhausted, the relief rolls grew. In the window of the Telephone Company the daily record of telephones in service gave a clue to the increasing distress in the city. In Chicago in one year, 1931, one hundred thousand telephones were dispensed with. But telephones dispensed with did not compare with other privations many families had to undergo.

A Work Relief Committee was one of the first committees that our commission set up. It was heartbreaking for people who had been self-supporting and who were willing to work to have to ask for aid, for relief. Work relief projects gave them the chance to earn the aid they received and helped to keep up their morale.

On this Work Relief Committee, Samuel Insull was chairman, Joel Hunter of the United Charities sat as representative of the employers, Dr. Martin Bickman from the Illinois State

Employment Service was administrator, and I, Agnes Nestor, represented labor.

We worked well together, even though at times it seemed odd that I happened to be the labor member on the committee when most of the projects dealt with work for men. Often I would find myself conferring with representatives of a painters' or street cleaners' union, or of some other union in trades engaged in solely by men.

Our committee began with the policy of paying the prevailing union wage for work done on relief projects. However, workers were restricted to earning only the equivalent of the relief allowed. The painters, for instance, could work fewer days than the street cleaners because the painters' hourly rate was higher. Thus we avoided the difficulties New York City encountered when it began paying a straight three dollars a day to relief workers and earned by this procedure the protests of the unions.

We called in union representatives to work out the method of selecting the men for work relief, as we did not wish to force the men to go through the humiliation of the relief rolls. The men drew names at their headquarters, each taking his turn at work. We had the full co-operation of all the union organizations, because they had no fear of our program's being a threat to their wage standards or a method of replacing regular workers.

For our projects we had to search for work which would not have got done without the relief fund. Money from the relief fund could be used only for public and non-profit work, or for work for non-profit organizations. Never did the streets and public buildings of Chicago get such cleaning! But we found other kinds of work, too.

I had some interesting experiences trying to head off a strike of street cleaners. Because the work had to be shared with others on the relief rolls, the street cleaners felt their members were not getting enough work. We managed, however, to iron out the difficulties, and the project became a satisfactory piece of work — if any relief work can be considered satisfactory. This sort of relief work was the beginning of what later became the programs of the WPA.

There was no place in our program for the women, and this distressed me. The Woman's Service Bureau, of which I was a member, was taking care of what it called "the unattached woman." But there were many women who needed work and could find none. In one instance, a large consignment of cotton material was sent from the U. S. Government to the Red Cross to be made into garments for people on relief. This sewing project was turned over to the Goodwill Industries. I persuaded the local work committee to allow those members of the garment workers' union who were out of work to take part in this project. We made an agreement with the garment workers for them to work ten days a month each, at four dollars a day. At the end of each ten days a new group would come on. Thus each out-of-work member could earn forty dollars a month, which to them was a great deal of money in those dark days. The names of those who were to work were sent in by the unions through the office of the Women's Trade Union League and cleared as on all other work projects. In this way we could be certain that those receiving the work were not already receiving relief. We decided to broaden the program to include other sewing trades whose members were experienced operators, and this helped to make the plan workable. Some of the members of these unions told me that they did not know how they could have gone through this period except for that work relief which we provided.

THE ADVISORY COMMITTEE for the Employment Bureau was another Chicago committee of which I was a member during this time. Britton I. Budd was chairman of this committee, and my old friend John Fitzpatrick was serving with us. We decided to take a registration of the Chicago unemployed not on relief and to use the various public schools as registration points. We appointed a Saturday morning early in November of 1931 for this project. The public school teachers were giving their time to help in this registration, and our committee had agreed to visit the schools that morning to see how the registration progressed and where additional help might be needed.

As only one room in each school was being used, there was makeshift heat. One of the schools I visited had a gas burner arranged to heat the room, and, as I waited for the teacher in charge to finish a registration, I stepped back a foot or two toward this burner. In a moment someone called out, "Lady, your coat is on fire!" To my consternation I found the entire back of my coat burned!

The Commission on Unemployment and Relief had been conducting a drive asking everyone who was working to buy something to help get the wheels of industry rolling again. I had just bought this new coat, which I badly needed, and now it was ruined. The outer cloth of the back of the coat was burned away till the white flannel lining was all that was left in that region. I had to take out-of-the-way routes to get home. I was fortunate that it was a Chicago-made coat; the manufacturer was able to match the material exactly and charged me only twenty dollars for putting in a new back. At the office of the Commission on Unemployment and Relief they teased me by telling everyone that I had bought a new coat and then had taken it back and had the company make it over just in order to give workers additional employment.

On that Saturday in November, 1931, 61,250 men and 9,964 women registered with us as unemployed and not on relief. Of the women, 3,809 were clerical workers, 2,831 domestic and personal service workers, with the remainder falling into some eighteen other groups. The clerical workers, we saw, were as hard hit as the industrial workers.

George F. Getz, chairman of the Commission on Unemployment and Relief, told us labor members that when first the commission had been set up his business associates had warned him, "Look out. You have five labor representatives on that commission!" Against our five there were about forty businessmen among the fifty members. Mr. Getz and the businessmen learned to work with us labor representatives and discovered that we could all work together on our common problems. They soon found out, too, that they needed the labor representatives' experience.

In February, 1932, the Illinois Emergency Relief Commission was set up to deal with the ever-growing problem of relief and our work ended except for the Advisory Committee which was then set up.

OUR WOMEN'S TRADE UNION LEAGUE had set up an Unemployment Relief Committee to deal with the special relief problems of unemployed women workers of our league. One day we found out that some of the women of the dressmakers' union were living in unheated rooms. On weekdays these women would go to their union headquarters to register for work; not that there was in their minds any hope of work, but the union headquarters was a warm place to spend the day. On Sundays, however, the union offices were closed. Seeing this, our league arranged open house at our club house every

Sunday with games and refreshments. Weekday evenings we held classes and even dancing parties to cheer up our unemployed during those trying months. At least we could give them warmth and a pleasant time.

Many of the girls in the garment workers' union, we found out, were going without lunch and spending their lunch money for carfare to and from the union headquarters in the hope of getting jobs. We embarked upon a project to get lunches for these girls. We tried first to work out a plan for a lunchroom, but that plan did not prove practical, the union offices being scattered over too large an area. Finally we went to the Illinois Emergency Relief Commission and asked for meal tickets for our unemployed garment workers. With such work as they had been able to get, and by using up their savings, these girls had managed to keep off relief. The commission agreed to give out the tickets but wanted them handled through a social worker. We objected to this; we wanted the tickets given out through the union secretaries who knew which girls were without work and who could be trusted to issue the tickets. The proposal was shifted back and forth, even getting to the Woman's Service Bureau. Victor A. Olander and William H. Saxton, corporation counsel for the city of Chicago, helped us get our plan approved by the commission. Our way, the girls received tickets which they could present at certain restaurants for forty-cent lunches, and they did not feel they had to lower their pride by being "charity cases" in order to survive during this terrible period.

PROLONGED UNEMPLOYMENT brought on the breakdown of industrial standards. One case I remember proved quite a confusing one. Certain cotton-garment plants in the city were working their women workers ten hours a day and even seven days a week, with the women earning barely enough to live on. In some cases these women had even to apply for relief. These women had no union organization, and, with so many out of work, they were afraid to complain about the long hours and low pay.

One day at a meeting of the Woman's Service Bureau, the question came up as to whether it was fair to give relief funds to a woman who was working thus full time but not earning enough to live on. Upon further investigation we learned that the plants in which these women were working were making the garments which our Woman's Service Bureau purchased for its relief clients; we could then understand why we had been able to purchase the garments so cheaply. We found ourselves caught in a vicious circle. The women did get relief funds. Those were desolate times!

From everywhere in the city complaints poured into our office about the low wages being paid women who were working in unorganized trades. We felt we should do something about these trades. I called together a group of women interested in this problem, and we decided to issue a call to all women's and civic organizations to join in a movement to secure a minimum-wage law for women workers. New York State passed such a law in 1933, and President Roosevelt sent a letter to the governors of all the other states suggesting the passage of a similar law. It was a legislative year in Illinois. We organized what we called the Illinois Joint Committee on Industrial Standards, with Hazel Kyrk of the University of Chicago as co-chairman with me. Governor Henry Horner, acting on the President's letter, sponsored an Illinois minimum-wage law for women. We supported and worked for the bill, and it was passed by the Illinois Legislature toward the end of the session.

June of that same year, 1933, saw the passage of the National Industrial Recovery Act with its famous Section 7(a) guaranteeing workers the right to organize, and a new organization movement started and at once swept the country.

This period saw the beginning of many new unions and a restored membership in many of the unions which hard times had thinned out. My International Glove Workers Union, which had been at a low ebb in its activity, began organizing again, and even Gloversville, where the union had been dormant for years, became fully unionized.

Our Women's Trade Union League began to get calls to organize workers faster than we could answer them. The cotton-dress workers, who during the depth of the depression had been protesting their working conditions, struck and were unionized. It was the beginning of a permanent organization in that branch of the trade.

The unionized dressmakers, who during the prosperous years just before 1929 had made some gains, had during the depression lost almost all their shops. They reorganized their union and called their third strike. The workers responded enthusiastically. Within two weeks they had won their twenty-year-old struggle. They returned to work with a recognition of their union, a guaranteed minimum wage, a shorter work week, and machinery for settlement of disputes.

Then the milliners staged a general strike, and they too won, going back to work under agreements for all the shops in the downtown area. The struggle had been long and discouraging. Victory was heartening for us who had gone through those long, hard years.

MEANWHILE, MY OWN ACTIVITY was now shifting to Washington, where "codes of fair competition" were being set up. Though these were employer's codes, representatives of the unions concerned were called in to examine the codes, and a Labor Advisory Board under the National Labor Administration had been appointed to help. On this Labor Advisory Board, my friend Rose Schneiderman was the one woman appointed to serve with William Green, John L. Lewis, David Dubinsky, and Sidney Hillman. Rose spent all her time in Washington during the life of this National Labor Administration.

Under the National Industrial Recovery Act a minimum hourly wage rate and a 40-hour week were established until the various industries could work out and secure approval of their separate codes. This procedure was designed to give the workers some protection while the separate codes were being formulated and approved.

My International Glove Workers Union was concerned about two codes — that for the leather and wool-knit glove industry, and that for the cotton-cloth glove industry, which at that time was almost entirely unorganized. This cotton glove industry was located in small towns, seventy-five per cent of them in the Middle West. Four companies owning twenty-six plants and employing about five thousand workers comprised almost half the industry. The industry had always paid low wages, as low as eighteen cents an hour. While the codes were being formulated, the minimum rate for skilled women workers was raised to thirty-two-and-a-half cents an hour.

Once the codes had been approved by labor and industry groups, public hearings were conducted; then the codes had to be approved by the National Industrial Relations Administration and signed by the President. I cannot enumerate all the hurried trips I had to make to Washington to represent our union in this matter. The leather- and knit-glove hearings were always lively, the friction being mainly between the Eastern and Middle-Western manufacturers. In the cotton-cloth glove industry the main contention was between the manufacturers of the North and those of the South. The manufacturers of the South wanted a differential in wages which the manufacturers of the North, as well as the unions, opposed.

The leather-glove industry of Fulton County, New York, proposed that a general minimum-wage rate be established. This proposal was supported by the manufacturers of the East but opposed by those of the Middle West.

The code for the leather and wool-knit industry was approved November 4, 1933, and that for the cotton-cloth industry December 30; but the wage schedule for the leather-glove industry was not approved until September of the next year. I was in Washington the day this order went through. Elisabeth Christman, whose office was in Washington, was ill, so I took her a copy of the order and sent wires to our locals.

Difficulties arose as soon as the codes had been approved, for the manufacturers contested them. To settle these difficulties, code authorities were set up, and the unions were given representation on these committees but without voting power. Elisabeth Christman was appointed to the Leather and Wool Glove Code Authority, and I was appointed to the Cotton-Cloth Glove Code Authority.

I was not certain what sort of reception I would get at my first meeting of my code authority, because employers who were members of the committee were from non-union plants. I thought they might even object to my being there representing the International Glove Workers Union at a meeting of heads of non-union glove industries. But to my surprise I was cordially received and given every consideration during my term with the group.

One day the employer members of the group were talking about the forthcoming meeting of their association. One member suggested that Professor E. H. Hahne, the Government representative, be invited to address the association. Then Mr. B. Elsey of the Indianapolis Glove Company, said, "I think Miss Nestor should be invited to address our convention, because our members think she has horns and I would like them to see that she does not." But they did not invite me; nor did they invite Professor Hahne.

The Enforcement Committee for Illinois under the Leather and Wool Glove Code Authority was another interesting organization. On this committee employers and workers had equal representation. I worked on this committee until the late spring of 1935, when the National Industrial Recovery Act was held unconstitutional. All Federal Government regulation of industrial standards was then ended until the Fair Labor Relations Act was passed in 1938.

I liked the National Industrial Recovery Act. But of course labor should have had an equal representation with employers in the workings of the measure. Under the measure, responsibility for enforcement was placed upon the employer. We had good employer compliance in the glove industry, however; we had only to collect a little more than seven thousand dollars for back wages from twenty-seven employers in sixteen states.

24

Chicago's "A Century of Progress"

THE CITY OF CHICAGO would be one hundred years old in 1933. Back as early as 1926, Captain Myron E. Adams had been vigorously promoting the idea of a centennial celebration. Later, Mayor Dever appointed a Ways and Means Committee to plan for such a centennial. On the committee, made up of thirty-five citizens, there were four women members — Mrs. Harold Ickes, Mrs. Catherine Waugh McCulloch, Mrs. Julius Benedick, and I.

But before very much actual planning for the centennial had been done, two untoward events occurred. Captain Adams, who had been one of the first to promote the idea of the celebration, died. Then Mayor Dever's term of office expired, and there was elected in his place William Hale Thompson who, at first, was not favorable to the centennial idea.

Then Charles S. Peterson, a prominent Chicago businessman who had gone abroad, came back filled with enthusiasm about a "world's fair," and this gave the idea of the centennial a new impetus. Finally, in December of 1927, Mayor Thompson called a town meeting in the council chambers to consider the plan. As I was entering the room for the meeting, I met Victor Olander who also had been on Mayor Dever's committee, and we took seats together near the rear of the room. Then just before the meeting was to begin, Helen Bennett, a well-known Chicago journalist, came through the room apparently looking for someone. When she saw me, she exclaimed, "Oh, Agnes, come up front. Ruth wants you." The "Ruth" to whom she referred was Ruth Hanna McCormick. I was rushed to the rostrum and found myself acting as secretary to this first large gathering to plan for Chicago's great centennial celebration.

Work for the centennial was started immediately. A corporation was formed called "The Second World's Fair Corporation," and it began to raise money for the project. Later the name of the project was changed to "A Century of Progress," and a board of trustees was elected, with Rufus C. Dawes as chairman and Major Lenox R. Lohr as manager, to handle the affairs. On my way to work one day I read in the newspapers that I had been elected to this board of trustees, and on reaching my office I found my official notice of this election. I was appointed to head the centennial's Women in Industry Committee. There were many other special committees of interest to various groups, with a group of well-known society women forming the Social Functions Committee.

As a trustee, I attended all the monthly meetings of the board and was included in all the special affairs when distinguished visitors were entertained at the "Fair," as we continued to call it. One special visitor I particularly admired, and whom I met many times later on, was Miss Frances Perkins, then Secretary of Labor. She was given a reception when she visited the fair in the spring of 1933. She told me later that she would never forget the military salute which she received as she approached the Trustees Building, a salute which was her due because of her Cabinet rank. In the Trustees Room she saw our conference table and was so charmed by it that she said she would have one like it in the new Department of Labor

Building then under construction. The table was narrow at one end, widening toward the other where about five could be seated. Around this table everyone was in sight and could see everyone else without shifting position.

Two years later, Governor Horner appointed State Director of Labor Martin P. Durkin and me to represent Illinois at the opening ceremonies for the new Department of Labor Building. As we toured the beautiful building, I saw in Miss Perkins' conference room a striking table, the replica of the one she had so much admired in the Trustees Room at our Chicago "A Century of Progress." Since then I have taken my own seat at that table many times, helping to work out problems which concerned working women.

Chicago's centennial, at its opening, seemed like a fairyland to me. I had attended the San Francisco Fair of 1915, when the A. F. of L. convention had met in that city. But our Chicago "A Century of Progress" seemed to excel the western fair in every respect. The centennial ran through 1934. No other such celebration had been known to end without a deficit. Our centennial made a record by paying all its obligations and closing with a profit of $276,084.00. This profit was apportioned to certain non-profit educational enterprises, of which the Chicago Museum of Science and the Adler Planetarium stand today as examples.

Five mayors had been in office in Chicago during the seven-year planning of the centennial. Mayor Dever did not live to see the centennial open. Mayor Anton Cermak, who defeated Mayor Thompson, met a tragic death in March of 1933, two months before the centennial opened. Frank J. Carr served temporarily until Edward J. Kelly was elected by the city council and became host for the city.

At the close of the celebration, each member of the board

of trustees which had planned the project received a hand-
somely-bound book of views of the centennial, the book itself
such a fine example of typographical art that it should be
placed in a museum of Chicago history.

THE YEAR THE FAIR CLOSED, Mayor Kelly appointed
me a member of the Chicago Recreation Committee. Long
before, in the early days of our social work in Chicago, our
Women's Trade Union League had instituted summer camps
for working women at River Park Grove near Palatine, in the
Cook County Preserve. We had managed to get the carpenters'
union interested in the project and also some lumbermen. We
had tiny cottages set up with front screened porches. Here the
factory girls could come for fresh air and relaxation, great
medicine for worn-down nervous energy. We provided horseback riding, tennis, golf, archery, and hiking. Our rates we
made fantastically low. A full day at camp cost 15 cents.
Lodging for the day and night was 50 cents. A week at camp
was provided for $2.50. Food was either brought by the girls
or could be bought at a small commissary not far from camp.
Mayor Kelly's recreation work was an activity in the like of
which I had long been interested.

A Divided Labor Movement

AS THE DEPRESSION was lifting in 1934 and 1935, once more the future looked bright for organized labor. The National Labor Relations Act of 1935 guaranteed the workers' right to organize, and the A. F. of L. membership reached over three million, the highest since World War I. Then there came what seemed to most of us a tragedy indeed, a split in the labor movement.

The A. F. of L. convention of 1935 met in Atlantic City with over one hundred national and international unions represented. Then through a number of resolutions the question of industrial organization came before the delegates and became a fighting issue. At stake were the millions of unorganized workers in the steel, automobile, and rubber industries. A resolution that, in disregard of the A. F. of L. constitution, these industries be organized on an industrial, rather than on a craft basis, was defeated on the convention floor by a vote of 18,000 to 11,000. The vote was based upon each organization's membership, and the minority vote was swelled by five international unions which cast 7,000 votes. Of this 7,000, 4,000 votes were cast by the United Mine Workers.

Dissatisfied with the majority vote, eight international unions then met to consider ways and means of carrying out industrial organization in defiance of the convention. Thus was born the C.I.O., the Congress of Industrial Organizations, which soon flared into a roaring organizational activity, and another labor movement was started.

This split of the labor movement into two major national movements soon had repercussions in our International Glove Workers Union. Fulton County, New York, where the union had taken on new life under the NRA, with a flourishing organization resulting, seemed doomed to have a split in its ranks. In 1934, our Chicago convention had seen the largest delegations since the start of the organization. At that convention I had felt that at last our prospects were bright. We were invited to hold our next convention at Gloversville, and that was like a dream come true. I had been hoping for long years that something could be done to stabilize the union at Gloversville, for there had been troubles in that region since the disastrous strike of 1903. However, worse was still to come.

In Gloversville the Table-Cutters' Branch of the local union had become dissatisfied with certain administrative policies. In 1936 this branch withdrew their affiliation from our International Glove Workers Union and remained independent. Then, two weeks before our 1937 convention was to meet at Gloversville, the Operators' Branch, the largest group in the Gloversville union, withdrew its affiliation. With such dissatisfaction existing in the Gloversville local, we hurriedly changed our convention city from Gloversville to Johnstown, the twin glove city three miles away.

Upon my arrival in Johnstown, a joint committee from the Table Cutters Union and the Operators Union, now both independent, came to see me. They wanted to meet to work out some sort of agreement. But there was also still another problem weighing on our minds. En route to the convention,

I and some other officers of our International Glove Workers Union had held a conference in New York with Sidney Hillman on a proposal that our International Glove Workers Union affiliate with the Amalgamated Clothing Workers' Union. In return, the Amalgamated Clothing Workers' Union pledged to fully unionize the glove industry. This proposal was brought before our convention. We had not been prepared for it, and the entire time of the convention was taken up with its consideration.

Joining with the Amalgamated Clothing Workers' Union would mean leaving the A. F. of L., for the Amalgamated Clothing Workers' Union was one of the original C.I.O. organizations. It would also mean that our small craft-organized union would be subordinated and lost in a much larger union tending toward industrial organization. However, without the now independent Operators Union and Table Cutters Union of Gloversville, many felt that our International Glove Workers Union would be so small as to leave us no hope but to join with Amalgamated.

The action of the convention on the proposal was finally to refer it to our affiliated locals for a referendum vote of the membership. But with our convention meeting as it was in May, and the vote to be taken in June, there was little time for full consideration of the proposed step. The picture looked gloomy. As for me, I could not bring myself to support the proposal. It was one of the most agonizing periods of my professional life. Joining with Amalgamated meant to me joining with an organization which had no connection with our glove trade and in which our identity would be completely lost. I went home from the convention clinging to the hope that the proposal would be turned down by the referendum vote, and that all would come out right.

The big locals in the Middle West voted almost solidly against the proposal. But when the vote of the New York locals came in, it was found that the proposal had carried by a small margin. Almost at once there came a letter from Mr. Kennedy, secretary of our International Glove Workers Union, saying that there had been a conference with Mr. Hillman, that Mr. Hillman suggested that the affiliation with Amalgamated begin July 1, that our office in Washington be closed, our belongings shipped to the office of the Amalgamated Clothing Workers' Union in New York, and that he, Mr. Kennedy, was to be the director of our "Glove Worker Department of the Amalgamated Clothing Workers' Union."

I re-read Mr. Kennedy's letter. It was a stunning blow. I had received the letter on Friday, and this submerging of our union was to be effective the following Tuesday. But no formal agreements had been made concerning the rights of our members within this larger organization. Our local unions had received only a memo based largely on long-distance telephone conversations with Mr. Hillman's secretary. The entire arrangement, on the face of it, had been worked out much too loosely. The legal aspects of the whole matter had been violated completely. And in our own section, the Middle West, there was overpowering dissatisfaction with the arrangement. But what, I wondered, could there now be done?

I put a call through to Washington to A. F. of L. President William Green.

"You know about the Glove Workers?" I managed to say.

"Of course, I know," replied he.

"What about the members who do not want to go into Amalgamated?" I asked. "Can we keep our charter?"

"Yes!" replied he, emphatically, with no hesitation.

"Very well," said I. "We have no funds, no equipment; but we will start from scratch."

I saw what I had to do. The Amalgamated Clothing Workers knew the garment industry, but we who knew how different was the glove industry would have to sacrifice even old friendships to hold on to the gains we had sacrificed so much to obtain.

Mr. Green assured me that the A. F. of L. would help and asked me to recommend an organizer whom he could put on their staff for our trade.

That evening the Milwaukee local was holding a meeting. I wired our vice-president, Thomas Durian, telling him his local could stay in the International Glove Workers Union and asking him to come to Chicago the next day. Together we called an emergency meeting of our officers and worked out plans for an emergency convention to meet in Milwaukee in the fall to elect new officers and to make plans for rebuilding the union. I notified Mr. Kennedy that we were holding the A. F. of L. charter for those of the locals who wanted to remain in the International Glove Workers Union, and that those who wanted to join the Amalgamated Clothing Workers would have to do so direct.

The Milwaukee convention that fall elected Thomas Durian general president and Anton White, a young worker, secretary-treasurer. I was elected to serve as vice-president. We all left that convention with a renewed hope, a crusader spirit. Soon our International Glove Workers Union had been built into a fine organization with a membership greater than when the Fulton County locals were included. We raised our per capita tax and were soon on a self-supporting basis with an extended program and staff.

I saw Sidney Hillman once during the years following. I met him in a railroad station in Washington, D. C., and we exchanged a few words. Following his death, his wife, Bessie

Hillman, when on a trip to Chicago, came by to see me. I knew she felt bad over the break between Sidney and me, for we all had worked together during those early struggling years. But she understood.

As for the rest, the Amalgamated Clothing Workers knew the garment industry, but we knew the glove industry. They could not realize how difficult a struggle it would be to organize glove workers. Or what detailed knowledge was necessary in negotiating agreements in the glove industry. They put a necktie worker in charge of their Glove Worker Department!

26

The Women's
Eight-Hour-Day Law!

IT WAS PASSED in 1937, our Illinois Women's Eight-Hour-Day Law. We knew that year we had lined up enough votes to see it passed, but until the roll had been called in the house there was uncertainty; so often we had stood hopeful in that gallery only to hear at the last moment that we had lost, sometimes by only a single vote.

In the senate the bill had been shepherded through by Senator Francis J. Loughran. In the house the sponsor was Representative Edward P. O'Grady, and when the last vote was announced he was the proudest member of the house that day. He turned to share his honors with me, calling on me to take a bow from where I sat in the gallery.

My own emotions were mixed. The victory did not seem as thrilling as that of the passage of the Women's Ten-Hour-Day Law more than twenty-five years before. We had been so young then, and in between there had been so many defeats. Also, so many of us who had begun the fight were gone.

That night we celebrated with a "Victory Dinner." We tried to include everyone who had had a part in the long fight. There was Mrs. Halas who had succeeded Elizabeth Maloney as my working partner at the legislative sessions at Springfield. She and Mary White, one of the younger workers and president of the Bloomington Telephone Operators' Union, had been beside me in the house gallery that day. There was Mary Dempsey of the Waitresses' Union, Kate Crain, and many another whom I knew well. But I seemed to be the sole survivor from those early days, the only one who still remained after the many years of the fight. Many a trip I had made to Springfield, many a thrilling moment there had been, and many a heartache.

Because there had always been such a big lobby opposing it, our eight-hour bill had seemed the most controversial measure facing each biennial of our Illinois General Assembly. Always the hearings had been lively. Always incidents had occurred in connection with it to make news.

From the beginning the labor movement had supported us, first with Edwin R. Wright as president and James Morris as secretary of the Illinois State Federation of Labor, and later with John H. Walker as president and Victor A. Olander as secretary. The state directors of labor, Barney Cohen and Martin P. Durkin had given us much support. They now saw that our bill was on Governor Henry Horner's desk for his signature in time for the bill to become law on July 1. Mrs. Halas and I stayed in Springfield and witnessed Governor Horner's signing of the bill, and we received the pen he used.

Meanwhile, the day after our "Victory Dinner," the *Chicago American* took the following note of our achievement:

Eight-Hour Bill Feted At Dinner
by William H. Stuart

Five hundred labor leaders and supporters of the eight-hour day for working women in Illinois sang and spoke in jubilee accents at a "Victory Dinner" at the Chicago Women's Club last night.

It was a celebration to mark enactment of the women's eight-hour law after a 27-year battle, given under auspices of the Illinois State and Chicago Women's Trade Union leagues.

Mary Halas was toastmistress and Agnes Nestor was historian and chief spokesman for the cause, and from many lines of industry, business and professional service they gathered their friends to celebrate.

SING VICTORY SONGS

One song sung in a mighty chorus was to the tune of "Working on the Railroad." Its words:

> We've been working down in Springfield
> Twenty-seven years.
> We've been working down in Springfield
> Just to get the members' ears.

> When the House would heed our story
> Some senators were goats.
> Twenty-seven years we labored
> Just to get twenty-six votes!

There was a song to the tune of "The Old Gray Mare" telling how working conditions were not what they used to be—that they were much better.

Then there was a refrain to the tune of "On Wisconsin" eulogizing Agnes Nestor:

> Agnes Nestor! Agnes Nestor!
> Fighting as of yore;
> Just that we may work eight hours,
> She'll work twenty-four.

> Now there's rest for Agnes Nestor,
> She'll have time to play;
> We're here to cheer and cheer
> The eight-hour day.

There were lines after "Rosie O'Grady" putting into the picture State Representative Edward P. O'Grady, who several times sponsored the bill:

> Good Eddie O'Grady
>> He worked with a will.
>> He's a friend of each lady
>> Who tried to pass the bill.
>
> Now we all are happy
>> After the fight and the fuss.
>> And we love good Eddie O'Grady,
>> And Eddie O'Grady loves us.

Among those at the speakers' table were Louie E. Lewis, President R. G. Soderstrom of the Illinois Federation of Labor, United States District Attorney Michael L. Igoe and Mrs. Igoe, State Senator Richard J. Barr and Mrs. Barr, Mrs. Lottie Holman O'Neill who through the years sponsored eight-hour laws, Representative Edward P. O'Grady, and Sophonisba Breckenridge of the University of Chicago.

CREDITS CAUSE HELPERS

Miss Nestor, telling of the long fight, gave credit to a score who helped in the early years. Among them were Jane Addams, Alice Timius, Mary McDowell, Federal Judge William H. Holly, and Elizabeth Maloney.

R. G. Soderstrom put a high estimate on the help the labor movement had received from the Women's Trade Union League and in particular from Agnes Nestor and Mary Halas.

Our bill signed by Governor Horner, Mrs. Halas and I traveled back to Chicago happy. Over twenty-five years we had struggled down there at Springfield, and at last our purpose had been achieved — the Illinois Women's Eight-Hour-Day Law! The then Secretary of State Edward J. Hughes rushed the printing of the new law and surprised me with one of the first copies off the press, sending it special delivery so that I could have it over the July 4th week end.

Another victory of that year had been the state ratification of the Woman Suffrage Amendment. Dr. Anna Howard Shaw at the time was ill in a Springfield hospital recovering from an attack of pneumonia. The day the amendment was ratified, I went to see her and announced: "Well, Dr. Shaw, Illinois ratified the Woman Suffrage Amendment today!"

But she did not seem at all carried away by the news. "You know," she said, "when you keep it away too long, the joy of victory is gone — it comes too late."

She seemed to have none of the fire of enthusiasm with which I had expected her to greet the news. Her long crusade was over. But at least she lived to know that she had won. She died that summer.

27

Education for Working Women

ABOUT 1914, in connection with our Women's Trade Union League's program of education for working women, Mrs. Edward Trowbridge gave a course in short story writing.

The next morning the Chicago newspapers featured the incident, jokingly remarking that working girls were now going to write their own short stories. Usually we had to work hard to get publicity for any of our projects, but this time we were beseiged by the newspapers, one paper even offering to publish the girls' stories.

With us, however, this education program was no joking matter. Another project we started at about this time was a course in creative arts. In this course pottery making became one of the most popular features. Girls who all day long had worked under tension in factories could here relax and have outlets for their creative abilities. Working in clay, with no time limits, and with the joy of making things of their own designs, the girls found new possibilities within themselves. One girl, a waitress, said that after working all day at her job she became so nervous that she could not sit half an hour reading, but that in this pottery class she could sit for two hours enjoying it so much that she completely forgot the passage of time.

We sought to provide opportunities for these working girls to explore some of the cultural avenues which had been denied to them. And in this connection, my old boss of the glove factory, Mr. Eisendrath, came forward one day with a most enlightening comment. Grace Abbott told me that she had asked him one day if it did not make him feel good to see me, who had once worked in his factory, rise to a position of prominence in the labor field. His reply was that it saddened him somewhat, because it made him wonder how many other girls there might be in factories who given opportunity might accomplish big things.

In 1917 we worked out a plan with the Chicago Board of Education for the use of classrooms of public schools in which to hold classes for working women when these classrooms were not in use otherwise. One particular course which I helped to work out was a course in the history of the trade-union movement. We had the late Professor John R. Commons of the University of Wisconsin, one of the outstanding economists in the country, open that course.

The next year I helped in organizing our School for Active Workers in the Labor Movement. We selected a few women in trade-union work to come to Chicago to give short courses in this field, including academic field work. Arrangements were made for the girls to enroll at the University of Chicago in the courses on Labor Problems and the History of Trade Unions under Professor H. A. Millis. It was something new for working women, without the required prerequisite academic background, to attend the university classes. But we were trying to give the working women the kind of study they desired and would find useful.

Meanwhile, our Women's Trade Union League itself carried on classes in public speaking and parliamentary law and other subjects. One instructor in parliamentary law I remember organized his class so that one night the class acted as a city council, another night as a state senate, still another night as the U. S. Senate, and so on. In this way his class not only practiced its parliamentary law, but also the class learned the workings of our various governments, and all in a most interesting manner.

In 1921 I attended the small meeting at which the Workers' Education Bureau was organized in Chicago. That meeting marked the beginning of a national movement. That year Bryn Mawr College pioneered with its Summer School for Working Women, opening its classrooms for a ten weeks' course. Dr. Martha Carey Thomas, president of the college, sponsored the school, heading a national committee of trade-union women and Bryn Mawr alumnae. I served on both the local and the national committee for this new kind of school.

That first summer school accommodated one hundred students, and they came from all parts of the country. Miss Hilda W. Smith, dean of Bryn Mawr, directed the pioneer work of this summer school, and her idealism, her fine understanding of people, her devotion to the purpose of the school, gained the success of this initial year.

A summer school for working women at Bryn Mawr College of course drew a barrage of criticism. "Why did Bryn Mawr want working women there?" "Could any good come of such an undertaking?" These questions were fired by many. But by the second year, when the school had established itself and its value, most of this criticism quieted down.

During the second and third years of the school, the summers of 1922 and 1923, I served as assistant director of this new venture, representing the trade-union women on this summer school staff. Around us we could behold a most democratic diversity in our student body. Some came from metropolitan areas like New York City and Chicago. Some came from towns which were mere dots on county maps. Some were from New England, some from the Middle West, some from the Deep South. All were American, though some were foreign-born. I used to say that there was as much educational work going on from the mere mingling on the campus as from the teaching in the classrooms.

Sometimes, at our summer sessions, an unconventional note would get sounded on tradition-laden Bryn Mawr campus. One summer, Dr. Thomas, president of the college, gave a garden party for the students. Dr. Thomas was a stately person, a woman of whom the regular college students stood much in awe. One of our trade-union women students, however, knew the warmth and kindliness within Dr. Thomas and was unacquainted with the awe the regular college students felt. She was a dressmaker from New York who had returned for a second summer session. She greeted Dr. Thomas at the garden party by impulsively throwing her arms around Dr. Thomas' neck and kissing her. No student had ever before dared demonstrate toward Dr. Thomas such appreciation in such a manner. But we all saw that Dr. Thomas was not displeased. A graduate of the regular college, seeing the scene, commented: "I dare say we used the wrong approach to Dr. Thomas! We, too, should have tried to embrace her!"

Of our hundred or so students in this new summer school, many of course belonged to trade unions. But some there were who belonged to company unions, and some others had been drawn from Y.W.C.A. industrial groups. I became interested in a girl named Louise who came from Oregon. Louise belonged to a company union and believed that the only successful form of worker organization. Louise was young, attractive, with the ability to become a leader. The trade-union girls thought it a pity that so fine a girl should be on the wrong side. They determined to win her over.

Toward the end of the term, Louise was sitting at my table for meals, according to our rotation plan of seating arrangement. There arose a discussion concerning a strike, and my ears perked up in surprise as I heard Louise defending the strikers. Later I asked one of Louise's instructors, "What happened to Louise?" "She has had opportunity to learn first-hand about trade unions," replied the instructor.

Another striking case was Sophia, a glove worker from Chicago, who attended the two summer sessions while I was at the school. Sophia had come from a foreign country to America at fourteen. The little education she had, she had obtained at night schools. She attracted attention at the school when she wrote a paper in her English class on "My First Day's Work." The editor of the school paper printed it. Her instructor, Dr. Mitchell, was so impressed with the qualities of Sophia's mind that he insisted she should be given opportunity to go to college. We were able to secure a scholarship for Sophia from the Friendship Fund of the Charles R. Crane family, and Sophia was allowed to choose the college she wished to attend. She chose the University of Wisconsin, and after one year in preparatory school at Bryn Mawr she was able to meet the college entrance requirements.

Sophia had told me that working in the factory she had used to dream of going to college, but that then the possibility of such an education had seemed only a forlorn dream. Our summer school put her ambitious feet on the pathway to her goal.

Zona Gale was at that time a regent of the University of Wisconsin. When Sophia had entered the university, I wrote the celebrated author, suggesting that sometime when she was in Madison she might look the girl up. A few weeks later Sophia received a formal invitation to attend a reception at the home of the president of the university. There she found herself in the company of the university's elite — and of the famous Zona Gale. Such was Zona Gale's way of responding to my letter and of meeting Sophia.

I was present when the tenth anniversary of the Bryn Mawr Summer School for Working Women was celebrated. Since those first years there had been many changes, but the girls seemed much the same. I watched them during their anniversary program and joined in their party in the gym. I recalled the heated debate of those early years which the girls had had over the question of whether they might wear bloomers in the classrooms. Now I saw girls running about the campus in shorts! Ten years before, smoking had not been permitted. Now the girls had their own smoking room. But underneath it all, they were the same fine girls, with the same burning enthusiasms.

On the staff of the college I found my childhood friend, Harriet Ferguson. Harriet was she who had had the star roles in our backyard theatre in Grand Rapids. We spent all the time we could manage talking over our early childhood days.

After seventeen years, the Summer School for Working Women was moved from Bryn Mawr to West Park, New York, and became the Hudson Shore Labor School, a co-educational and year-round workers' school. Meanwhile, during the intervening years, many other schools for workers were started, and many other colleges and universities recognized the need for special courses in labor and industrial relations. This growing interest in labor relations is a heartening inspiration to us who pioneered through those early struggling years.

28

As We Go Marching On

TWENTY-FIVE YEARS of labor and heartbreak it had required to put through an eight-hour workday law for women in Illinois. It seemed only a moment till that law was threatened.

I was on my way to Washington to attend a board meeting of the National Women's Trade Union League, December 7, 1941, when the news of the Japanese attack upon Pearl Harbor came over the radio. Once again our country was at war, and almost at once there arose a clamor for a relaxation of the labor laws. In Illinois Governor Dwight H. Green called a state-wide conference of trade-unionists to consider the matter.

Women were now going into war work, and a relaxation of the labor laws would mean night work and increased working hours for them, with, in some cases, the loss of the one day's rest in seven. The need for increased production was the excuse given by those who sought to by-pass the laws. But we who had fought so long, and who had lived through World War I, knew that this was not the way to increased production. Consequently, and from the very first, we set ourselves in opposition to the clamor — and in the interest of production!

A relaxation of the labor laws prevailed "administratively" in many plants for a time. These plants began to find the long

hours so fatiguing to the workers that they abandoned the
seven-day week. After the first year of war, eight Federal
Government branches — the War Department, the Navy Department, the Department of Commerce, the Department of
Labor, the Maritime Commission, the Public Health Service,
the War Manpower Commission, and the War Production
Board — issued a "Recommendation on Hours of Work for
Maximum Production," stating that one day of rest for the individual approximately every seven days should be the universal
and invariable rule, and that only in extreme emergencies and
for a limited period of time only, should workers or supervisors
be called upon to forego the weekly day of rest. The "Recommendation" pointed out that the eight-hour day and the forty-
eight-hour working week approximated the best working schedule for sustained efficiency in most industrial operations; and it
asked those plants keeping their workers on the job in excess
of forty-eight hours a week to examine their present situation
with respect to output, absenteeism, accident, illness, and
fatigue.

We of the Women's Trade Union League and other interested organizations hoped that this warning would be heeded
and that the clamor for the longer work week would cease. At
the next session of the Illinois Legislature, several of us went
to Springfield to demand bills compelling an eight-hour working day and a forty-eight-hour working week for war plants in
the state. We were backed by the Illinois State Department of
Labor and by the Illinois State Federation of Labor. Rueben G.
Soderstrom, president of the Illinois State Federation of Labor,
made a strong fight for our side. But when the bills were first
presented, they were defeated by so large a vote as to cause
many to presume the bills were dead. The bills, however, were
saved from extinction by a motion for further consideration,

thus leaving them on the calendar for another roll call.

I left Springfield that night to attend a meeting of the executive board of the International Glove Workers Union. The next day, to my surprise, I learned that our bills, presented again in the Illinois Legislature, had been passed by the house. If only our bills could now get through the senate! There our champion was Senator John E. Lee, the staunchest labor supporter in the whole of the Illinois General Assembly.

Senator Lee fought well in the senate and almost alone. And it looked as though he might win. Then the opposition presented a message from the Navy Department asking for increased working hours for increased production, and our cause was doomed.

That message from the Navy Department puzzled me. The Navy Department had signed the "Recommendation on Hours of Work for Maximum Production." I sent a telegram to Assistant Secretary of the Navy Ralph Bard, asking if his Department had changed its policy on hours of work and telling him of the bills just defeated in the Illinois Legislature and of how his message had been used to effect that defeat.

Mr. Bard replied at once. No, said he, the Department had not changed its policy. He enclosed a copy of the telegram he had sent to Springfield and which had been used to defeat our bills. The "copy" contained twenty-two lines. The message which had been put on the desks of the senators at Springfield had contained only twelve lines. At Springfield part of Mr. Bard's message had been deleted, leaving only that part which might be interpreted as favoring our opposition. I sent Mr. Bard a copy of the short message which had been used at Springfield.

I heard nothing more of the matter for some time. But our program finally bore fruit. As soon as V-J Day came, Illinois

State Director of Labor Robert L. Gordon declared the relaxation of labor laws program ended. Henceforth, he announced, the greatest caution would be pursued in issuing permits to employers to waive compliance with the law.

Following the war, the Women's Bureau of the U. S. Department of Labor, under the direction of Frieda S. Miller, made a study of the effects of the long factory working week on the production efficiency, attendance records, and home life of the women during the war years. It seemed time to seek an irrefutable answer to the question of what schedule of working hours would best maintain a stable, healthy staff of women workers to carry on a sustained, high-quality production over an extended time.

Many women workers, the study disclosed, not only did industrial work but also had home duties to perform. A too-long working day, a working week which was too long, produced a fatigue from which the working woman did not fully recuperate; and this fatigue showed itself in illness, irritation, and a general inability to carry on both home duties and factory work efficiently.

"As the months of war lengthened into years during World War II," the report disclosed, "illness and absentism became more common, and production slowed down."

This highly important report should be referred to in case of another emergency like World War II. But, alas! all too often all warnings are forgotten when come the times they would be of greatest value.

POST-WAR PLANNING

THE AMERICAN FEDERATION OF LABOR, at its convention in 1942, directed its president, William Green, to appoint a committee on post-war planning. Manufacturing, which was reaching to a new peak, was expected to decline once peace had been achieved. Tremendous cut-backs were expected in such industries as aircraft manufacture, shipbuilding, machine tool and machinery making. The making of munitions, it was felt, would cease completely. Government employment, it was thought, would be severely cut back. What was feared was the threat of mass unemployment such as had existed in the thirties. Employment, it was envisioned, would overshadow every other issue.

The committee A. F. of L. President William Green appointed consisted of David Dubinsky, John Childs, George M. Harrison, Richard Gray, George Q. Lynch, Rueben G. Soderstrom, Milton F. Webster, and myself, the only woman member. We got to work at once and worked through months of meetings. Many of the problems we discussed did not arise. The end of the war, for instance, saw full employment. But one of the problems we were much concerned with was the employment of women after the war, and this problem did confront us in a variety of forms.

The war years saw the total number of women employed constantly rising, and at an accelerating pace. Normal increase of women in industry in peace time had been at the rate of 300,000 a year. During the war this increase was at the rate of a million a year, till at the end of the war the number of women employed stood at twenty million!

The A. F. of L. Post-War Planning Committee concerned itself with many problems. A special committee making its report under the auspices of the general committee was appointed to consider the problems of these millions of working women. Of this special committee I was chairman, and serving with me was Rose Schneiderman, Sallie D. Clinebell, and Florence Thorne. In our report we sought to give an all-round picture of women's part in the war industries. We knew that the end of the war would bring a shifting of a great portion of this mass of women workers from the war industries to other fields. With most of these workers un-unionized, they might grow into a threat to the work standards in their new occupations. We called attention to the need for organizing these workers, the need for setting up work standards for them, and the need for awakening their responsibilities towards the unions.

We foresaw also that there would be the necessity for re-educating these shifting workers for their new positions. There would also be the need for developing within this mass of women workers new leaders who could carry on and enlarge the work of organization and improvement of the working standards for women workers.

THE WOMEN GO MARCHING ON

IN MY MOTHER'S working day, less than two million women were employed in industry, "ten years of age or older," as the census then listed women workers. (Since 1914, the census counts only those "fourteen years old and over.") In 1897, when I first went to work, there were five million women employed in industry. Today, there are twenty-odd million working women, and industry is constantly looking to hire more. I found it hard to get my first job in a factory; but today "Girls Wanted" seemed to be a permanent sign in many industrial plants, and we see industries branching out from the big industrial centers and locating in the smaller towns in order to find new supplies of working women, particularly for the sewing trades.

Women workers have entered in increasing numbers into

fields new to them, particularly into what is called the durable goods industries. Women are now also heavily employed in many industries of recent origin, like radio, electronics, and other fields unheard of years ago.

Meanwhile, the past fifty years have seen a vast improvement in the working conditions of the working woman. But these improvements in working conditions did not come about of themselves. They were gained through heartbreak and bitter struggle, through legislative action and through the force of the women's trade unions. They were gained through the sloshing damp feet of the shivering "foreign-born" picket, through working women unjustly jailed and sitting out their sentences, through bold hard bitter work by those whom conscience would not let stand by idle and watch injustice dealt to the down-trodden and the helpless.

The struggles of my own early days for the Saturday half-holiday, the eight-hour day, and the seventh-day's rest, the five-day week, and the pushing up of the wage scale, these have now given way to the struggle for what we call "welfare plans." Vacations and holidays with pay are now regularly included in agreements, as are also hospitalization benefits; and some organizations are striving hard for sick benefits and pensions.

But even the gains we have made are not secure. There are, there always will be, threats to these gains — as even now can be seen in the restrictive legislation which has recently swept through the legislatures of several states and even through Congress.

All of which means that the women workers of America must remain ever alert to protect their own rights; all of which means that the women workers must continue to develop new leaders with foresight, with insight, and with courage.

Some of the gains of recent years came so quickly to many that they do not fully understand the struggles made by the women before them to make these recent gains possible.

In recent years there has been a great increase in the membership of women in trade unions. But the trade union movement has changed with mass organization; and the form of separate unions for women, which in my early days made for the development of leadership among women and a more militant group of women leaders, has been lost. Few separate unions for women now exist. In the great mass organizations with their mixed memberships, the women are lost and do not play their full parts. It is for this reason that it is wise to look back and take courage, *and example,* from women leaders such as Mary McDowell, Jane Addams, Anna Nicholes, Margaret Dreier Robins, Elizabeth Maloney, Elisabeth Christman, and the host of others who through the first half of our century struggled so hard to improve the working conditions and the very life of working women.

Most of that great group are gone now. Mary McDowell died in 1936, in her eighties. Margaret Dreier Robins died in her seventies in 1945. Both had been early presidents of the Women's Trade Union League of Chicago and active during its most stirring years.

Jane Addams passed away in 1935, at the age of seventy-five. Mary Halas died suddenly in 1941. Her death to me was a great shock. We had worked closely together. Keenly I felt her loss. She had been president of the Illinois State Women's Trade Union League and had worked with me at Springfield. Mary White succeeded her both in the league and in legislative work at Springfield.

Our stalwart friend, John Fitzpatrick, died in October of 1946. His death seemed to mark the passing of an era in our labor movement. He had been president of the Chicago Federation of Labor from 1904 to the end of his life. A blacksmith by trade, a native of Ireland, he had come to Chicago as a boy, had grown up and lived until his death in a simple home "back of the yards." When I think of him, the qualities which stand out in my mind are loyalty, good faith, courage, and simple kindness. He had such a jovial Irish turn of mind and playful humor that often it was not readily ascertainable whether he spoke in earnest or in jest, as when long ago he used to tell the story of my ducking a policeman in a water trough during my first strike when I was a little factory girl.

[Editor's note: Agnes Nestor died December 28, 1948, in Chicago at St. Luke's Hospital. From 1913 until her death she was president of the Women's Trade Union League of Chicago. At her passing, the labor press mourned that "The woman who works has lost her best friend."]

THE END

Name Index

Subject Index